Readers praise

LEAP!

"When a friend gave me *Leap!*, I thought, 'Not another book for women about how to grow old. What the hell does that have to do with me?' Three hours later, I was deep into the book—that had everything to do with me. I'm a man with a successful career, but my kids are grown, my once athletic body creaks with every push-up, and, most important, I have no idea what I want to do with the rest of my life.

"Reading the stories in *Leap!* of people my age, famous and not so famous, embracing getting older, stirred and reenergized me. I've bought the book for a number of men, who all gave me attitude until I pushed them to read it. Now they're LEAPing with me—not quite dunking the ball like we dreamed we did forty years ago, but feeling like we could."
—BENJAMIN BYCEL

"I loved *Leap!* All those wonderful stories—every one had something to say to me. The most important was: We can do creative things for ourselves now. It doesn't have to be for the recognition anymore. Thank you for writing this."
—JILL EIKENBERRY

"You may not have been aware when you wrote *Leap!* that it would be not only a guide for aging boomers, but also a healing message for those in grief. My twenty-two-year-old son drowned in a boating accident not long ago. I have read 'grief' books people recommended—but they were not terribly satisfactory.

"So I picked up *Leap!* from my stack of unread books. It has done more to focus my mind on what to do under these tragic circumstances than almost all the other things I have tried. I am thinking about changing my job and living as your book suggests. My son's premature death has shown me that life is too short and uncertain to do anything else.

"So many thanks for writing something that has been a true inspiration and source of comfort."
—Michael Barclay

"I know your book is intended for Boomers, but I think it speaks to my generation (I am thirty-two), because we are all trying to find purpose in this life. More important, I know it speaks to the people of New Orleans. I have never dealt with trying to find meaning in my life as I have post-Katrina. Once you go through a life-changing experience, you have a hard time looking at life the same way."
—Luetta Marchant

"My husband died four years ago.
I retired.
I'm off hormones.
My lover dumped me.
I'm getting deaf.
I think this is 'the Narrows.'
I am reading your book."
—Rogers Barde

"*Loose Change* was one of a handful of books that always went with me no matter how often I moved. Now *Leap!* will, too. I'm newly divorced, entering the workforce in my early sixties. For the first time, I have to make a living. I'm trying hard to embrace the change and uncertainty. Reading this book was a release from the guilt I'd felt in falling below 'standards' I was 'supposed to have achieved' at this time of my life. Your writing really comforts me. Keep publishing: I need you!"
—Ellen Alterman

"After a cerebral hemorrhage at fifty-five, I have spent the last year asking, 'Now that you did not die, Laura—what the hell are you going to do from this point on?'

"I laughed out loud at parts of your book, and got tearful as well. Most of all, you are able to articulate what many of us were unable to before.

"Oh—and thanks for not being too 'granola.' I have read many pieces that are over the top with goodness and positive bullshit.

"Thanks for giving us HOPE!"

—LAURA NEVILLE

"FINALLY someone is explaining to me that I'm not alone in what I'm going through. This is especially important for a guy, since we aren't talkers, I've heard!"

—DEL MARTINIS

"I just finished *Leap!* What joy! You made me laugh, cry, and contemplate. I retired from thirty years of teaching and have recently lost my father, my brother, and my eyesight. (I have only partial vision in one eye.) Empty inside and at a loss for what to do, your book inspired me. The people you interviewed were so familiar from books, articles, and excerpts that I felt I was home again—reading *Leap!*"

—CAROL ROSS

"*Leap!* is an education, a joy, a deep gasp, architecture for new and bolder perspectives, and above all an inspiration. Know that six copies are going out today to friends who are also sitting in mud and somewhat envious of my newfound energy and boldness due to *Leap!* Thank you!"

—GARY GROUNDS (NAME CHANGED AT REQUEST OF SENDER)

"When I saw your name on the cover I said, "Oh my god—*Loose Change*!" I was thrilled that you had tackled this topic—one which I was ignoring because to tackle it meant to throw my life into chaos, or at least to acknowledge the chaos my life had become.

"You are not an author to offer answers. What you do is more compelling—you reach out to the reader through story and personal narrative, and in the end allow us to connect with who we were and how we want to live now."

—TANIA REIS

LEAP!

LE

AP!

What Will We Do with the Rest of Our Lives?

Sara Davidson

Ballantine Books New York

2008 Ballantine Books Trade Paperback Edition

Originally published in hardcover in the United States by Random House, an imprint of The Random House Publishing Group, a division of Random House, Inc., in 2007.

BALLANTINE and colophon are registered trademarks of Random House, Inc.

Portions of this work were originally published in different form in *Mirabella* and *O: The Oprah Magazine*.

Published in the United States by Ballantine Books, an imprint of The Random House Publishing Group, a division of Random House, Inc., New York.

LIBRARY OF CONGRESS CATALOGING-IN-PUBLICATION DATA
Davidson, Sara.
   Leap!: what will we do with the rest of our lives? / Sara Davidson.
     p. cm.
   Includes index.
   ISBN: 978-0-345-47809-2
   1. Middle-aged persons—Life skills guides. 2. Baby boom generation—Life skills guides.
  3. Middle-aged persons—Conduct of life. 4. Baby boom generation—Conduct of life.
  I. Title.
  HQ1059.4.D37 2007
  305.244—dc22   2006049527

Printed in the United States of America

www.ballantinebooks.com

9 8 7 6 5 4 3 2 1

Text design by Laurie Jewell

For Andrew and for Rachel

Leap, and the net will appear.

—attributed to John Burroughs, Jimmy Buffett,
and unnamed Zen masters

CONTENTS

LEAP!

1

The Long and Winding Road

When I walk through the stage door of the Roseland Ballroom in New York, I hear an unmistakable riff—the long electric piano solo that spirals up and down until it can't go higher or become more intense and then it resolves as Jim Morrison comes in to sing: "The time to hesitate is through . . ."

"Light My Fire" by the Doors was the number one song in America in 1967. But onstage at Roseland almost forty years later are Ray Manzarek, the original keyboard player, Robby Krieger, the original guitarist, and between them, replacing Jim Morrison, is Ian Astbury, a singer in his thirties who looks so much like Morrison that the image of the three suggests *The Picture of Dorian Gray.* Ray and Robby are in their sixties, with silver hair and deeply lined faces, but Jim doesn't seem to have aged—he looks frozen at twenty-seven, the age he was when he died.

The Doors of the Twenty-first Century, as they call themselves tonight, are doing a sound check for a concert celebrating fifty years of rock 'n' roll. Ray stands at the electric piano, wearing a black Issey Miyake shirt with pleats over gray pants. His hair is slicked back, and he's rail thin from lifting weights, swimming, and yoga. "I feel juicy," Ray says into the microphone, testing the level. "I feel juicy now. I got filth running through my blood, Robby. It's gonna be a dirrrrr-ty night." It's also going to be a loud night, and I make a note to come back later with earplugs and my glasses.

The Doors created and released albums for only four years, 1967 to 1971, but they've been embraced by succeeding generations, and my son has the lyrics to a Doors song on his blog. After Jim's death, Ray kept making music on his own and wrote two books, none of which connected with a mass audience, but that was all right. He hadn't played a Doors song in thirty years when in 2002 the Harley-Davidson company asked the Doors if they would re-form the group to perform at an L.A. concert celebrating Harley's hundredth anniversary. "Robby and I said, 'Let's do it!' " Ray recalls, but John Densmore, the third living Door, said his ears were too badly damaged to play drums. Their manager brought in another drummer and, to sing, Ian Astbury of the Cult.

Playing for thousands of inflamed Harley-Davidson riders at the California Speedway was "so much fun," Ray says, that they went on the road as the Doors of the Twenty-first Century, until a lawsuit forced them to drop the Doors name and perform as Riders on the Storm.

Backstage at Roseland, I ask Ray how he deals with the fact that his most well-loved work was done more than thirty years ago. He waves his hand, dismissive. I tell him I have the same issue on a smaller scale. "My first book was a bestseller—it was number two in the country and made into a miniseries. I've written five books since then and hundreds of articles and screenplays, but none has had that impact. I used to feel upset because people would meet me and say—"

"I know what they tell you," Ray says. "You were big once upon a time, and you don't have it anymore. Well, thank you very much, really nice of you to point that out. Have you ever had a success? No, you haven't. I see, you . . . LOSER!" He shrugs. "What can we do with this society? We're vicious that way."

"How do you handle it?"

"You don't. You get pissed off and say, Fuck you. Fuck you! You got the nerve to say that stuff to my fucking face, you fucker?"

He imitates the guy confronting him: " 'Well, Ray, you know, a lot of people have said you're just doing it for the money.'

"Like who? Is he there with you? Put him on the phone, let me talk to that asshole.

" 'No, no, no, there's nobody here. I'm just saying . . .' "

Ray sighs and tells me, "You have to put up with shit like that."

I say, "I spent a lot of time feeling that I wasn't fulfilling my early promise, whatever that was. Now I've come around to the fact that I wrote a book that's still in print after thirty years. That makes me feel . . . humble."

"Exactly," Ray says. "Here's the point. Did you do one thing? Yes, you did. You got any friends from high school who did *one thing*? You got any friends from college . . . Do I have any friends from UCLA film school who did . . . *one* . . . *thing*? No."

"You did more than one thing."

"Whatever."

"You don't have those demons?"

"Oh sure, absolutely. I'm more competitive than you are, and you're obviously very competitive. We're competitive animals. That's the nature of being human, and that's what drives us to accomplish great things. You live your life to the fullest, but at some point, things are snatched away from you. Death is going to happen."

I ask if he still takes psychedelics. "No. That's for your twenties and thirties. Once you open the doors of perception, they stay open."

"Not for some," I say. "The doors clanked shut when they became workaholics and tried to be superparents."

"If they've forgotten the message, well, now that the kids have grown and retirement is approaching, let's reinvent the gods. That's what Jim Morrison said. 'Let's reinvent the gods—all the myths of the ages.' The problem for Jim was that he had no idea how far he could go, how high he could get, before he was eased out.

"Psychedelics do a strange thing," Ray says. "You accept that death is going to happen. Your friend is gone, you've danced for a while—you danced feverishly and madly around a bonfire and had that ecstatic joy and now the dance is over and all you can say is: So be it. Another kind of dance begins."

. . .

I had this conversation with Ray Manzarek toward the end of a three-year period when everything I touched turned brown and died. Everywhere I'd go people would ask, "What are you doing now?"

"Different things . . ."

If I'd told the truth, I would have said: I'm doing nothing. For the first time since college, I have no work. After twenty-four years and several award nominations, I can't get hired to write for television. In Hollywood jargon, I can't get arrested. I can't sell articles to magazines or books to publishers and I don't know how I'll earn money. The phone doesn't ring, and I have to crank myself up to go out and hustle and why, dear God, do I have to hustle at this age? It's humiliating.

During this same period, my lover of seven years, a cowboy artist I'd expected to spend the rest of my days with, rides off with no discussion. My children, who've occupied my first thoughts on waking and my last before falling asleep, are going off to college. As long as they lived with me, I got up at seven and made pancakes, drove them to school, soccer, Little League, ballet, music lessons, helped them write their papers and do research on Egyptian history and carve pumpkins for Halloween. No more. My kids, my lover, and my livelihood are being yanked from me at once and there's nothing I can do. When I tell this to a friend, Peter Simon, the photographer, he says, "Oh, honey, you've got money problems and no sex. That's not good."

Not good at all. I can't sleep, either. I fall asleep but wake at two, my feet jackknifing. Why hasn't my agent called me back? I read or watch a movie, hoping my eyelids will close, but they don't. Three A.M. I have stomach pains—it's the cowboy, I can't seem to untangle him from my body and I miss him so intensely I want to call and tell him he can name his terms, just come back. It wouldn't work.

My doctor suggests I see a hypnotherapist, Guy Birdwhistle. His name is so ridiculously cheerful that I make an appointment. In his waiting room, I sit on a couch beside the trickling portable waterfall that's de rigueur for New Age healers. When Birdwhistle opens the door, I'm shocked: He has the face of a teenager, wears a crisp blue shirt and tie, and speaks with a British accent.

"How old are you, may I ask?"

"Twenty-nine," he says, showing me to a chair. "How can I help you?"

Good question. I don't think he's lived long enough. I ask how he became a hypnotist. He says he was working at Fred Segal, the trendy clothing store, "and I was having terrible anxiety attacks. I went to a hypnotherapist and got relief, and thought, I want to learn to do this."

What the hell. I can't sleep, I tell him, my identity is being stripped away, and a spiritual teacher I've worked with, Nina Zimbelman, tells me that my life as I know it is over.

"What's wrong with that?" He smiles.

I start to cry. "I'm afraid I'll die, I'll disintegrate."

"What's really happening is, your life is beginning. It's that simple.

When you embrace doing nothing, all sorts of things can happen. If you struggle, you'll be yanked kicking and screaming, so you might as well give in. You're on vacation."

Okay, I'll take the rest of the day off. Instead of driving home to fret and make calls to people who won't return them, I stop at Manderette, a Chinese restaurant on Melrose that serves exquisite food and where I usually can't get a table. But at three P.M., nobody's in Manderette except a fortyish man and woman playing cards. They're on vacation, too, I assume.

I'm actually eager to go to bed. I play the hypnotherapy tape that Birdwhistle made for me, drift asleep but bolt awake at four with fear in my chest. What am I supposed to do for the next thirty years? I've raised my kids, written bestsellers, had deep love. . . . Why am I still here?

• • •

Why are we still here? When I look around, I see that others are going through similar transitions and that as a group we're being stripped of our relevance, our primacy. We're turning fifty at the rate of one every seven seconds, and the advance guard, the icons who set the tone—Bob Dylan, the Beatles, Joni Mitchell, Angela Davis, Tom Hayden and the Chicago Seven—are well into their sixties or would be if they were alive. We did not plan for this; we did not know that at fifty-five we might have thirty more years of vigorous health, lust, and a desire to contribute and create.

Let me define what I mean by "we," because the boomer generation—usually described as people born between 1946 and 1964—is not one culture or even one generation. It includes people turning sixty and considering retirement and others who've just hit forty and are having babies. Of those born during those years, 52 percent voted red in the last presidential election and 47 percent voted blue. When I speak of this group, I'm speaking about a cohort of various ages who were infected by the ideals of the sixties, who believed we should make love, not war, had a passion for improving the world and a transformational agenda. This cohort, whom I've been writing about for three decades, are mostly middle class and can get emotional when they hear "Sgt. Pepper"—they remember where they were and how they felt when they first heard it—or see a film clip of Bobby Kennedy saying: "Some men see things as they are and ask, 'Why?' I dream things that never were and ask, 'Why not?'"

We come together periodically for what I think of as geezer rock concerts, such as the one at Madison Square Garden in 2003 for a Simon and Garfunkel reunion. The audience rose when Paul and Art came onstage and sang "Old Friends." Paul had written the song when he was twenty-eight, imagining what it would be like to be with Art when they're seventy, sitting on a park bench, not talking, "lost in their overcoats."

On this icy night in December, Paul and Art are sixty-three and don't look anything like those silent old men. Paul is sexy and commanding as he plays electric guitar, and Art still has an Afro, that annoying ethereal smile and angelic voice. Before long, twenty thousand people are singing and dancing and time is elastic: We're seventeen, with long hair and beads, singing "Feelin' Groovy," and we're thirty, wearing a power suit and singing "Fifty Ways to Leave Your Lover," and we're fifty or sixty and a chill passes through us. Suddenly seventy seems just a breath away.

There's a new life stage—after fifty and before eighty—and we're the ones whose mission it will be to figure out what to do with it. When my life began to unravel, I set out to interview friends and strangers who led me to others who are making their way, experimenting and asking: What's the next part of life about? How do we make the leap?

Most of us are addicted to work and have spent more hours at our jobs than any other activity, except for those who've been full-time parents, which is another kind of job. But what happens if we don't work so much or at all? People tend to fall into three groups: The first are being squeezed out of jobs and feel like Willy Loman, clawing to stay in the game; the second are quitting work or starting new ventures because they don't want to repeat what they've done the last thirty years; and the third group are riding square in the saddle and want to keep going. Mort Zuckerman, in his sixties, publisher of the New York *Daily News,* told me, "Nobody I know wants to stop working at this age because nobody feels it's old and guess what, it isn't."

If we're creative, what happens if our work no longer sells for as much or at all? Will we keep doing it anyway? Probably, but how will we make our funds last until we reach one hundred, a real possibility? How much money is enough, how much achievement is enough, or have we found that recognition is like a drug and you can never get enough? What if we still strive for excellence and distinction? Tirzah Firestone, a rabbi, says, "When you're being lowered into the ground, recognition will mean nothing. Nothing!" What will matter? Isn't this the question to ask? What will matter when the dealin's done?

I'm determined to learn what it will take to do the next stage of life well. How do we move ahead with grace and purpose, take risks, laugh and love without condition, be provocative, and gain some serenity and understanding of what our time—and our cohort's—has meant?

What I've found is that there will be no single answer or solution, as everyone will go at this differently. Many models will arise, just as there were many lifestyles in the sixties: political activism, hippie communes, getting back to the land, as well as traditional jobs and families.

Some are making choices they would not have predicted. I've spent my life in New York and Los Angeles and could not have imagined that at fifty-nine I would move to Boulder, Colorado, where I knew no one. Or that Ed Wayne, a Texas good ol' boy, would sell his oil valve business and build a hospital for kids in Serbia. Or that Gloria Steinem, who famously announced she would not take a husband or have children, would get married at age sixty-six.

We're inventing this on the fly. Tom Hayden believes we can revive our activism. "When you're done with the work you've had to do and raised your kids, you can be a freer person than you've been since you were twenty. We may have thirty more years to give the system hell!"

Thomas Moore, author of *Care of the Soul,* says giving more than receiving now is "the best way to work on the soul." Many will do just that, but what if serving meals to the homeless or treating AIDS patients in Uganda is not your thing? How can you feel you're contributing and not going out in a vessel of selfishness?

In Eastern cultures, this part of life is traditionally reserved for deep spiritual work. Householders give up their possessions, drop their names, and set off to seek truth. What would be the equivalent for us? Go on retreat, join a monastery, join the Peace Corps, build a community so we can grow old along with our friends?

What about having a face lift? Some say it's a vain absorption with the superficial, but I know meditation teachers and yoga instructors—people who advise their students to look beneath the surface—who've had face lifts.

Is there a test we can take, some kind of psycho-affinity-aptitude test that will tell us what we should do? Afraid not. Counselors say we should "surrender," "let go," "ride the horse in the direction it's going instead of trying to force it to go the way you want, because that approach won't work anymore." But what does this mean? Surrender to what? And how is surrender different from giving up—leaving the field in defeat?

What happens to love, and sex? In our youth, the birth control pill was unloosed and the sexual revolution began. Is it an accident that just as we hit prime time, Viagra came on the market? Some of us are on our third or fourth marriages, and others, whom I view with awe, are celebrating thirty years with the same spouse. Some announce that they're finished with sex, while others stand with the actress Joan Hotchkis, who declared at sixty-seven in a one-woman show: "I refuse to go unfucked to my grave!"

• • •

What it comes down to is: What do you really want to do? What will make you feel most alive? That you've used your time well? That your being here has mattered?

When I started work on *Leap!*, I did not know what, where, or with whom I wanted to be. At the blackest hour, if you'd asked what I wished for, I might have said: A partner I love, a show on the air or a book on the bestseller list, recognition from my peers, and closeness with my children, who're healthy and thriving. In short, I wanted my old life back. But as I followed the lines of research, another view began to emerge. A curtain fluttered in the wind and there were glimpses of something moving that would slip from sight and return.

It was like looking for whales on a boat trip I took with friends, Dr. Andrew Weil and Kathy Goodman, up the Inland Passage of Alaska in 2000. For a week we were cut off from phone and mail, unplugged from electronics. The sea was green and still and the silence absolute. Then out of nowhere we heard a rumble like a jet taking off: *Sheeeeeeooooooh!*

A burst of white steam, and a whale broke the surface, arching up and curving back down as if it were a wheel that was revolving. In seconds we were in a soup of whales—seventy or eighty blowing like jets. *Sheeeeeeooooooh! Sheeeeeeooooooh!* We grabbed binoculars for a shockingly close look: the foaming spout, then the hoary back emerging, and the tail rising last, hanging motionless in air before slipping into the sea, causing us to moan in pleasure.

Then the whales were gone and we were in limbo, floating somewhere in Frederick Sound and somewhere in our lives. Somewhere in our fifties. Somewhere near the end of raising our children. Work was up in the air, relationships were shot to hell, and we did not know what we were going home to.

So it begins.

2

The Narrows

When I felt my identity was being ripped away, I looked for books, poetry, anything that might shine a light, and the most instructive words I found were in a tape, *The Crown of Age,* by Marion Woodman, the Jungian analyst. Marion tells a story from when she was in her forties and everything in her life started to break apart—"everything was gray." She knew she couldn't teach school as she'd done for twenty years and decided to go to the Aurobindo ashram in India to try to understand what was happening. But she never made it to the ashram. She contracted dysentery in a Calcutta hotel and was so weak and delirious she couldn't get out of bed for nine days.

When her fever began to abate, she decided, as a first step in reentry, to go down to the lobby and write a letter to her husband. She sat on a couch and before long an Indian woman in a gold-trimmed sari came and sat beside her, smiling. Marion moved along the couch but the woman moved with her, putting a warm brown arm around her shoulders. "I couldn't understand why she didn't sit on the rest of the couch. She kept cuddling against me. I kept moving, and as I moved, she moved," Marion says. They couldn't speak each other's language, so Marion went on writing her letter. "When *we* finished," she says, she rose and made her way back to bed.

The same thing happened for the next four days, and on the fifth, when Marion came down to the lobby, an Indian man approached her and said, "My wife won't have to come sit with you anymore."

"I beg your pardon? What are you talking about?" she asked.

"The lady is my wife. I saw you were dying, and I sent her to sit with you."

Marion Woodman had felt she was dying not so much from dysentery as from "a terrible anguish of the soul." After listening to the tape, I called to interview her and she said in a gravelly voice, "Everything I'd known and believed about myself was being stripped from me." I was relieved to hear that such stripping—when the supports that prop up your identity are kicked away—happens to others, "usually at fifty-five or sixty," Marion says, "but I've seen it happen at forty." She describes it as a time of multiple blows: Your body is losing its beauty and strength, your kids are not turning out the way you'd hoped or they're living in Hong Kong, your partner may be gone, "and your childhood faith no longer gives you the assurance that there's life after death," she says. "You have to ask yourself, Why am I being stripped? You may think: I'm lost, I don't want to struggle on. I don't like what I see in the mirror. I'd rather die in full flight. Then a new energy comes in and says: *I am going to live.*"

• • •

When I spoke with Marion, I was not receiving any new energy. I was still kicking the door, trying to get back in and recover what I'd lost. Other writers had managed to do this: Marc Cherry had been washed up, shunned by the networks, and embezzled out of thousands by his agent when he wrote *Desperate Housewives* and made it to the A list. But no matter how hard I worked, how many ideas I developed and pitched, I could not write the comeback, breakthrough, fuck-every-goddamn-one-of-you script. I could not sell a project.

When my TV agent stopped returning my calls, I decided reluctantly to hire a new one. I'd been with the big three—ICM, CAA, and William Morris—and found they're all about the same. At the beginning, they make a flurry of calls and pump you up with flattery. Michael Peretzian, the vaunted literary agent at William Morris, answered the phone when I called, "Hi, talented!" But when assignments get scarce, so do the guys in suits.

I drew up a list of agents I wanted to interview, and had my lawyer send them scripts. The first told me on the phone, "I checked around and I can't sell you to the networks. You don't have edge."

I asked what he meant, since people in the business use "edge" in every other sentence. I assumed it meant some combination of darkness, bizarreness, and pushing the envelope. The script I'd sent him, *Bloodhound Red,* had plenty of bizarre darkness: a deaf gay hero, a woman being tortured, and a lovable and loyal bloodhound that gets its throat cut while its owner is forced to watch.

The agent thought a moment. "I have a script I just sold where there's a corpse with its penis cut off on page two. That's edge."

Every agent on my list passed. I came to understand it was not "edge," it was my age—fifty-seven—that made people feel I was out of touch with the eighteen- to twenty-nine-year-olds they were desperate to attract. Never mind that David Chase was in his fifties when he created *The Sopranos,* which pulls in that age group. I joined the class-action lawsuit being brought by TV writers against the networks for age discrimination. The plaintiffs include about 180 writers, such as Tracy Keenan Wynn, who wrote *The Autobiography of Miss Jane Pittman* and *The Longest Yard,* and Ann Marcus, an Emmy winner who co-created *Mary Hartman, Mary Hartman.* Most can't get jobs, and some can't even get an interview.

The dangerous part about this kind of rejection is that it makes you lose your nerve and start to believe what they're saying: You can't write, you're old news, your ideas are bad, and you might as well slink off into the nearest hole and die.

As I was sinking, people I loved were deserting me. Zack, the cowboy who'd given me unwavering support for seven years, became mean and cruel. He didn't show up for dinner one night, refused to answer his phone, and kept to himself for a month, after which he called and said it was over, he didn't understand why but "that's where it's at." How could he turn his back on the deepest love either of us had known? It was as final as if he'd died, only he hadn't and I dreaded the possibility of running into him with another woman.

At the same time, my house was no longer safe. My teenage daughter had turned on me with a hostility that spread through the rooms like something black and inflatable. She cooked her own vegan meals, and when I tried to talk with her she shot me a scornful look and punched up the death metal rock. With no one to laugh and talk with, to make love and find comfort with, I'd sit at the computer from morning till night and have to eject myself forcibly—grab the arms of the chair and push up—to go to bed.

Lying awake, I stewed over the decisions I'd taken, the foolish words I'd said, and the hash I'd made of opportunities. I'd failed at work, at love, with my kids—at everything. This is what the Buddhists call the second arrow. The first is the bad thing that happens. The second is what you do to yourself because of the bad thing that happened.

Carly Simon

Anxious to find reassurance and know I was not alone, I began looking for contemporaries who were going through some kind of stripping. I needed to see that people could survive, find a way through. Were there strategies I could learn? Had anyone left a trail of bread crumbs?

A friend told me Carly Simon had been dealing with multiple blows. I'd known Carly in New York when we were in our early twenties, and I'd thought she was dazzling, totally original, and somewhat lost. She was playing with a band that wasn't gelling, working in a kids' summer camp, and hanging out with a guy who was breaking her heart. Then she signed a contract with Elektra and her first album rose to the top of the charts.

Before she became a star, we'd compared notes about rock singers we lusted after, and suddenly she was having affairs with them. She was being fetched in a limo to meet the Rolling Stones backstage, or flying to the Caribbean for a tryst with a movie director and I hung on every detail. My husband, a radio host, and I were fighting and I believed the marriage was keeping me from all the fun and high times Carly was having.

Years later, we met in Los Angeles and our positions had reversed: I was divorced and Carly had just married James Taylor. "You remember those years," I said, "when I was married and you were single and going out with those exciting men? I couldn't wait to hear about it and was insanely jealous."

Carly laughed. "Sara, the most exciting part about it . . . was telling you."

* * *

I had not seen Carly in twelve years when I called her in the summer of 2004. I'd heard that she'd been diagnosed with breast cancer, had a mastectomy and chemotherapy just as she and her second husband were drifting apart, her career was in the cellar, and her kids were going off on their own. She was living on Martha's Vineyard, where she'd spent summers as a child and later built a house on a storybook piece of land not far from the sea.

When I reach her, she says she hikes and photographs her land every day and arranges the pictures in scrapbooks. "I love a gray day," she says. "I love storm clouds and fog. On a sunny day, I will tolerate it if there aren't too many of them. But when it's gray, I feel, Hallelujah!" She sings it out. "My absolute favorite thing is the mist—the deep mist when no planes are landing. I love the isolation of the mist and how the landscape looks. How the blues come out of gray tile. How the purples come out."

She tells me she's "supposedly retired. I've had so much rejection I couldn't bear it anymore. I was not allowed on the David Letterman show. I've always been on *Letterman*. When they turned me down, I thought, That's it."

"I understand, babe," I tell her. "I eat rejection for breakfast, lunch, and dinner."

"I'm sorry," Carly says. "Sorry for you, sorry for me. There's gotta be a different way. People are so scared of getting older, they pretend it's not happening."

She doesn't appreciate it when someone tells her, "Oh, you look so young!" She would rather they say, "You're beautiful at your age," which she is. She still has sensual lips, elongated tawny legs that fold and twine about each other, an endearing self-mocking humor, and a dramatic presence that draws eyes.

She never liked touring, but in the decades after her major hit albums, she continued writing songs, making CDs, and creating music for movies, winning an Oscar for "Let the River Run" in *Working Girl*. She knew, though, that she was racing the clock. "In the music business, they're always looking for the younger, the hipper, and women of a certain age get disappeared." After she turned forty, she says, "I was just trying to keep my head above water."

In her fifties, she underwent surgery for breast cancer at the same time she hit the skids professionally. She'd been recording with Arista records since 1984, and in 1997 they offered her a new contract as a "heritage artist." An antique. But Clive Davis, the head of Arista, promised to supervise her next CD, which would become *The Bedroom Tapes*. Carly imitates Clive telling her, in his deep New York street voice, "I'm gonna do for you what I did for Caaaah-los." Carlos Santana, whose career he'd revived by hooking a new young audience on Santana's music.

For a month, Clive listened to Carly's work and gave her notes. Then he was forced out by BMG, the German company that owns Arista, reportedly because they thought that at sixty-seven Clive was too old for the record business. He was allowed to take ten artists with him when he left to start a new company, "but he didn't take me," Carly says. "In came L.A. Reid," a black hip-hop producer who cofounded LaFace Records with the R&B singer Babyface. Reid showed up at one of Carly's sessions and said he'd been a huge fan and she was in safe hands, he was going to push *The Bedroom Tapes*. A few months later, a friend at Arista called Carly from a sales conference and said, "You should know: Your record is dead in the water."

Carly arranged a meeting with Reid after making many calls that he didn't return. She flew to New York and asked all the department heads to be present. "During the whole meeting, L.A. Reid watched television," Carly says. "It was devastating. And of course I took it personally. I'd just finished chemo and was down for the count. Fighting for my life, and fighting to keep some kind of status and respect."

She lost her apartment on Central Park West when the owner raised the rent from $7,000 to $24,000 a month. "I wasn't making money, I was losing money," she says, so she moved to Boston because it was more affordable, her husband, Jim Hart, was teaching poetry at Harvard, and her kids wanted to attend the Berklee College of Music in Boston. "I thought if I created a house beautiful on Beacon Hill, we could all be together," she says. "I was desperately trying to keep things together." After she remodeled the building, her family gathered there for Christmas in 1998, but two weeks later, Carly received a letter from a neighbor demanding that she play music only between the hours of nine and five.

"I left," she says. "I can't sing and play on a schedule, and I didn't want to start a war. So I moved, lock, stock, and barrel, to the Vineyard," which had a glittering summer population but was nearly deserted in winter. She lived by herself except for visits from Jim and her kids, Ben and Sally Taylor. "I liked being alone because I didn't have to be up for anybody, making dinners, feeling my identity rested on whether I made a good fillet of flounder." The drugs she was taking for cancer made her so depressed that at times "I could barely get out of bed. And I had to fight against feeling discarded like a dog, which was harder than dealing with the chemo."

"You had reasons to be depressed," I say.

"The blows came too fast: wham, wham, wham," Carly says. What helped her was the music. She worked on *The Bedroom Tapes* in Sally's old bedroom, installing electronic equipment and learning how to lay eight tracks and mix them. She had a drum machine and could spend all night experimenting with rhythms because no one was listening. "I was doing what I'd done thirty years before—just making sounds I liked. I had to try to keep pleasing myself. That was the only star I could follow."

It also helped to laugh. "If I could giggle—whatever made me giggle—that felt good. And the walks I would take. Oh God! My love of the trees and flowers I'd planted and the fog—that never stopped."

Then she was called to help a friend of her son's, John Forté, a black musician who'd won a scholarship to Exeter but at twenty-eight was arrested for drug trafficking. He and Ben had lived with Carly one summer, and Carly was the person Forté phoned from jail. "There's nothing better than feeling you're needed," Carly says. It was Forté's first arrest and nobody had been harmed, but he was given a minimum mandatory sentence of fourteen years. Carly began studying mandatory sentencing and trying to get Forté released early. "I called all the senators on the Judiciary Committee," she says. "I couldn't get any help from the Democrats. The only one who called back was a Republican, Orrin Hatch, from Utah, because he was a songwriter. We'd have long talks about . . ." She laughs. ". . . bridges of songs."

Three months after our phone call, when I speak with Carly again, she's engrossed in writing a play about Forté, and planning to go to Los Angeles for the installation of a star with her name on it on Hollywood Boulevard. Her tone and attitude have changed, which surprises me. "You're not retired anymore?"

She gives a disarming laugh. "That was a whim. I'm hardly retired." She's signed a contract with Disney to write music and be the voice of Winnie-the-Pooh in movies, and she's composing songs for herself.

Then Richard Perry calls. Richard, the superstar producer with whom she started collaborating thirty-three years ago, with whom she made "You're So Vain" and other hits, and who's always been in love with her voice and probably her, asks if she wants to record some romantic standards. He sends her an arrangement he put together of "My One and Only Love." She records a vocal track and sends it back to him in California. They do four more songs, making the artistic decisions and funding the enterprise themselves with no record company executive looking on. When it becomes clear that they have an album they're both happy with, they sell it to Columbia, and the week it's released, it hits number seven on the *Billboard* chart. The trade papers announce: "Pop music icon Carly Simon is back on the nation's top ten with *Moonlight Serenade,* her breathtaking new album."

How sweet it is. In the video that comes with *Moonlight Serenade,* Carly and Richard drink martinis and dance cheek to cheek. "A couple months ago I didn't know I was going to be doing this record," Carly says on the video. "And now it's finished."

In another moment, talking with me, she reflects, "For better or worse, I'm enough of a public figure that I count. But when you've been hit again and again, you keep your dukes up." She says she tries not to keep them up, because her power as a songwriter has always been her vulnerability—"my willingness to expose how it is."

This vulnerability runs like a vein through *The Bedroom Tapes*. She sings about the scar from her mastectomy; she tries to carry the scar with pride, but when a man calls wanting to see her and she tells him about it, he never calls back. In another song, "We Your Dearest Friends," she imagines her friends getting together for dinner without her and gossiping that Carly may still think she's a star, but it's over. "It's been a long time since you had those famous lovers."

Carly says she wants to learn "how to walk down the ladder gracefully. I have this image—I'd like to get smaller and smaller in a relevant way."

"Do you know anyone who's walked down that ladder with grace?" I ask.

"There are plenty of people who've huffed and puffed down the ladder, who've clawed and tried to cut off the feet of people going up."

She says it was her mother, Andrea Simon, who "made me not afraid of age." Andrea was a tiny woman with the carriage and voice of a grande dame. I remember seeing her in the mornings on Martha's Vineyard, walking her Dalmatians and appearing fully clothed on Lucy Vincent beach, where she'd sit and chat with her son, Peter, and his friends, all of whom were naked. Carly says, "My mom would hold out her arthritic hand and say, 'Isn't this beautiful!' There was beauty in a withered hand. She was so joyous and enthusiastic in the way she greeted age—that was a gift she gave me."

I've never had such an example, but if Carly can welcome age with grace, maybe I can follow. We both work in an industry that glorifies and panders to youth, both love the creative process and want to keep at it. What helped Carly find her way back to sunlight, or to the gray mist she loves, was giving aid to someone in trouble, laughing, making music, and, above all, following her own star and not seeking approval from the marketplace. She kept doing what she believed in, trying to please herself.

I felt inspired to look for that inward star, especially when outside doors were closing. I was moved by the concept of walking down the ladder gracefully, although the reality may be problematic. How does one become smaller and still remain "relevant"? I suspect this begins with facing the fact that it's time to walk down, but my eyes have been habitually trained upward. The first story I wrote, at five, was about a boy who longed to climb trees. My shoulders are hitched forward, my orientation is toward rising rather than descending, and changing this—accepting and reversing the orientation—feels like turning a train around.

Tom Hayden

Not long after speaking with Carly, I learned that Tom Hayden had left public office, not by choice, after eighteen years in the California legislature, where he'd been called "the conscience of the Senate." When I'd first met Tom in the sixties, he was living in a black ghetto in Newark, New Jersey, with a collective of SDS members doing community action. Years later, he was one of the few who crossed the bridge to work on the inside and found it exhilarating—if intricate and knotty—to create and shape public policy. "When you're doing it, you feel passionate, engaged, purposeful, and turned on," he says, "until you get beyond it and see you've been locked in a prison, which all jobs are." His addiction to politics was so strong that he might have stayed in the state senate until he dropped, but term limits forced him to retire in 2000.

The following year, at sixty-two, he ran for a seat on the L.A. City Council and immediately became the front-runner in a crowded field. He'd won seven elections in the same area of Los Angeles, but in a runoff he faced an attorney, Jack Weiss, in his thirties, who campaigned under the banner "A New Generation of Leadership." The race was fierce; Tom was ahead, he fell behind, he surged ahead, but when the ballots were counted, Tom says, "I lost by about two hundred fifty votes out of fifty thousand. The election might have been stolen, because in some precincts there weren't any votes. But it was over, and I had to reconcile to the fact that it was over."

The loss was "shattering—you feel it in your bones," he says. Two months later, he collapsed from heart failure and had a quintuple bypass. When the hijacked planes crashed into the Twin Towers on 9/11, Tom was lying in a hospital bed struggling to regain his health and his appetite for life. Looking back, he says, "I left my heart at the office. I used up all the energy I had in that campaign, and when I lost . . . my heart gave out. I haven't had fire in the belly for campaigning since then."

He was depressed and started seeing a male therapist who specializes in working with men recovering from heart surgery. Tom changed his diet, started exercising an hour every day, and gradually, he says, "I got better. When you feel well and healthy, you can lapse into this illusion that you've pushed the reverse button and you're back to forty-one. But you're not."

He had to design a new role that would not include campaigning. "Hypertension is what you need to run for office, and that can be a killer when you're older." He's learning there's a difference between being intense and being competitive. "I'm still intense. I'm speaking out for global justice and against the war in Iraq, but those things don't give you the same kind of extreme stress that campaigning does. If I'm thinking, It's me versus you, in every encounter—that's what makes my chest go tight."

Tom still has a boyish, lopsided grin, although his hair is white and his goatee salt and pepper. He can be playful or sarcastic, empathic or bluntly critical, all with Irish charm and wit.

I ask if he's made peace with giving up electoral politics. "I'm feeling my way, just as I did when I was in my twenties," he says. "This is new territory—your life is accelerating to its end." He says he's caught between two forces: the drive for power and achievement—the activist impulse—and the desire to be more reflective, spend time with family, travel, and mentor young people. "There's a transition you have to go through and I'm not done with it. In my view, people have to put it down—put their career drives down." Tom believes this is especially tough for men, "who want to lead, organize, and minister."

Not just men.

The choice to shift away from activism, Tom says, "was made *for* me by heart failure." He drew up a list of countries he wants to visit that he couldn't while he was a senator because he didn't want to be away from his constituents: India, South Africa, all of Latin America. He's become a professor at Occidental College, where he teaches the history of social movements: "who starts them, how does that spirit get awakened, and how do they move from the margins into the mainstream?"

He still campaigns for other people running for office. "I care intensely about the elections," he says, "but let somebody else break his heart about them."

Like many who've survived a catastrophic illness, he feels the time ahead is a bonus. "I'm glad I have some years when I can sort of wrap up my life, instead of being abruptly put on a stretcher and carried away drooling." He laughs—gallows humor. "I don't think there's any greater satisfaction while you wait for the boxcar than experiencing wisdom about your life and times, and being able to write or just talk about it."

I ask if he ever feels he hasn't accomplished as much as he'd hoped. He's silent. "Yeah." He breaks into a smile. "But I'm sixty-four, I'm still alive, I have a great family, and I'm free to do almost anything I want. What kind of weird little elf of ambition is trying to make me unhappy by saying: You could have accomplished more? I swat it!"

We laugh. Tom has two children from his marriage to Jane Fonda, two grandchildren, and when he was sixty, he and his wife, actress Barbara Williams, adopted a biracial baby, partly because Barbara hadn't had a child and was unstoppable in her desire to raise one. I ask Tom, "Is it different being a father at this age?"

"I'm a more experienced father, and I love kids," he says. "But if I was four, would I want a twenty-four-year-old dad or a sixty-four-year-old dad? You can evaluate the pros and cons for yourself."

The framework for the years ahead is clear to him. "I want to read, write, and mentor." He takes a breath. "But not a day goes by when I don't have conflict about it."

I tell him there's a wave of people who'll be forced to make a similar transition. Most major law firms have a mandatory retirement age of sixty-five, no exceptions. "There's going to be a mass of type-A, smart, ambitious, workaholic people suddenly cut loose. What will they do?"

Tom smiles. "This could be interesting. A lot of men will go into deep depression and that's dangerous. But on the bright side, because we're so numerous and healthy, we could revive our social activism and give the system hell."

What about the people yelling at us, "Get off the stage!"

Tom cracks up. "I used to think it's time for us to do that, but I'm re-vising my view here. I think the last chapter could be our finest."

I like this view. It hasn't happened before—revolutions are generally made by the young—but we've rewritten other rules. "We'll need lead-ership to energize people. . . ."

"We have voting power," Tom says, "economic power, and we have ideals that were compromised by a thirty-year run in the system. Now we have another twenty or thirty to restore those ideals and stand for something we're proud of."

He pauses. "I hope!"

When I repeat Tom's assertion that we could "give the system hell" to Danny Goldberg, who was then CEO of Air America Radio, Danny says, "Tom is a saint. He never gives up. He has money, he doesn't have money, he has a government office, he doesn't have an office, he's in the zeitgeist, he's out of the zeitgeist, but wherever he is, he's relentless and fearless."

I agree that Tom is a hellacious leader, but he did stop running for office. When he speaks about the need to "put it down—put your career drives down," I flinch; I can't accept this. I'm drawn to the example of judges, scientists, businessmen, and artists who make significant contributions in their sixties, seventies, and later. How would I put down the drive I feel in my very spine to excel and play the game at high levels? Maybe I could garden and tutor children for a few months, but thirty years?

Money, Honey

Then there's the issue of money. Every month or so, I huddle with my financial consultant and do the numbers. We calculate what will happen if I take my retirement pension early. If I sell my house and move down, how many years could I go without earning? He assures me that if I downsize the house and don't spend more than I currently spend, I'll be okay, but I have trouble believing him.

Destitution, writes Anne Lamott, "has been the most historically consistent nightmare of our species." Even affluent people are frightened of sinking into the gutter. A friend who's a psychologist suggests a way to deal with this: Spend two hours imagining yourself a bag lady or bum. Picture yourself in the street. When I try this, I realize I could call my sister or a friend and they would take me in.

The people I'm writing about are never—I repeat, never—going to end up destitute, though many fear it. Some will need to keep earning as long as they can; some have the privilege of not having to worry about money; and some are teetering at a point where if the roof collapses or they're diagnosed with cancer, they have no insurance or savings to draw on. But they have family, friends, people to call, and they won't be out on the street.

Donald Washington, who's in the latter group, came close. I knew Donald at the University of California at Berkeley, where he was a witty and charming screwup who could pull A's if he wanted but nearly flunked out. After graduating, he shocked his friends by enlisting in the army and going to Vietnam. He said he wanted to test himself, but we thought he was walking a tightrope, daring fate to let him fall. After his army tour he settled in New York and started tending bar at Malachy's, one of the first singles bars. Don made the customers laugh and feel welcome, and when he changed bars, which he frequently did, many went with him.

His dream was to open his own place, and he was constantly refining the concept, enrolling partners, and scouting locations, but he could never quite pull it off. He raised a daughter by himself before it was fashionable, and between jobs he would pursue different ventures— getting a real estate license, starting a microbrewery—but he'd always end up back behind the bar. When he was fifty-five, the saloon where he was working was taken over by a chain, and Don quit. "They were looking over my shoulder, measuring what I poured." For the first time, he found it hard to land another job, and then, in rapid fire, his father died of a stroke, his girlfriend Kristen died of melanoma, and his loft was converted to a co-op, which he couldn't afford to buy. He packed his things in the Chevy convertible he'd owned for twenty years and drove to Miami, where his daughter was living and had offered him a room. When the Chevy broke down, Don abandoned it and started riding the bus, which is what he was doing when I met him in Florida. "I'm usually the only guy like me on the bus," he says. "It's all domestic workers and the elderly, but hey, it's okay. I've downsized my life. I'm working part-time, my dad left me a little dough, and I'm gonna save up to get my own place."

When I see Don standing outside A Fish Called Avalon, the restaurant in South Beach, I'm surprised at how unchanged he looks: tall and lanky, with blond hair going gray, wearing his uniform of 501 jeans, a T-shirt, and basketball shoes. "We're the new old," he says. "We keep on truckin'." He describes the Job-like period he's been through: "I took hit after hit. My biggest fear was homelessness. I had no cushion at all, because I'd lived from job to job. I felt humiliated; at fifty-five, I've got to ask people for money, for help."

A friend dragged Donald to a meeting of Debtors Anonymous. "I didn't want to sit in a room with broke, bad-luck people," Don says, "but I identified with every person there. It turns out money is harder to talk about than drinking."

I didn't know, I say, that there's a 12-step program for people addicted to . . . what? Being in debt?

Don nods. "Living in financial chaos, surviving from paycheck to paycheck, expecting there'll be someone to bail you out." He acquired a sponsor and had to keep a log of every penny he earned and spent. "I was like a five-year-old, writing down numbers. Then I had a PRG—pressure relief group—where you go through all your numbers with your sponsor, look at where your money went, and come up with a plan to get out of debt."

He's just about there, he says when we finish dinner and walk along Ocean Drive, passing young men and women with tattoos snaking around their arms and flamboyant tropical clothes. "I could think, Jeez, I've peaked, I'm finished," Don says. "Or I could think: Anything can happen because you know what? Anything *has* happened." He says there's a plus side to hitting bottom: "It makes you fearless. You know you can survive."

Into the Narrows

Every culture has a legend about the descent to darkness, when you're sucked down or feel you've taken the wrong train—the one that says "Underworld." It's often called an initiation, because those periods when we're shattered and in pain are what transform us. As I spoke with dozens of people who'd managed to make it out of the pit, I realized that each of us goes through the stripping according to our character. Those given to gloom will see no hope and want to check out. Those who step in shit and look for the pony will view it as an "opportunity." A comedy writer, Robin Schiff, went through the fall with wild exaggeration. She told her life story to everyone, she says, "including the checkout guy at the market." My way, so far, was to kvetch and feel sorry for myself.

The people whose stories I've told—Carly Simon, Tom Hayden, and Don Washington—all experienced stripping and had a conversion, whether it was deciding to walk down the ladder gracefully, becoming fearless in tackling debts, or, in Tom's case, putting his career drives down. After listening to them, I saw that nobody seems to escape, no one has a dispensation. Your child gets cancer, you get cancer, your business fails, you lose your house or your marriage, and you're brought to your knees by what seems a landslide of failure.

Everyone must go through the narrows—the transition to a different phase of life—and if you don't do this voluntarily, the world or your body will force you to. Maybe your knees wear down and you have to stop running, or you find you can't drink as much and stay out as late without paying. You're compelled to shift gears, and you won't come out unchanged. Like the insect in the cocoon, you'll be turned to soup and reforged, but it won't be sudden and complete like the butterfly emerging with new wings.

I did not submit willingly, and when the landslide came, I could not see bottom. I had no idea when or if I would stop falling. Seeing that others had survived gave me a thread of hope but did not spare me from groping, wounded, through the blackness. I was still waking up each day with raw fear that bears down on the chest, cramps the stomach, and shuts off the capacity to feel pleasure. Each of the people I interviewed had found a unique route through the tunnel that enabled them to see daylight. I would have to find mine.

3

Sweet Surrender?

You wake up in a room that's filled with packing crates. In an hour, the oversize truck will lumber up to your house, the ramp will be lowered like a drawbridge, and men in uniforms will descend. By this time you've given away your orchids and ferns, put your cat in its carrier, and placed your keys on the empty kitchen counter. You've lived in this house for fifteen, twenty, or thirty-five years, and for many painful weeks all you've been doing is triage. With every lamp, every dish, every swim fin, you've had to decide: Does it go to your kids, to your new place, into storage, to Goodwill, or into the dumpster parked in front that you've filled with hundreds of pounds of papers? You've come across old letters and nude pictures of a boyfriend you haven't thought about in decades, which flooded you with memories and tears.

. . .

There are few times when you're free enough of commitments and tethers to move to a different state. The last for me had been in the seventies, when I'd left New York and settled in California. During the twenty years I was raising my kids, I would not uproot them from their schools and friends. I would not go off by myself on an assignment or trip that took more than two weeks, and I would not quit a profession that paid well. Suddenly I had none of those anchors.

My daughter, my youngest child, was preparing to leave for college, and although she rarely wanted to speak with me, we were connected. After she'd gone, I knew I couldn't sit by myself in the house with nothing to do. It had become clear that the strategy I'd always used successfully—initiative, doggedness, and hard work—was not producing results. Life was not yielding to "intelligence and effort," as F. Scott Fitzgerald wrote in "The Crack-Up." I heard people say this stage of life requires a different approach: listening, surrender, and letting things unfold. But I detested the notion of surrender; it felt like giving up and refusing to try anymore.

I started to think about moving, but where? I did not want to return to a place I'd already lived, which ruled out New York, Boston, and San Francisco. I considered Tucson, where a friend owns a spectacular ranch, but it seemed remote. Seattle was too rainy and gray. Hawaii, where my sister lives, seemed small and out of the loop.

I was sitting one night listening to music when the word *Boulder* came to me. I'd never been to Boulder, Colorado, and didn't know anyone there, but Nina Zimbelman, the spiritual teacher who'd told me my life as I knew it was over, had been urging me to pay attention to intuitive messages and "knowings."

"How can you tell if it's a knowing and not just a random thought?" I'd asked.

Nina said a knowing "seems to come at a deeper level, and if you lean into it, you'll see whether it flows." If you don't run into roadblocks, if you step into the current and it carries you, it's probably a knowing. She added, though, that acting on intuition doesn't always produce what you'd call a happy result. "Sometimes you need to have an experience that you wouldn't volunteer for."

I decided to "lean into" Boulder. I checked the Internet and found that it's nestled in the Rockies, less than an hour from a major airport, with three hundred days of sunshine a year and access to sports I love—skiing, hiking. It also has a thriving spiritual community with teachers from every tradition, a Buddhist university—Naropa—and the University of Colorado, which has a School of Journalism and Mass Communication.

I wrote to the dean of the school, sending my bio and several books and asking if he needed someone to teach literary journalism. Months later, I received an e-mail from a professor, Len Ackland, who said he'd be "willing" to meet with me.

This did not sound auspicious, but I flew to Boulder to check it out. Len was wearing jeans and hiking boots when we met in his office. He explained that many people want to teach in Boulder because it's such a desirable place to live. The only job he might be able to give me was as an adjunct instructor, teaching freshmen the basic course. "You can leave your résumé," he said, holding up a file bulging with résumés. But he said a reporter for the local paper, the *Daily Camera,* had taught the course before and done a good job. "She's ahead of you."

I thought: I've written for *The New York Times* and the *L.A. Times, Harper's, Esquire,* and *Rolling Stone,* covered presidential elections, and reported from overseas, and I have to take a number behind the reporter for the *Daily Camera*? But this was the way my life had been going.

The books I'd sent were sitting on Len's desk. "If you're not going to read these, I'll take them back," I said.

"My wife might want to read them," he said.

I scooped them up and turned for the door.

"Wait," he said. "There's a woman who teaches critical writing, Jan Whitt. Maybe she can figure out some way we could use you."

He led me down the hall and introduced me, but Jan, a stylish blonde, said brusquely, "Sorry, I can't talk now. I'm late to meet students." As she swept past me she said, "I have office hours tomorrow at nine. If you come right at nine, maybe I can see you for a few minutes."

This certainly was not "flowing," but what the hell. I held out the books. "I know you won't be able to read these, but you can look at the jacket copy and see what I do—"

"No! No! I don't have time for that. . . ."

Her eyes were flicking from the books to my face, and then she stopped. "Oh, my God. Are you . . . *that* Sara Davidson?"

"I presume so."

She ushered me back into her office. "Forget the students. I teach you in my classes. I feel like William Faulkner just dropped into my office and I didn't recognize him. We have to find a way to bring you here."

In five minutes, I'd gone from being a piece of shit who has to take a number behind the *Daily Camera* to William Faulkner.

Jan introduced me to the associate dean, Meg Moritz, who arranged for me to come to the school as a "Hearst Professional in Residence." This gave me a date and a reason—other than intuition—to arrive in Boulder, and from that point, things did flow.

Jan drove me around town, and there was one street I immediately wanted to live on—Mapleton Avenue—in a historic district with cozy Victorian houses, a grassy center divider, and four rows of maple trees leading up to a canyon with a wealth of hiking trails. "You and everybody else," Jan said. "It's the most desirable street in Boulder, and one of the most pricey." When I checked the listings, though, I immediately found a furnished house to lease on Mapleton at a reasonable rent. It was owned by a woman painter, Henrietta Mueller, who'd moved to a retirement community but couldn't bear to give up the house. She'd built a second-floor studio with twenty windows where I could write, looking out at the Flatiron Range. People I met in Boulder were incredulous at my luck. It was perfect.

Boulder, I learned quickly, takes political, environmental, and spiritual correctness to extremes. I've been a seeker for years, eager to travel any road if it might lead to wisdom but also quick to find the flaws, humor, and absurdities in what's being claimed. I've studied Judaism, Christianity, Hinduism, and Buddhism and gleaned much of value but never been able to swallow the dogma. I tend to shrink from people who stare at crystals and channel entities or who won't use a clothes dryer because of its impact on the environment.

I felt awkward and amused at first, trying to learn the behavior code in Boulder. In many houses, you're expected to leave your shoes at the door. When I walk into a restaurant, the Kitchen, they place a green bottle on the table with a card: "This is our house water—Eldorado Springs. The Kitchen is 100% wind-powered and our used oils are recycled for bio-diesel." At a fast-food "burrito joint," a sign states that all the meat is organic—"another step along our *Food with Integrity* journey."

Everyone's on a journey and no one has problems, they have "issues." "Relationship issues." "Health issues." When a new friend, Donna Zerner, takes me to the Arkansas River for a raft trip, she says, "I told the outfitter about our diet."

"What about our diet?" I ask.

"We don't eat wheat, dairy, meat, corn, or sugar."

"I eat all that! What made you assume . . . ?"

Donna looks shocked. "Everyone I know eats this way."

I'm a heathen here.

When I call a gardening service, they offer a "free astrology reading for new clients." When I go to an internist whom many have recommended, he has green tea in the waiting room, and his new patient questionnaire asks: "What inner barriers might you have to following a program for health?"

I've never liked dogs and Boulder is a dog town. People seem to have two or three, and they're not well trained. On the street you hear shouts of "Heel!" or "Come back here!" and the dogs don't do either. The Humane Society consistently runs short of dogs for adoption and has to fly them in from Wyoming and New Mexico. The city council determined that you're not the owner of your dog, you're its guardian, and if it harasses a prairie dog by chasing it, you'll be fined $1,000.

A café downtown, Colorado Canines, serves espresso for humans and "homestyle entrées and smoothies" for dogs. There's a do-it-yourself dog wash and a flyer advertising camping and rafting adventure trips "for Dogs and their people," with a picture of a dog roasting a marshmallow on a stick held between its teeth.

In Los Angeles I was considered a jock, but in Colorado I'm a wimp. I see people running in the mountains during a blizzard wearing shorts. My next-door neighbor says, as he wheels out his bike in freezing rain, "We're frontierspeople. We don't care what the weather is, we go." I observe there's a dress code: a North Face fleece jacket, black warm-up pants, and hiking boots—the equivalent of Prada and Manolo Blahnik in Manhattan.

I'm entranced, though, by the muscular presence of the mountains, the vast open sky, and the climate. One day it snows, but the next day the sun is so strong that I go native—wearing nothing more than a fleece shirt in January. In the fall, the maples turn red and gold, and the aspens! The color is like no yellow I've seen—so intense that the trees seem to give off light. As I walk up Sunshine Canyon, there are ribbons of quaking gold among the evergreens and I have to stop and take in a breath.

What surprises me is how quickly I meet people I like, and after a few months, I have more friends than I had in Los Angeles after twenty years. One of the first I met was Joan Borysenko, who did pioneering research at Harvard Medical School on mind-body interactions and writes books like *Inner Peace for Busy Women*. A mutual friend had given me her number, but I phoned four times before she returned the call (she was busy) and said she could meet me briefly between a haircut and a doctor's visit. She walked into the house on Mapleton Avenue, sat down at the table, and after ten minutes put her hand on my arm and said, "We're obviously going to be friends for life."

She invited me to her house in Gold Hill for dinner—the first of many where we talked and laughed until it was too late and I was too wasted to drive down the mountain so I slept in the guest room. I came to call them "My Dinners with Joan." People describe her as "drop-dead beautiful," with flawless skin and expressive blue eyes animated by playfulness and warmth. She loves to be in love and seems not to have gone five minutes without a husband. When we met she'd just divorced her third. After spending time with her I felt—as most do—appreciated and nourished.

We were having breakfast one morning at the Dushanbe Tea House, which was built and shipped to Boulder, board by board, from Tajikistan, when I told her I was about to turn sixty and not happy about it. Not only was sixty unequivocally old, but what was there to look forward to? The run-up to seventy, eighty, loss, deterioration, and death?

"We need to do a ritual for you," Joan said.

I don't think so.

"We'll make you feel better about what's coming. You'll have escorts."

Right. I laughed, but as days passed I warmed to the idea. We invited five other women I'd met in Boulder and my sister, Terry, who agreed to fly in from Hawaii. The cavalry was coming. But what would we do at this ritual? Joan said she would organize the event, and it must be a surprise. I thought about inviting men, but Joan nixed that. "Men would *not* be into this." In fact, when I told my friend Dan Wakefield what we were up to, he howled with laughter.

· · ·

It's snowing when I walk into the home of Chris Hibbard, a psychologist who lives with her husband near Wonderland Lake. The seven women waiting for me tie a blindfold over my eyes and walk me down a staircase. I wasn't expecting a blindfold. What are they going to do? Undress me? Nah, they wouldn't do that.

"Take off your shirt," Joan says. "We're going to dress you." I slip off my sweater—not easy with the blindfold—and they pull a garment over my head and tie something around my shoulders. They're fiddling with my hair and ears, and when they lead me back upstairs, music comes on: the Motown wall of sound and Diana Ross and the Supremes singing "You Can't Hurry Love."

They pull off the blindfold, my sister drapes a lei around my neck and holds up a mirror: I'm wearing a long blue formal gown, a royal purple velvet cape, diamond earrings, and a child's toy crown. Everyone is laughing. "You look gorgeous. You look regal." They've dressed me as a queen, like Elizabeth with a velvet cape and attendants who bow and call her "Your Majesty." I'm embarrassed and feel like a goofball. My athletic socks don't match the gown, so Chris slips them off and brings out high-heeled black slippers.

We sit around a coffee table on which there are roses, candles, sacred objects, and profane gifts like red thong panties. Joan begins by welcoming everyone and turns to me. "You've already lived a full life." She describes the stages: being a baby, a little girl with a lunch box going to school, having your first crush, your first French kiss, going to college, starting out as a cub reporter, achieving success, suffering setbacks, getting married, having children, and going through the cycle again with them. Tears roll down my face. I see the train of my life chugging by: I'm in the hospital giving birth, I'm holding my son's tiny hand as we wade into the ocean, and then he's waving to me as he drives away to college.

"Now it's time to let go of all that," Joan says. "Time to become empty." She asks me to describe "where you are in your life and what you'd like from this gathering."

I look around. I barely know some of these women, and if I'm to respond truthfully, I must say what I've told only my most intimate friends: I can't write. Every time I come up with an idea for a book, my agent shoots it down: "It won't sell." I try to pitch a series of magazine articles, start a newspaper column, make a pilot for a radio show, and one by one every project gets rejected.

"Maybe you're supposed to do something else," Chris says.

"I've thought about that—starting a new career, but what? Something in the health field, working with kids? Nothing calls me."

Joan, who's a few years younger, says, "I'm watching you and it frightens me because I can identify. I had great success with everything I touched when I was younger. Now it's harder to get work and there are more setbacks."

I'm aware, I tell Joan, "as I'm sure you are, that these problems would be a gift—cake and ice cream—to people who face grinding poverty, hunger, dead-end jobs, serious illness and no access to medical care. My health is great and I've never felt so strong."

"As lives go, you got a pretty good one," my sister says.

"I agree."

Tirzah Firestone, a rabbi who has the charisma of a rock star, tells me, "The image I'm seeing is of a field that's being plowed so it will be fertile. But it's winter and . . ." She raises her palms. "Nothing is growing above the ground. You need to be patient, accept that this is a fallow time, and in the right season, something important will arise."

She stands, saying she has to leave early to wash the body of a woman, a musician, who just died of breast cancer at thirty-seven. The contrast between my birthday and the funeral of a thirty-seven-year-old is chastening.

Before leaving, Tirzah opens the oven and takes out a challah she prepared in the morning and baked at Chris's house—a bread so rich with eggs and honey it tastes like cake, filling the house with its aroma. We sit down to a potluck feast: butternut squash soup, brisket and mashed potatoes, guacamole, pizza with goat cheese and sun-dried tomatoes, fresh pineapple from Hawaii, and dark chocolate almonds. We eat like heathens and someone puts on Mick Jagger: "I can't get no satisfaction . . ."

After dinner, we sit on the floor before the fireplace. Leslie Morgan, a surgeon who studies belly dancing, tells me to close my eyes. "Do you want to ask for help with anything?"

I think a moment. "I'd like help on the solitary path I'm cutting."

"Can you feel the angels in the room?"

"No." I doubt that there are angels flying about, and we're entering the fringe zone now, and yet I feel enfolded in warmth. I'm struck by the care and thoughtfulness that everyone contributed to this day: Terry picking flowers in Honolulu to make a lei, Tirzah baking challah, Chris kicking her husband upstairs so we could take over her house, Joan shopping and preparing since dawn. The week before, Joan had sent me an e-mail suggesting I complete these sentences:

1. I realize that life is both precious and short and that I have lived the majority of my years. When the angel of death comes to my door, I will be ready to go because . . .

2. The thing I will miss the most when life is over is . . .

3. In the years to come, I will be grateful for . . .

When I'd read the first question, I'd thought: I'll be ready to go because . . . I've had love. Love was the answer to all the questions.

* * *

We end the evening with crafts, making beads for a necklace out of rose petals that Joan boiled and blended into a paste like clay. Chris brings out a chocolate cake and asks me to make a wish, but I'm wished out. It's time to ask, What does God, spirit, whatever name we assign to the force that weaves itself through the world, want from me?

"Good question," says Janet Quinn, a professor of nursing at the university. "Just surrender and you'll hear."

Surrender! The word I hate. I tell her I don't understand the distinction between surrender and capitulation. When I was hitting the wall in television, I went to a career coach who suggested, "It might be time to say, I lost the battle. Nobody wins every battle." But I can't do that.

Janet, who has blue eyes and a passion for horses that arrived late in life, says that's not what she understands by surrender. "I've been working with this, and what's come to me is that giving up makes you small. It's defeat, being vanquished, a victim, whereas surrender is an expansive state, something active and pulsing. And you do it every moment. You don't just surrender once and that's it." She throws out her arms as if running to meet a lover or embrace a child. "You open yourself to the unknown."

I stare at Janet; the snow has stopped falling on the blue spruce outside the window, and I know what she's saying is true. I think of the bronze statue by Cyrus E. Dallin, *Appeal to the Great Spirit*, which stands at the entrance to the Boston Museum of Fine Arts. It's an image that's been widely reproduced: An Indian sits on a horse bare chested, his head raised toward the sky and his arms extended with palms up— open, vulnerable. There's yielding and sublimity in his posture, and in this light, surrender is an act of courage, blind courage, opening yourself and calling: Whatever comes, I accept.

4

The Body Electric

Ah, but how can I learn to stop worrying and love the bomb—my aging body? Today I found gray in my eyebrows, and what are those . . . jowls? A friend used to say, when we were in our thirties, that there had to be an age—sixty, seventy, eighty?—when we could "give up and pig out." But I fear this is not to be. I weigh myself every day and try mostly in vain to eat smaller portions. My first husband used to say, "A thin girl is a happy girl," and that still holds for this reporter.

Whoopi Goldberg says she was shocked when she found that "my ass is bigger." She looked behind her and said, "What's that? I'm being stalked by my own ass."

What to do? Work out compulsively? Have your hair dyed and cut in the latest twenty-something style or go defiantly gray? If I start wearing a Wonderbra and have my eyelids done, will I feel embarrassed, as if I'm cheating, trying to deny what's happening, and failing to make the transition gracefully? Or is it natural, even admirable, to want to look as attractive as you can for as long as you can?

In the spring of 2004, I was given an assignment to explore physical aging with women who've been famous for their bodies. I'd managed to resurrect my magazine writing career, although it still felt tenuous since only a few were giving me work. I was intrigued when *O: The Oprah Magazine,* asked me to interview actresses and supermodels who'd owned "the *it* body" twenty or thirty years ago: Cheryl Tiegs, Christie Brinkley, Farrah Fawcett, Iman, Jane Fonda, Jayne Kennedy, and Raquel Welch. These women had lived by their looks, and the loss of their near perfect youthful figures must have felt catastrophic—like me not being able to write. How did they adapt? Had they learned, as Carly Simon's mother did, to see beauty in a withered hand? Had Jane Fonda—always on the edge—found a way to accept her aging thighs, and if so, could she please tell me how?

The Vagina Army

I'm sitting with Cheryl Tiegs in the living room of the estate in California where she lives with her son and two Labradors, Beluga and Truffle. At fifty-seven, she still has the tall, big-breasted, blond freshness that landed her on the cover of the *Sports Illustrated* swimsuit issue three times and on the cover of *Time* in 1978 as "the All-American Model." Thousands of pubescent boys learned about love staring at a poster on their bedroom wall of Cheryl in a shocking pink bikini.

After talking on the phone for the *O* interview, Cheryl invited me to her home. She speaks, at first, as if she's programmed for positive thinking. Everything is "easy" or "a pleasure." Her mantra is, "Do something about it." She says there are days "I feel beautiful and days I don't, and when I don't, I do something about it."

Like what? I ask.

"Go out and exercise. It gets the endorphins going and brings a glow to the skin." She adds with a laugh, "I come from a land of Minnesota farmers. This body does not come about totally naturally. It wants to hold weight."

She's devised a regimen: three sessions of yoga, two of cardio or weight training every week, and not eating bread, pasta, potatoes, dairy, or sweets. Ever.

Isn't it onerous having to live like that? I ask.

"It's a pleasure. It's the easiest thing," she says.

"It's not so easy or we wouldn't be having an epidemic of obesity."

Cheryl says it's easy if you're motivated. She likes to wear short skirts and tight jeans. She recently posed for the swimsuit reunion issue of *Sports Illustrated*, which Christie Brinkley, at fifty, had found nerve-racking. For Cheryl it was "totally easy. Putting on a bathing suit doesn't scare me."

"You're a better woman than I."

She gives me an appraising look. "Are you in shape?"

"I think so. I hike, I ski with the masters race team, and I can ski as fast as my twenty-one-year-old son."

"Well, you are, then," Cheryl says.

"I won't wear a bathing suit."

"Why not?"

Where to start? Varicose veins . . .

"You can get those zapped," Cheryl says.

"No, no . . ."

"Yes, you can."

I shake my head. "It wouldn't help."

"I had a friend, an actress, and she *did something about it.* She went to a vein doctor. You should go before it gets out of control."

"You don't understand. It *is* out of control." I tell her I went to a doctor twenty years ago who injected the veins and made them disappear, but they came back and multiplied.

"I'm so sorry," she says. In that case, "just wear a sarong and put the accent on your breasts."

Well, the breasts . . .

Cheryl concedes that even hers are "not as firm as they used to be. There's nothing you can do about that. So let's worry about the things we can do something about."

"Such as . . . ?"

"Exercise, diet, and emotional happiness."

Okay. What can we do about emotional happiness? I ask.

"Dance. Have sex."

"I remember sex."

"Sex is fun, and it makes you feel beautiful," she says.

Cheryl has been married four times, starting at twenty. Her first husband was fifteen years older than she, but her recent relationships—as with many of us—have been with younger men. "I'm sincerely and honestly grateful for every marriage I've had," she says.

"You are?"

She wrinkles her forehead. "Except the last one. I'm having a hard time wrapping my mind around being grateful for that."

Before I can pursue this further, she asks if I'd like to have lunch. I follow her to the kitchen, where a woman from the Philippines dishes out stir-fried vegetables, and we carry our plates on wooden trays to the dining table. Cheryl says she feels chilly, although it's May, and wears a turquoise sweater, jeans, a diamond pendant in the shape of a C, and high-heeled sandals that make her at least six feet one. The house is formal and baronial, with large, dark-wood furniture, monogrammed linen towels in the powder room, and a portrait of Cheryl by Andy Warhol. The only casual note is a set of drums in the living room that belongs to her twelve-year-old son, whom she had with her third husband, Tony Peck.

I ask about her fourth husband—the one she's not grateful for—a high-profile yoga instructor, Rod Stryker, who'd changed his name from Nimrod Gross.

Cheryl's face tenses for the first time. "It's complicated. I don't even consider that one a marriage because he didn't know what marriage was all about."

Had he been married before?

She shakes her head no.

"That's a warning. . . ."

"Hello! I had thought, Oh great, no baggage, no ex-wife and kids. Wrong!" She says Stryker was kind and sweet at the beginning and became the "coldest man I've ever known. There'd be times in this house when we wouldn't speak for three days. If we passed in the hall, we were not allowed to touch."

This sounds like an affair I had with a vaunted Buddhist teacher, I tell her, whom we'll call Sam. "He was brilliant and handsome, people came from all over the country to study with him, and he was the most depressed man I've known. He wouldn't let me use the word *love*—it made him squirm."

"I know that one," Cheryl says. "*Spiritual* does not necessarily mean stable or happy."

"Sam had irritable bowel syndrome, and every meal was like a gauntlet: Would he get through the food without doubling up in pain? Sex could also be followed by pain. He knew there were emotional causes but said he had no insight into what they could be. And he's teaching others to attain self-knowledge!"

"Yes, I've been there," Cheryl says. "It's a nightmare."

We're into it now, eating our vegetables with chopsticks and trashing the gurus.

Cheryl says she'd listen to her ex-husband's words in class and believe he meant them. "You'd think someone who teaches about love, kindness, and having an open heart would *be* kind and loving and openhearted."

"They're teaching what they need to learn," I say. "A friend who was a monk for ten years told me: 'Never fuck a spiritual teacher.' Which I ignored. He said many of the teachers he knows commit themselves to that life because they can't handle intimacy."

"I think that's true, but it shocked me." Cheryl says the man she's involved with now, Dan Buettner, is the opposite—warm and open. He's in his forties, holds world records in long-distance cycling, and is writing a book on longevity. Cheryl met him when he was dating a friend of hers who no longer speaks to her. "He adores me, laughs with me. As far as I know, he can see no wrong in me."

"This is the kind of guy you want. . . ."

"Hello! I am so happy," she says, and we're back to the woman who finds everything "easy." She's not troubled about approaching sixty. "I know my life is going to be wonderful because my life has *been* wonderful all these years." She admits that it takes more maintenance to look good. "We're fortunate because there are vitamins and topical creams you can use that make you less wrinkled."

"That may be," I say, "but it's time to face the fact that someday— and it'll come soon—we'll have wrinkles. . . ."

"I'm not sure I agree," Cheryl says. She has a line of cosmetics, Ageless Woman, that includes Softox (now called Deep Wrinkle Relaxer). "It's the answer to Botox. If you use it twice a day for a month, you can reduce the appearance of wrinkles. I'll give you a sample."

"But creams or no, we're going to look different. Your animals grow older, dogs get gray hair."

Cheryl considers this. "They're not using Softox."

• • •

I was still laughing at the image of the dogs using Softox when I drove out the gates of Cheryl's home. I tried using Softox on a wrinkle by my eyebrow but gave up after a week. Who wants to be rubbing cream twice a day into every line and wrinkle, along with flossing teeth and stimulating gums and applying three different moisturizers to the eyes, face, and hands?

The other stars I interviewed were attempting to stop picking and appreciate how well their bodies have carried them down the years. But there were surprises. Iman, the first African to become an international supermodel, was spotted when she was eighteen by Peter Beard, the photographer who'd been Cheryl Tiegs's second husband. Born in Somalia, Iman was an exotic sensation when she arrived in New York, where people described her as six feet tall, "half of which is neck." In fact, she's five feet nine and says, "I hated my neck. Women in Somalia are extraordinarily beautiful, and I felt I didn't measure up." She says no one else thought she did, either. In her high school, there were about four hundred boys and thirty-two girls. "For the prom, every girl had more than one date, but I didn't have a single date. My father actually paid my cousin to take me." At forty-eight, married to David Bowie, Iman says she can stand in front of the mirror and not "pick pick pick. I just say, *Aiiii!* and move on."

Raquel Welch, unlike Cheryl Tiegs, says, "It's a drag, I resent not being able to eat sweets and carbs and having to be so disciplined to stay in shape." I'd expected Raquel to have a vapid, bimbo voice, but she speaks with exaggeratedly good diction, as if she's a spokesperson for Revlon. Her body "made it possible for me to have a whole career," she says, "but it was a one-note appreciation."

She says that at sixty-three, it's a "losing battle" trying to keep the shape you had in your twenties. "You've got to kiss all that sweet good-bye." People still ask her to pose in a bikini, but she declines. "I should kill myself to get in shape so everyone can see whether I'm still hanging together pretty good? What's the point? I'm a mature woman, and I have so much more to offer. I never felt the body was my strongest suit."

What was? I ask.

"My dancing," she says. "Camille Paglia always said the reason I made such an impact was because of the way I moved."

Jane Fonda says she hated her body and "lived in my head" until her agent dragged her to see Eve Ensler perform *The Vagina Monologues.* Jane had been asked to do the play but read one page and said, "I don't think so. Hanoi Jane has enough problems."

Watching Eve's performance, Jane had one of those radical conversions that have been her pattern. She was a sex symbol in her twenties in *Barbarella,* then became a left-wing feminist who went to Hanoi during the Vietnam War, then was a workout guru, then gave up acting and became the wife of Ted Turner, and now she's marching for the vagina. "I have become a very involved member of the vagina army. Because the vagina is a metaphor for self-love, for owning one's power, which is one's body."

She says the most revolutionary act we can take "is to stand within our bodies and say, 'Here I am. Deal with it!' "

I ask, "Are you able to do that?"

She laughs. "I'm trying. It's not an easy process."

All the actresses and models are busy—making movies, pursuing business and charitable ventures—and seem happier and less nuts than at the height of their fame. They still have bodies you'd trade a lot for. None will admit she's had plastic surgery, but I assume that most of them have. It's the norm in the entertainment business, and it's becoming more the norm in the wider population as people find that they can keep their bodies fit with training but there's no effective exercise program for tightening the face. Every year, an increasing number—including men—are weighing the cost and risks of cosmetic surgery against the anticipated benefit.

The Kamer Lineage

Dr. Frank Kamer will not confirm or deny that he's worked on Barbra Streisand, Frank Sinatra, Robert Redford, Elizabeth Taylor, Madonna, Dolly Parton, or Jennifer Aniston—all of whom are rumored to have been patients. Dr. Kamer takes extreme steps to protect the privacy of clients, keeping their records under pseudonyms and consulting with them after hours in a private hotel suite. He will say, however, "I've operated on just about all the greats of Hollywood."

A balding man with thick black eyebrows, Dr. Kamer wears elegant jackets and speaks in a booming baritone. He pioneered and perfected the deep-plane face lift, which results in a look so natural that even on the big screen it's not apparent that surgery has been done. Instead of cutting and tightening the skin—which can create tension and make the face look stretched—Dr. Kamer works on the underlying muscles, cutting and lifting them and then draping the skin over them with no tension.

Every year he trains two young doctors in his technique who then become part of the Kamer lineage, which is bankable. "I've trained half my competition," Dr. Kamer says with a laugh.

A number of years ago, when my eyelids began to droop so that each one hooded half my eye, I walked, or I should say crept, into Dr. Kamer's office in Beverly Hills for a consultation. There's often a six-month waiting list for new patients, but I knew a friend of the doctor's who used her influence to move me up. I'd consulted other surgeons who were less expensive, but my friend said, "Why get hamburger when you can have filet mignon?" The beef analogy was unfortunate, but I took her point. This was my face, and a mistake would not be easy or even possible to repair.

I studied the interior of Dr. Kamer's office, with its beige linen walls and antique chairs. I would not engage a surgeon whose waiting room was garish or cluttered. I wanted to see evidence of his aesthetics, his sense of proportion and form, and Dr. Kamer's office was serene, classically beautiful, and understated.

I walked across the deep pile carpet, hoping to disappear into one of the blue suede chairs. . . .

"Sara!"

I turned and saw, on the cream silk couch, two women who'd been my classmates at L.A. High School.

"Isn't this fun?" one said. "In thirty years we've never bumped into each other. Now we meet at the plastic surgeon's office."

Fun indeed.

Three weeks later, after my eyelid surgery, a friend picked me up and drove me home. I fainted on the way to the bedroom, and when I came to I was nauseated from the anesthesia. My eyes turned black and blue, and my face became so swollen it looked like a pie pan. As I lay in bed with ice packs over my face, I thought, If I'd known it would be this bad I never would have done it.

My daughter refused to come into my room. When we passed in the hall she covered her eyes. "I have no respect for you," she said. "I don't want my friends to know you did this. I'm ashamed. I want a mother who has wrinkles and is wise, not someone trying to look young with a plastic head." She burst into tears.

This was the period when my daughter was angry and ashamed of everything I did or said, including "Good morning." But her words stung and I couldn't sleep that night. How could I explain my feelings to my daughter, when her beauty was just coming on, like the flower opening, and whenever I saw her I took in my breath because she looked so fresh and effortlessly lovely? I was at the point where the rose is beginning to wilt, and I wanted to enjoy—for just a time longer—having my eyes fully visible. Four weeks later, when the pain and bruises had receded, I felt happy when I caught sight of myself in a mirror. I asked an actor I'd known for twenty years, "Do you see anything different about my face?" He drew back, then looked closer, puzzled, studying me from several angles. At length he said, "Your hair?"

    • • •

When I began working on *Leap!,* I went back to Dr. Kamer and asked if I could watch him perform a face lift. I wanted to see the procedure from the surgeon's view, so I could understand the mechanics, the risk and repercussions.

A face lift with Dr. Kamer may cost $20,000, and although he's never lost a patient, death is a possible side effect with all plastic surgery. Every few years a well-known person dies during a procedure, as did Olivia Goldsmith, author of the *First Wives Club,* and people cluck: She died for a better chin? Dr. Kamer says, "People shouldn't cluck, it could happen to any of us." He knows the surgeon and anesthesiologist who worked on Goldsmith and says they're highly respected clinicians.

No accurate statistics are kept of fatalities resulting from cosmetic surgery. A prominent New York surgeon, Darrick Antell, MD, tells patients that the incidence is "extraordinarily low, but obviously not zero." Anesthesia seems to be a greater risk than surgery: The patient may stop breathing, have a cardiac incident or allergic reaction to the medication. Some deaths result from patients withholding information. Dr. John Joseph, who trained with Dr. Kamer, says that one of his male patients went into heart arrhythmia on the table. Dr. Joseph called the paramedics, and the patient was rushed to the Cedars-Sinai cardiac care center. When he recovered, he told Dr. Joseph he'd had a heart condition for seven years. "I didn't tell you because I knew you wouldn't operate on me."

Dr. Joseph said, "Next time you want to kill yourself, go buy a gun. Don't involve me."

Dr. Kamer had a patient go into tachycardia because she'd taken cocaine. "People are stupid. They think cosmetic surgery is like going to the beauty parlor." Dr. Kamer says he turns down 50 percent of the people who come for consultations because "they're ill, they're crazy, or they don't need it. People come in with advanced cancer and tell me, 'I want to look good in my casket.' "

How do you judge whether people need it? I ask.

"They don't need it when I say they don't need it," Dr. Kamer says.

He declined my request to observe a face lift, so I approached Dr. Joseph, who'd operated on a woman I knew with admirable results—her face looked soft and natural. Dr. Joseph had a patient scheduled who was willing to let me watch, but he warned me, "If people saw a videotape of this surgery, they'd never have it done."

His staff call him Dr. J. He's forty-nine, short and trim, with brown eyes and thinning hair. "I consider myself bald," he says. "In the seventies I had a ponytail." His face is round and smooth—not a wrinkle— because he's tried on himself most of the procedures he does: Botox, liposuction, collagen. When he's not operating, his foot taps the floor continually, "but when I walk into the OR, it stops."

I arrive at his office in Beverly Hills at eight A.M. and find him wearing green scrubs, clogs, a head lamp, and magnifying eyeglasses. He introduces me to the patient, whom we'll call Rosalie, a pharmaceutical saleswoman who's fifty-five. She turns her head to look at me from the table and says, "I've been working up to this for ten years." She chose Dr. Joseph because he'd operated on a friend of hers and "she looked fantastic afterward," Rosalie says. "I kept putting it off for myself, but last month I was at a convention, and after working for twelve hours straight, I saw myself in the mirror under bright light. My God! That was it! I called Dr. Joseph the next morning and set the date."

Dr. Joseph draws lines on her face with purple marker to guide him as Jackie Lustig, the nurse anesthetist he's worked with for sixteen years, starts an IV. Dr. Joseph tells Rosalie, "You'll be sleeping like you're in your bed at home." Instead of general anesthesia, Dr. Joseph uses a combination of IV sedatives and local anesthetic so the patient is breathing on her own. The advantage, he says, is that "you're not inducing a coma. The anesthetic is short-acting, and you can see the face better because you don't have a tube down her throat." While Jackie is an RN who's licensed to administer anesthesia, some plastic surgeons will use only MDs, who charge higher fees. Dr. Joseph says he trusts Jackie, and "if you look at national morbidity and mortality rates, comparing MD anesthesiologists with nurse anesthetists, there's no statistical difference. It comes down to the individual. I know MDs I would never let put me to sleep. Jackie has put my mother to sleep."

While Rosalie is being moved to the operating room, Dr. Joseph tells me face lifts are "the most stressful thing I do. There's more at risk and more variables to deal with." The night before, he goes over the case and creates a plan, but "you want to be flexible enough to change it." His plan with Rosalie is to laser the wrinkled skin below her eyelids so it will grow back fresh. Then he'll suction fat from her jowls and tighten the muscles in her neck and face.

He says you don't need to be an artist to do cosmetic surgery. "If I try to draw or sculpt, it won't be pretty. You need a good eye—a sense of aesthetics—good hands, and good judgment." He says he learned from Dr. Kamer that it's better to do less than more. "If you do less and it's not enough, you can fix that. It's like cooking a steak—if it's too rare, you can throw it back on the fire."

Again, the beef analogy.

Jackie, who's slender with curly dark hair and an intense, watchful expression, says to the patient: "Can you hear me? Sweetie, can you hear me?"

Rosalie has her eyes closed and does not respond. Dr. Joseph begins numbing her face, using an extraordinarily long needle that's used for epidurals and spinal taps.

"This isn't the surgery, Rosalie, this is him injecting medicine to numb things up," Jackie says. "Everything is going beautifully. You're a great patient."

Dr. Joseph slides the needle into her cheek and moves it around, up toward the eye and down to the chin. It's the only part of the surgery I can barely stand to watch—the needle wiggling around like a snake under her skin. Dr. Joseph explains to me, "I'm infiltrating local anesthetic, just like the dentist. We numb everything. Otherwise she'd have to be under a general."

From speakers on the wall, Gato Barbieri is playing jazz saxophone.

Dr. Joseph starts to laser the skin under Rosalie's eyes, and Jackie switches off the oxygen flowing to the patient's nose. Smoke rises from Rosalie's skin, and there's a smell like charred meat.

What's that smoke? I ask.

"Burning skin," Dr. Joseph says. The area he's lasering is turning ash white. "We switch off the oxygen and don't have drapes in the room because they might create a pocket of gas that could explode. It's happened."

To you? I ask.

"Not even close."

He finishes lasering, and Jackie turns the oxygen back on.

"Jackie and I have been together sixteen years; it's like we're married," he says. "We can read each other's thoughts. I can tell what she's feeling by her breathing."

Jackie says, "If I'm anxious, he'll turn around and say, 'Jackie, are you happy?' Even my husband can't do that."

Dr. Joseph makes two tiny holes under Rosalie's chin, "so I can get at the jowls." With a narrow syringe, he extracts a small amount of fat—yellow like chicken fat. "That's all I'm gonna do. See—the skin is flat now." One side of Rosalie's face is flat while the other has a slight bulge at the bottom. The skin under her eyes is now becoming an angry red.

The surgical nurse hands Dr. Joseph a towel, thin like a tea towel, and he sews it to Rosalie's scalp to "keep her hair out of the way. In the olden days they used to shave your head for a face lift. Today you don't do that . . . patients wouldn't let you. . . ."

"Not in Beverly Hills," Jackie says.

He prepares to make the incision, which will be a foot and a half long starting at the temple in the hair, winding down and around the ear to the back of the head. Once the incision is made, he starts lifting the skin up from the underlying muscles; it reminds me of pulling the skin off a chicken breast before cooking it. He inserts his finger and pushes, separating the skin until he has a continuous flap or pocket "so I can take my hand and swoop it all the way from the back of the head to the temple." He likes using his finger because "it's the safest and best instrument a surgeon has. You get the most tactile feedback. An instrument will cut through anything, right or wrong, but with the finger I can tell, if I'm pushing too hard, that it's not the right place. If I push with the right amount of pressure and it separates—I *know* I'm in the right place."

I see thin yellow threads running between the muscle and skin. What are they? I ask.

"Blood vessels," Dr. Joseph says. "The hairiest part comes next." He has to work his way around the nerves that control facial movements, down to the SMAS (superficial musculoaponeurotic system)—the tissue encasing the muscle. Using a needle, he slides a thread through the tough tissue of the SMAS and tugs on the thread, which pulls up and tightens the jaw, as if he's lifting the string on a marionette's jaw. "Some people say you only need to lift the skin," he says. "One high-profile surgeon in Santa Monica gets fine results with that technique." But Dr. Kamer, he says, is more aggressive, lifting the muscles themselves because he believes that will produce a more long-lasting result. Dr. Joseph has tried both and takes the middle way—lifting the SMAS.

For decades, plastic surgeons have been arguing about which technique gives the best results. It's problematic to measure the effects of any technique because there's no control subject, and ultimately it's a personal aesthetic call: What looks best? In 1995, a test was done by four surgeons in the American Society of Aesthetic Plastic Surgeons (ASAPS): Sam Hamra, of Dallas; Dan Baker, of New York; John Owsley, of San

Francisco; and Oscar Ramirez, of Baltimore. They operated on two sets of identical twins at the same time in the same facility in San Francisco. Each surgeon had a different philosophy and technique, and the twins were the closest they could come to a controlled experiment. After six years, independent observers could not detect any differences in the results. No one procedure emerged as clearly superior to the others. Malcolm D. Paul, who was president of ASAPS, said, "All results were lasting . . . and the patients in the study were happy."

The key question that remains is how deep to go. Dr. Antell did his own study on identical twins, operating on eight sets using the skin-only technique on one twin and "some variation of the SMAS technique on the other," he says. This led him to conclude that it's best to do the minimal surgery. "The risk of complications and problems, generally speaking, increases the deeper you go."

What the surgeons agree on is that face lifts are improving, and no matter which technique is used, Dr. Antell asserts, if it's done well, "it will last forever. You'll continue to age, but you'll always look ten years younger than if you hadn't had the procedure."

There are numerous cases, though, where people come out looking ghoulish—as if their skin is pulled too tight—regardless of which technique is used. Dr. Joseph believes the success of cosmetic surgery rests on the talent of the doctor, not the technique. "It's the Indian, not the arrow."

* * * *

Before Dr. Joseph completes his work on the SMAS, he asks Jackie and his two nurses, "Is that enough, what do you guys think?"

"I think it's enough," Jackie says.

Dr. Joseph tells me, "This is where the art comes in. Pulling at the right angle, knowing when to stop."

"He makes it look easy," Jackie says.

Rosalie speaks up suddenly. "Am I gonna look beautiful?"

"Yes," Jackie says. "You're doing great."

"Is Dr. Joseph happy?" Rosalie asks.

"Very happy," Dr. Joseph answers, and to Jackie, "On that note, dial her down. I want her to be deeper."

Jackie injects morphine into the IV line.

How come she's able to talk? I ask.

Rosalie herself answers, "The conversation is interesting."

Dr. Joseph and Jackie exchange a look.

"She won't remember this," Jackie says. "Can you hear me now, sweetie? Are you in any pain?"

There's a long moment. No answer.

Dr. Joseph says, "Here's where people make mistakes—when you put Humpty-Dumpty back together." He says everyone has a sideburn, a natural hairline below the ear, and if you pull the skin up so far that there's no hair showing, "it looks like a Barbie doll. You also check behind the ear to make sure the hairline is even, no zigzag or break. The test is—can you wear your hair pulled up and not be busted?"

He gently lifts Rosalie's skin with a forceps, lays it over the new muscular structure, and cuts off the excess before stapling it closed. He cuts the skin with a knife as if slicing a pizza. So much of what he does reminds me of cooking and sewing that it's surprising there are so few women in the field. Dr. Joseph and Dr. Antell believe this is because the training takes longer than most other specialties, and getting a practice up and thriving is so time-consuming that it effectively precludes having a family.

After finishing the first side, Dr. Joseph takes a break, retreating to the pre-op room to sit still and "focus the chi." He operates three days a week and does only one face lift a day, although some surgeons will do two. He takes Fridays off to play golf.

Raised in the Midwest, he says, he always wanted to do plastic surgery. "It's fun, clean, and creative; it's not cancer or trauma." Because it's elective, he says, "you're out of the health insurance loop, and the patients are not as litigious."

When he walks back to the OR, Jackie says, "I'm not happy—she's obstructed." Rosalie is making gurgling, snoring sounds. Jackie inserts a nasal tube in one nostril, and we hear air rush in. "I like that sound," Dr. Joseph says. "You happier, Jackie?"

"Yes."

He sews a towel to the other side of the scalp and repeats what he did on the first side. It goes faster because he knows Rosalie's anatomy now, but "no one is symmetrical," he says. "I treat each side as if it's a separate individual and pray it comes out even." When he's finished, he turns Rosalie's head from side to side and feels her cheeks with his fingers. He thinks there's a bleeder under the right cheek that could cause a hematoma, and asks for the staple remover. "I'm gonna find it, fix it, and get outta Dodge," he says. "It's just a nuisance, not serious." When he starts opening the incision, blood streams out and he probes for the source. "Okay, where are you?" He finds a small artery pumping blood and cauterizes it.

"What's her BP?" he asks Jackie.

"One twenty."

"There's another arterial spurter. . . ."

"Dr. J! Put her in the center! I got a problem," Jackie says.

I scurry out of the way.

Dr. Joseph straightens Rosalie's head, and Jackie moves behind her. "Get that light out of my way and pull the drape back on her chest. Give me the tongue blade. . . . Where is my tongue blade?!"

A nurse hands her the tongue blade.

"Get out of my way!" Jackie says.

"Nobody's in your way," Dr. Joseph says softly.

"Turn on the suction and hand me the end," Jackie says in a loud voice. The nurse hands her the oxygen tube, and Jackie puts it in Rosalie's mouth, holding her tongue in place.

Rosalie's blood pressure returns to normal.

"All's well that ends well," Dr. Joseph says calmly. He explains later

that narcotics "slow down the patient's ability to breathe, so we venti-
lated her by mouth. She was not actually dying. All you have to do is
give her oxygen until the morphine wears off."

He turns to his staff. "Now, where were we?"

He finds the second arterial bleeder and cauterizes it.

Rosalie starts to fidget on the table.

"Just lie still, sweetie," Jackie says. "We're almost finished."

Dr. Joseph feels her cheeks again with his fingers. "She looks good.
We're done except for putting in the staples."

Afterward he orders in salads from a deli and we eat them in the pre-
op room with plastic forks. "Except for that one minute," he says, "the
surgery was uneventful."

* * *

The following day, I have lunch with Dr. Kamer on the patio of the
Peninsula Hotel, across from his office. He flips a dark glass shade down
over his regular glasses and studies the menu. He's wearing a light blue
shirt, a blue-and-orange tie and tan jacket, and everything works together. This is his day to consult with clients, which he finds more
draining than operating. "Surgery is like art—you go in and draw a picture and nobody's around. You get into the Zen of it, whatever that is."

When he began doing cosmetic surgery in the late sixties, he says, he
was driven—"just driven"—to seek excellence. "The first time I saw a
nose job—the way it just changes a little girl's life or a little boy's life—
that blew me away. I love it, I really love it."

He's sixty-nine now and recently gave a keynote lecture at the Royal
College of Surgeons of England about the evolution of his face lift technique. "It was a great honor—to have them acknowledge that what I do
is surgery. Not cosmetic surgery. *Surgery.*"

In the lecture, he described how he'd progressed from lifting the skin
only to lifting the SMAS to doing the deep-plane face lift. He attended
the ASAPS conference in San Francisco when the twin study was done

and thinks that "it was a great idea, but you can't draw conclusions based on four cases. You need hundreds of cases, and there's no way to evaluate the aesthetics—that's in the eye of the beholder." He says that after doing more than ten thousand face lifts, three thousand of which were deep-plane, he's convinced the latter gives a longer-lasting result. When he starting out doing a less invasive face lift, he says, he had to redo 20 percent because the jowls would return.

"Whatever you do judiciously to an aging face, you will make it look better," he says. But when he shifted from less invasive face lifts to the deep-plane, "I went from having 20 percent of the patients unhappy to .01 percent."

As we walk back to his office after lunch, I ask if he's had any face work done. He looks shocked. "Do I look like I have?"

"No, but if it was a good job, it wouldn't be apparent."

The doctor laughs. "A few years ago I stopped looking at myself when I shave. I do it by feel in the shower, so I don't have to see the wrinkles."

Why don't you have one of your colleagues do a lift?

He shakes his head. "I'm too afraid."

* * *

Fear is one reason people disavow cosmetic surgery, but bias and philosophy weigh in with greater heft. A close friend who was a legendary beauty in her twenties says she won't have surgery because she's less concerned with wrinkles than with her health. "My heart, my knees—will they hold up so I can keep doing the things I love, like hiking and swimming? That's my priority."

The cost of a face lift is prohibitive for many, but some who could afford it decline on the grounds that it's a superficial fixation. They want to look in the mirror and say, "I'm proud of my scars and lines," and they point to figures like Georgia O'Keeffe and Jacques Cousteau, whose weathered features had grandeur because they reflected their character.

Carol Muske-Dukes, the poet and novelist, is blond, tall, and glamorous in her fifties. "Isn't age beautiful also?" she asks. If you try to erase the marks of age, "that's misguided. We miss out on seeing what our older faces look like. I think Diane Keaton looked beautiful in *Something's Gotta Give*." Keaton was fifty-seven, said she'd never had cosmetic surgery, and did her first nude scene because "somebody my age has to be naked in a movie."

Yet I know a minister, a meditation teacher, and a bestselling author of spiritual books—people whose vocation is to help others look beneath the surface and connect with what's essential—who've had face lifts. "You do this for yourself," the minister says, "the same way you choose to wear colors you think are flattering and new clothes that give you a boost."

Thomas Moore, who trained to be a Catholic monk and wrote *Care of the Soul*, surprised me by saying he supports people's efforts to look as youthful and beautiful as they can. "I think it's wonderful to be so concerned when you're older with the Venusian thing—with the body, with your own beauty. I'm very much in favor of anything you can do to keep your youth."

What about men who have an ear pierced in their fifties or women who wear a belly ring like their teenage daughter?

Moore smiles. "Sorry, I can't judge that. If you can get away with it, great. It's the attitude that matters. If you're doing it because you're afraid of getting older, that might not work. If you're doing it to celebrate beauty and a youthful heart, I think that's wonderful."

Gloria Steinem, who looks elegant at seventy, agrees with Moore. She wouldn't have plastic surgery because she thinks it can be "quite dangerous" but says that "painting, decorating, even piercing I can live with. I think women should be able to wear whatever they fucking please."

Fucking right. (Steinem is the only person I know who can say "fuck" and sound ladylike.) But I've seen that going to extremes to look young can be grotesque: Helen Gurley Brown posing for *Newsweek* in a miniskirt and black fishnet stockings, with her face stretched tight and her hair dyed coppery red. But I like her message. "I'm seventy-eight," she wrote, and "I had sex last night." She urges older women who have a younger, impoverished lover to "take him to Gucci. Take him to Armani." When it's time to undress, she says, keep the lights down or "back out of the room when it's over if you think your front is better than your back."

Clarity came to me in the talk I had with Thomas Moore. He's sixty-three and lives in rural New Hampshire, where "we have these barns and silos and old farm equipment out in the fields. As the barns begin to lean and the machinery rusts, suddenly the artists come out and paint them. I think that's true of people as well."

He says you can do "at least two things at once: age with grace—say, 'Okay, I'm going to be older and enjoy it'; and at the same time say, 'I don't want to lose my youth.' Our childhood is always with us, our adolescence is always with us, and it's good to be in touch with those phases as we age." Moore says one of his favorite stories is about Carl Jung. "He got connected with the boy he'd been at age six by playing with blocks. Can you see it? His patients would leave the great doctor, and he'd get down on the floor and build houses with blocks. He said it was the most important thing he did to reconnect with childhood." According to Moore, the fountain of youth is "always there inside, no matter how old our bodies are."

So it's not either/or. You can focus on developing the inner qualities that make people appealing and compelling as they age: charisma, humor, intellectual zest. And you can tend to the outer package, just as you'd refurbish a historical building so it doesn't look run-down or dilapidated. You can appreciate how strong your thighs are and wear a sarong to cover them, or a Hawaiian shirt to hide the gut. You can do whatever you fucking please, with the right attitude.

5

Change Is Gonna Come
or
Another Fucking Opportunity for Growth

When we step out of the car, there's a loud screeching of machinery—*hrrrmmm hrrrrrmmm*—and the smell of wood burning and smoke rising through the trees. The earth is wet and reddish brown, staining our shoes. I sit on a log and watch Billy Holder, a wizened man who's called "the artist with the bulldozer," drive straight at the trees and push them over. If a hemlock or fir bounces back, Billy digs out the soil around the bottom, loosens the roots, and down the tree goes. Two other workers strip off branches and throw them into a bonfire that's ten feet tall and burns around the clock.

I'm visiting Nina Zimbelman in the Smoky Mountains of North Carolina. She's bought, for her community, a mountainside of virgin land that looks as it did at the time of the Revolutionary War. She lets Billy decide where to carve out roads and clear sites for homes. Despite the smoke and noise, I can't stay awake. I'm falling asleep sitting up, probably because I'm terrified of what I've come to North Carolina to do.

I stand and walk toward the dozer. Billy throws a chain around a stack of trunks and starts hauling them down to the county road. The trees have dark brown bark, but where they've been cut, they look exposed, white, raw. I turn to Nina. "How do you feel . . . cutting down living trees?"

"It's for a purpose," she says. "Before you can have a new experience, you have to clear out the old."

I watch the trees being dragged behind the dozer, their branches breaking off with loud cracks.

"I identify with the trees."

Nina laughs. "You're in tear-down phase."

· · ·

Change! Tear it down! Start the revolution. Break the eggs to make omelets. When we were younger, we were breathless for change and expected it to keep rolling—a perfect wave in an endless summer. Change was carrying us in a direction we welcomed: participatory democracy, racial equality, more enlightened gender roles, and sexual freedom. Then we awakened to find that change can trigger a backlash and sweep you off to straits where you never intended to go. My first book was called *Loose Change,* and at the end, an activist who'd fought for a revolution that did not materialize said: "That's the lesson of revolutions. They don't turn out the way you expect."

These days I brace for change. A new version of Windows? I'm fine with the old, it does everything I want so why do I have to install a more complicated program? One of my friends bought a TiVo, but it's still in the box because he doesn't have time to learn to use it. I hate it when a favorite restaurant closes or a company stops making the slippers I've worn for years. But this is the tip of the iceberg.

Change has a different meaning from when we were young—more serious because it often brings loss of what you love and ultimately loss of all. The Buddha said a noble truth to reflect on is: "Everything I hold dear will change and be taken from me." In secular terms, Mike Nichols told his producer, after the colossal success of *The Graduate:* "We still have to die."

How we deal with change is the deciding factor in whether we weep or laugh, suffer or have joy, in the years ahead. You can resist or roll with change, cling to the rocks and get thrashed by the current or let it carry you to the sea. When a business owner I know watched his product become obsolete, he said, half-joking, "Here it comes: another fucking opportunity for growth."

The choice is between contracting or expanding, but it's not so simple. I know it's essential to let go, surrender, but how can I open my arms like the Indian on the horse at the Boston Museum of Fine Arts when I'm frightened of losing what I love?

Reb Zalman

One of the first people I talked with about change was Rabbi Zalman Schachter-Shalomi, called Reb Zalman. Friends and students view him as a model of how to be bold, warm, lively, and unpredictable at eighty-one. With smooth olive skin, white hair and beard, Reb Zalman wears suspenders and a knitted yarmulke. He's been married four times, had ten children, taught at three universities, written hundreds of articles and books, and been a friend to religious leaders from Thomas Merton to the Dalai Lama. He founded the Jewish Renewal movement to infuse new meaning into Jewish traditions, drawing on the Hasidic rabbinical training he received in Eastern Europe along with teachings from Buddhists, Native Americans, and Catholic priests. My favorite image of him is at a Simchat Torah service I attended, a celebration of the Torah being given to Moses on Mount Sinai. Reb Zalman danced around the room carrying the scrolls in his arms as George Harrison sang "My Sweet Lord."

When he was about to turn sixty, though, Reb Zalman had plunged into a depression that "no amount of busyness could dispel," he says. "My career was going pretty good and didn't justify the depression. But at night in unguarded moments, when I looked in the mirror, I saw I was changing—getting old. How would I deal with that? After age fifty, you've already procreated and done what you've done in the world. Why do we have to live? Salmon spawn and die. What are we needed for?"

He went off on a forty-day retreat in the mountains of New Mexico, living in a rustic cabin where he prayed, meditated, wrote, and took walks. When he came down from the mountain, he understood that a new vision was needed. The models that prevailed then for growing older were: the medical model, where it's treated as a disease; the die-in-the-saddle model, where you keep working and expire slumped over at your desk; and the recreation model, where you say, "I've deferred my own gratification and now it's my turn to play, dammit." Reb Zalman founded the Spiritual Eldering Institute to offer a different approach. He says the decades after fifty are a time for "unparalleled learning," making peace with the past, and becoming an elder who inspires younger people.

I don't look forward to being called an "elder," "senior," or "crone." An elder is respected in tribal cultures, but we don't live in tribes, and I sense that people who make a point about "honoring elders" are merely being polite. Reb Zalman concedes that "we need to find a better word." But Michael Meade, the poet and mythologist, says we can make "elder" work. "When I think of an elder, I see the tree," Meade says. "An elder is vital and creative, an elder has courage, humor, and salt. An elder is weird—that's a Welsh word that means you have a foot in two worlds, this one and the eternal. So the elder is truly weird."

Reb Zalman, after founding the Spiritual Eldering Institute, designed a workshop in which participants can review their lives, analyze what they've learned, and prepare to pass that wisdom down the line. He wrote a book, *From Age-ing to Sage-ing,* then turned over the running of the organization to others. His strength lies in coming up with a vision and gathering people to pursue it, then he'll move on to create a fresh project.

At seventy-nine, he began studying Arabic. "If I don't go into a new field, I'll get stale," he says. He thinks it's also important to learn new motor skills. "I went bowling with my son. Oy, my arm hurt because the bowling ball was too heavy, but there was also the joy—the endorphins—of knocking pins down." He laughs. When he was lecturing in Brazil, "they offered me a hang glider ride. Fifteen minutes later, I was in the air."

Weren't you scared? I ask.

"Of course I was scared! I was afraid my brake would fail and I'd fall, but that's also the thrill of it," Reb Zalman says. "You can be more reckless now than when you were younger. That's why we need an Elder Corps to go into the trouble spots of the world and work for peace. People say, 'You might get shot.' Okay, that's better than dying of a heart attack."

Here Come the Masters

One of the best approaches to change, as Reb Zalman indicates, is to learn something, because it requires you to take the initiative and get out in front of the wave instead of letting it break on you. Becoming a beginner again is like traveling to an exotic country: All your senses start firing.

Some people go back to college. Aimee Liu, who'd published four books, including *Cloud Mountain,* applied for an MFA program in creative writing when her youngest child was also applying to college. "I felt beat up by the publishing business and needed a kick start," Aimee says, "and the degree would enable me to teach." She and her son wrote their essays at the same time. "It was kind of cute. We compared applications and watched the mailbox for acceptances."

Barbara Weiss, a high school teacher in Washington, D.C., applied to the Fletcher School of Law and Diplomacy at fifty-four. She figured that years of herding teenagers would serve her in dealing with heads of state. In Massachusetts, Tracy Kidder, the Pulitzer Prize–winning author, enrolled in Italian classes at Smith College. "It's a gorgeous language, though useless," he says. "The undergraduates hated me because I'd memorize cantos from the *Inferno.*"

After moving to Colorado, I learned there was a masters ski racing program at the local resort, Eldora, and signed up. "Masters," I discovered, is becoming the PC word for "older." When I transferred my funds to a Boulder bank, they informed me they had a "masters account" with special rates for people over sixty. I like the concept of "mastery," which is fortunate because masters programs are hatching everywhere: masters running, masters baseball, masters basketball, and masters swimming.

I've skied since I was nineteen but never raced, so on the first morning I show up for training, I find that everything I know and all the gear I own are wrong. There are ten men (the oldest is eighty-one), one woman, and two coaches setting up gates for a slalom course. I'm wearing a teal Jean-Claude Killy one-piece suit I bought on sale in Aspen, but the team members laugh at it, calling it "a green body bag." They wear skintight racing suits with large spiderweb patterns, and over the suits they wear black shorts that are held up by suspenders, something like lederhosen, to keep their butts warm on the chairlift. They tell me my boots are inadequate—not high performance—and my skis are hopeless. The lone woman, Marcie, who's in her sixties and would later fall on the snow and break her pelvis, offers to give me her old helmet—required equipment.

There's no problem keeping up with the team when we ski down the mountain, but when we enter the slalom course, I start skidding and slowing down. For years I've been taught to stand up tall, be graceful, and expend minimal energy, "just put your weight on your big toe and you'll turn." But the racers assume an aggressive crouch, pushing hard to get their skis on edge and their bodies forward. We watch a video of Bode Miller, and his skis are almost vertical, cutting like knives across the snow. I have no idea how to get from my nearly flat stance to Bode's edge.

I decide I don't want to race in competitions and break my pelvis, I just want to learn to ski better and do this with a lively group. The coaches, Luther Tatge and Eliot Young, show me one thing at a time to change, and I make progress. At the end of the season, they talk me into entering a race, the Mountain Dew Vertical Challenge, being held at Eldora. Marcie says, "It's fun, and lots of people in it have never raced before." So I put on a bib with the number 69 and start to get nervous. This is a race, a test, and I don't fail tests. You're not allowed to take a practice run to check out the gates; you get one shot. I ski down the course more cautiously than I'd like, and the woman announcing the race says: "Sara Davidson from Eldora Masters Racing. Good time, Sara!" What is she talking about? I clock the slowest time—by six or eight seconds—of all my teammates. But at the awards ceremony I'm handed a gold medal. I came in first in my age group because I was the only woman in my age group.

Nevertheless, taking home the gold is like tasting blood. I'm now qualified to ski in the Mountain Dew finals and drive to Keystone, Colorado, for the event. They begin the race with the oldest women and work down to the youngest, then take the oldest men and work down to the youngest. Letting the older females go first gives us the advantage of skiing a course that's not rutted and grooved. We like that. The first woman is eighty-three and moves so slowly she's practically walking, poling around the gates as everybody cheers and says, "How cool is that?" One of my teammates, though, says it's patronizing: "letting them go first and cheering because they're moving at all." When they call my class, there are a dozen women in my age group, and I come in last. But next season, my coaches tell me, "you've got a shot at making the podium."

Two years have passed and I have not made the podium, but I'm constantly learning, and every morning when I train, flying downhill on freshly packed snow never fails to boost my mood. And there are other benefits. After my first season I took my two children and a few of their friends to Vail. I'd taught my son to ski when he was five, holding him between my legs as we coasted downhill, but by twelve he didn't want to ski with me. He'd stand at the bottom of the lift looking frustrated and say, "What took you so long!"

At Vail, he strapped on a snowboard and on the first run I beat him to the chairlift. "Have you noticed anything different about my skiing?" I asked.

He nodded and said under his breath, "Remarkable."

Because I'd been the worst on my team and could never close the gap, I'd assumed I was not improving much. My son announced he was going to ski the next day because skis are faster than boards, implying there was no way in hell I would beat him.

The next morning my son and I, both on skis, started at one end of the resort and worked our way up and down three mountains to the other end of Vail without stopping except to have lunch. I did not beat him, but he had to work hard to stay in front. He was pumped, cheeks flushed, when he drove our group home that night. "I hate to admit it," he told the other kids, "but I really enjoyed skiing with Mom."

Bebe Moore Campbell

There's another way of tackling change that I call the judo approach: absorbing the force of the blow and flipping it to your advantage. I met with Bebe Moore Campbell, who managed to do this when unexpected events put an end to the plans she'd made. Bebe, author of bestselling books like *Your Blues Ain't Like Mine,* has been called "one of the most important African-American writers of the century" by *The Washington Post.* She'd expected that in her fifties she'd be freer of responsibilities and could spend more time with her husband, travel, and read. But her twenty-seven-year-old daughter, an aspiring actress, moved back home with her toddler just as Bebe's eighty-two-year-old mother developed glaucoma and couldn't walk well and a loved one was diagnosed with mental illness. Bebe took them all in. "I've got four generations in my house," she says. "These are the most stressful years of my life." She's caring for them all while she works on a book and campaigns for better mental health care. She wrote her latest novel, *72 Hour Hold,* while she was "mostly in my car, transporting this one to the hospital and that one to nursery school."

Her granddaughter, Elisha, wearing pink overalls, watches cartoons as Bebe and I talk at the dining table of her home in Baldwin Hills, an upscale black neighborhood in Los Angeles. The house is elegant, with a granite kitchen, swimming pool, and three-car garage. All the rooms are filled with paintings, crafts, and sculpture of and by blacks.

Bebe, wearing purple lipstick and her hair straight to the shoulders, says she's under pressure to complete her ninth book. "I was part of the Terry McMillan crowd. The publishers had ignored black writers and particularly black female writers. Suddenly we were hot and had to hustle to get the books out and make that list." She says she's looking around "for what I'll do with the rest of life, because literature is a cruel business. You can work for years, and one savaging from critics and it's all over."

Elisha spills her juice and Bebe grabs a sponge to mop it up. Her book, *72 Hour Hold,* is about a middle-class black family "coming to grips with their child's mental illness," she says. "Having a mentally ill child is worse than segregation because of the stigma, the guilt, and because you're alone. With segregation you have a group." She learned about this firsthand when she and seven other black women who had mentally ill relatives "had to go west—to the white part of town—to get some training. Then we came back to our community because the need and stigma here are greater." She leads a weekly group for family members, where they discuss brain diseases, medications, and how to communicate with empathy. "We also have a group for the consumers. . . ."

Who're the consumers? I ask.

"The ones who consume the medications." Her own relative is stable, she says, "but it wasn't always like that—it was frightening."

Bebe says one of her friends told her recently, "We've been stars. Now it's our turn to be servants."

Serving whom?

"Serving the household. Serving the community. Serving our loved ones." Bebe says she's learning to shift from achieving to nurturing. "I want to give more to the personal life and a lot less to the work. I never thought that before."

She's come to not just tolerate but savor having four generations in her home. "I grew up with my mother, my grandma, aunt, and cousin in the same house—that was a part of black culture until recently. It's still part of Latino and immigrant culture." Family members divide the labor. Bebe cooks, finds the right preschool, and drives Elisha there and back, correcting her grammar and teaching her manners. Bebe's husband, a banker, plays with Elisha at night, and her daughter takes Elisha to movies and parks. "I don't have to see *Shrek,*" Bebe says with a laugh. "When I've cooked a good meal and everyone's sitting around the table, talking and laughing—that's satisfying."

I ask if her daughter and granddaughter might get a place of their own.

"No time soon," Bebe says. "I like 'em under this roof right now. It works." She has a ritual: The last thing she does at night is go into her mother's room. Her mother, a social worker and lifelong "church lady," never cooked, Bebe says. "My grandmother did that. But my mother sure can dispense the wisdom." Talking with her mother before she sleeps makes Bebe feel calm. "She's serene," Bebe says. "I want her serenity."

Two years after our talk, on November 27, 2006, Bebe Moore Campbell died at fifty-six, of brain cancer.

Paul Krassner

In my twenties, I was married to a man whose father had written hit songs and Broadway musicals in the thirties and forties. He couldn't bear rock 'n' roll and would say over dinner at Sardi's, "Where's the melody? There's no melody. And I can't understand the words." I had little sympathy, but twenty years later I heard myself voice the same complaint about rap: "There's no melody. And the lyrics are a horror." Plato wrote in *The Republic* that any change in the culture's music "is full of danger to the whole state." He understood the power of music to dispossess one generation and raise up the next. For most people, it's tough to love the music that replaces what you grew up with. On Match.com, the majority in the forty-five to sixty-five age group, when asked to list the kinds of music they like, respond: "Everything but rap."

Not Paul Krassner, the satirist and comic who founded the *Realist,* one of the first underground papers. He's been able to ride with changes, even in music, and he's outlasted his friends who took their lives: Abbie Hoffman, Phil Ochs, Lenny Bruce, and Hunter Thompson. Last September, Paul called from his home in Desert Hot Springs, California, to tell me he was coming to Boulder to perform with a rap group, Guerilla Word Fare. He said he'd be doing a new stand-up routine, *Geezerstock,* about aging rock fans who gather for a redux of Woodstock. "I'm finally playing the age card," Paul said. In the routine, he's the announcer onstage at the festival who says to the crowd: "I've just been handed an announcement. Do NOT take the brown antacid."

While most comics feed on darkness and rage, Paul, according to his editor at *Playboy*, is "the only Jew I know who doesn't get angry." Paul created the term *yippies* and still dresses like one, wearing T-shirts with political slogans and rumpled pants. He still smokes pot, still has lots of curly hair, and walks with a limp—teetering from side to side in a gait he calls "the Frankenstein walk." He says the limp is the result of being beaten by police during the riots that broke out in San Francisco after the trial and lenient sentence given to the man convicted of murdering Harvey Milk, the first openly gay person elected to public office.

On the Friday night Paul is supposed to perform at Trilogy, I can hear the rap music from two blocks away. At the door to the dance hall, I ask the man collecting tickets, "When is Paul Krassner going on?"

He shrugs, pointing to the only man in the hall with gray hair. "Ask him yourself."

I make my way through the room, packed with twenty-somethings who're dancing, drinking, and shouting to be heard above the assault on the eardrums that's passing for music.

Paul is slumped in an armchair beside a speaker. I crouch down to say hello.

He looks at me with the eyes of a dog about to be put down. "I'm freaking out," he says. "I can't do my thing here." He waves at the young crowd. "I can't do *Geezerstock*."

"Let's go out where we can talk."

We sit down in a booth in the Trilogy restaurant and Paul asks the waiter for soup, but they've run out. "This is a nightmare," he says.

"How did you get involved?"

He says the leader of the rap group contacted him and asked if he would collaborate on a music/spoken-word event. "We e-mailed back and forth. I said I would do a bit about being a child prodigy, playing the violin at Carnegie Hall, and they could play violin music in the background. The guy said, 'Yeah, great!' But there's no violin. There's no collaboration. I was brought here on false pretenses!"

Paul says the band wasn't at the airport to meet him, he had to track them down, and when they collected him an hour later, they asked, "Who were the yippies, anyway?" Paul hits his head. "It's like they were asking, 'Who were the Wobblies? Who was Boss Tweed?' "

They had told Paul they would pay for a room in a bed-and-breakfast, but on the drive to Boulder they said the inn was sold out. "They put me in their crash pad, in a room that has nothing but a mattress on the floor."

"They put you in a crash pad? Jesus."

"There's a light switch on the wall but no light, and no radio or TV, and I'm a media junkie!"

We decide to leave and go somewhere else for dinner when one of the owners of Trilogy comes up to Paul. "They're ready for you."

I follow Paul back into the dance hall, where the band is still playing. Doing the Frankenstein walk, Paul climbs the steps to the stage and waits. It seems this song—if it can be called that—will never end and it doesn't; they merely break off playing abruptly. The only black musician—the only black person in the room and possibly in Boulder—says, "Mr. Krassner," and shoves the microphone at him.

Paul comes out shooting—making fun of George Bush, comparing him to Hitler—but the kids are talking and paying no attention. Paul imitates Donald Rumsfeld, announcing that the atrocities committed by U.S. soldiers at Abu Ghraib prison were "abuse but not torture." Paul says, "Not only does the emperor have no clothes, he has a hard-on!" There's a raunchy cheer from the crowd, not for Paul but for the black musician who's gyrating his hips and fondling a girl at the side of the stage. Paul walks over and shoves the mike back at him, saying, "Thanks for your attention."

Then we're outside again. "I'm exhausted," Paul says as I drive him to the crash pad. "I've been up since five this morning." The bandleader had said he'd leave a key under the mat, but Paul lifts the mat and . . . why are we not surprised? No key. There's a torn-up upholstered chair on the porch and Paul gamely drops into it. The Boulder City Council recently passed a law that it's illegal to have a couch on your front porch. Too many students had set fire to couches, but the council didn't outlaw chairs. "I'll just wait here," Paul says.

"It's one in the morning; they could stay out till three or four."

"I'll be fine," Paul says. "It's a nice night. Don't worry, please. Thanks for the ride."

I walk to my car, but when I look back at Paul, dwarfed in the beat-up chair, I can't drive away. "You're coming to my house."

I settle him in my guest room, and the next morning I make scrambled eggs and bagels as Paul limps back and forth on the deck in the sunshine. "That gig was humiliating," he says, "but you gotta laugh. I've never been introduced like that—the guy just throws me the microphone. The only worse introduction I ever got was at the Montreal Comedy Festival. I told the emcee I was a social and political satirist, so he introduces me as 'Paul Krassner—a sociopath.' "

I laugh.

Paul deals with disaster, with all of life, by laughing. He explains how humor became "my religion. At age six, I was onstage at Carnegie Hall playing the Vivaldi Concerto in A Minor. My left leg started to itch, and it got more and more intense. So I stood on my left foot and scratched with the right, not missing a note. The audience laughed! It was like a symphony, with different tones and tempos, and I was hooked."

Despite the fiasco at Trilogy, Paul still connects with young people who delight in his bashing of people in high places. He writes columns for the *New York Press* and for Adult Video News Online. "It's a porn site. They said I could write anything as long as it has something to do with sex. So my column is called 'One Hand Jerking.' "

When Paul does stand-up comedy, a third of his audience are young people and a third have "very old ponytails. Someone always asks if I ever think about death. I say, I can sum it up in three words: Every fucking day."

Paul and his wife, Nancy, a video documentary artist (the pair remind me of the cartoonist and his wife in *American Splendor*), often joke about where they'll spend their last years. Nancy says, "We'll pass a trailer park and I'll say, That could be our last resort." Paul says there should be an old age home for humorists, "where there're really good drugs and lots of laughs."

Show me the way. I admire Paul's resilience: He's always lived on the margins, never compromised to fit the marketplace, but adapted on his own terms and maintained his humor. On the night he bombed at Trilogy, when he was in my guest room, tossing in bed, he told himself, "You'll laugh at this in ten years. In one year. In one week! So why not now?"

Tim-ber

After watching Paul, Reb Zalman, and Bebe meet change with fortitude and humor, I fly to North Carolina to visit Nina Zimbelman, who skates through transitions with more willingness and trust than anyone I know. A tiny woman in her fifties with dark brown eyes that miss nothing, Nina had previously lived in Egypt, in a villa near the Great Sphinx of Giza, where she'd been doing metaphysical research. She left Cairo sooner than she'd planned because she received what she calls a "knowing" to move to Robbinsville, North Carolina, a small town in Appalachia where her ex-husband had purchased land. Nina didn't want to leave Egypt and settle in hillbilly country; she thought she'd have nothing in common and no way to connect with people there. "It was like I was being put out to pasture," Nina says. But she'd learned to follow inner promptings even when she couldn't understand where they'd lead.

Nina had three students with her, but the *knowing*—which she hears as specifically as I get directions from MapQuest—was to buy a parcel of virgin forest, clear sites, and put up multiple houses. "It made no sense, because there were only four of us," she says. "But the knowing was to build homes and a separate unit—a commissary—where a dozen people could cook and eat." By the time I visited two years later, a community was growing and there were a dozen people eating together in the commissary.

Robbinsville is a conservative, red-voting community of about eight hundred with a median household income of $14,000. Houses are tucked in the hills on roads or "branches" where you'll see barns with JESUS IS LORD painted on the side and notices of gospel singing and summer Bible school. No one, including Nina, could have predicted that she'd find people there who were eager to take classes with her or that she'd meet and collaborate with Patricia (Trish) Johnson, MD, head of the largest medical clinic in the county, the Tallulah Health Center. Trish, who's as small as Nina, with blue eyes and curly blond hair, had studied qigong and was teaching it to her patients, calling it "Chinese exercise." With a gentle laugh, she says, "If my patients can't pronounce it, they won't do it." Nina and Trish, who privately refer to themselves as the "mighty midgets," were seeing clients together, using Trish's medical training and Nina's intuitive skills to learn the source of people's illness. They were having such success treating patients with severe chronic disease, including the town mayor, that word spread and they were booked with clients who'd never heard the word *metaphysical*. What they felt was Nina's love, which softened the sting when she hit them with the truth about themselves they didn't want to hear.

In previous years when I would visit Nina, I'd slip quickly into an unaccustomed state, where I'd feel at ease and safe and there was nothing under the sun to worry about. But that's not happening on this trip. The night I arrive, I can't sleep, heartsick and frightened that I'm alone with no direction home.

In the morning, Nina drives me to the land she's developing in an area called England Branch. She introduces me to Billy, who had walked the property with Nina and told her to buy it. A thin man of sixty-seven, wearing a red cap and navy overalls that hang on him, Billy drives the dozer up the mountain, zigzagging back and forth, pushing over trees until the patch he's working on is level. Sitting on a log, I lean back against a hemlock. Nina's talking, but my eyelids keep falling shut. Billy stops the dozer, walks over, and shakes my shoulder. "Ya wanna ride?" He climbs back on and pats the yellow seat beside him. "Sit raaat here."

I swing up beside him and we drive uphill, straight at a clump of firs and mountain ash that yield and crash before us. Dirt and leaves spray back in our faces. The machine tips and vibrates so violently I have to brace myself to avoid falling out the side and being caught in the wheels and gears. Billy reverses and we tilt downhill, which feels as if we're going to fall right over forward. When he stops and I get down, no longer fighting sleep, Billy asks, "Think yull make a bulldozer girl?"

"I don't know. How long does it take to learn?"

"Ya give me a twelve-year-old, and if he's sharp, I can train him in no time," Billy says. "But ya take a fifty-year-old man? He's never gonna learn."

"That lets me out."

Billy grins. "Hell, you ain't fifty."

Nina and I drive into town to eat lunch at the lone restaurant, which has a cafeteria-style buffet with stainless-steel containers of ground beef, grits, bacon, biscuits, and French fries. By the time we return to England Branch, Billy has carved a flat pad out of the sloping forest. Two hours ago we could see only trees, but now we look out on a vista of emerald mountains, dotted with puffs of mist for which they were named "Smoky."

"That was fast," I say.

Nina smiles. "That's how fast you can let go."

Sunday morning, two days later, everyone in the community gathers at the commissary to make omelets. They tell me I look different. Katy

Lynch, MD, a colleague of Trish at the clinic, says, "You looked so sad and worried when you got here."

"I'm still filled with fear."

"Of what?"

"The tearing down. . . ."

"That's because you can't see what's coming," Nina says.

"That's just it. I wish I could swing out over the chasm and check out the terrain before letting go of the rope."

Nina laughs. "You don't get to do that. You have to let go first, not knowing."

Like skiing the racecourse, I think.

"What's ahead can't be more painful than what you're holding on to," Nina says.

Katy offers to work with me using a neuromuscular process. We go off by ourselves, and I have only a foggy memory of the procedure: It involves holding out my arms and Katy pushing on them as she asks questions, to see what my unconscious muscular response will be. If my arms drop, it means "no," and if they stay in place, it's "yes." But I can't help trying to figure out the answer and help my arms along. "Let's try something else," Katy says.

She asks me to give in to the fear, "go into it completely, let it swallow you."

I start to hyperventilate.

"What's the core fear," she asks, "the one that lies at the bottom of everything?"

"I'll be destroyed. I won't exist."

"Is there a part of you that's not afraid?"

"No."

She asks me to strip off the fear, wherever it is. "Pull it off the body. . . ."

"I can't—I can't separate the fear from me. I'd have to kill the whole being."

"Peel it off," she says. "Rip off your skin, your muscles, your organs, whatever it takes."

I imagine yanking off hunks of flesh, muscles, and blood vessels and throwing them into a pile. But fear is driving through my chest like a cold spike.

Katy tells me to pull out the spike.

I picture straining and struggling with the spike, and with a terrible sucking sound, it comes out.

She asks, Is there any fear left?

Yes.

Keep peeling, she says, and at length I'm nothing but bones: skull, ribs, pelvis, tibia. I think of the Dalí painting *My Wife, Nude, Contemplating Her Own Flesh Becoming Stairs, Three Vertebrae of a Column, Sky and Architecture.* Dalí's wife sits with her back to us, her flesh soft and youthful and her dark hair falling to her shoulders. She's staring at a version of herself that's all stone. In place of her pelvis there's a flight of stairs, and in place of her torso are three columns through which you can see the sky.

I'm contemplating myself as a stack of bones, and yet there's something breathing, pulsing. No matter what's ahead—no matter what I do or don't do, no matter what comes to me or what's taken away—I'm going to die anyway. So what is there to be afraid of? Why all this terror and clenching? Like the trees before the bulldozer, I'm going down. I might as well yield.

6

Sea of Love

When Joan Borysenko began telling friends that she was going to be married for the fourth time, to Gordon Dveirin, an organizational psychologist who'd also been married three times before, the women's posse mobilized. Her colleagues on the mind-body lecture circuit cornered her at meetings and said, What the hell are you doing? I'm sure he's terrific, but you said good things about your other husbands at the beginning. What makes you think this will be different? You'll end up in divorce court and lose a fortune. One author who writes bestsellers about how to love told Joan, as Gordie rephrased it later, "Just keep him around as a pet."

None of them had met Gordie, but that was irrelevant. They were upset at what they considered the delusion of taking vows she'd already broken three times. How could the vows mean anything? The phrase most repeated was that marriage for a fourth time represents "the triumph of hope over experience."

That's not exactly true, I tell Joan, because experience changes us.

"It does change us," she says. "I know my friends mean well, they're trying to protect me, but they're all so cynical and most haven't had great experiences of love."

A few months earlier, Joan herself had raised the question of why she's compelled to get married. We were in Gold Hill, having dinner at her home, which sits on a mountainside with panoramic views of the Rockies. The house always seems under construction because Joan loves "projects" and creating beautiful spaces. The rooms are filled with statues of goddesses, Buddhas, hand-painted fabrics, flowers, photographs of friends and family, and three clamorous dogs. Joan likes to cook, and as she forms and pats crab cakes with her hands, she says she wants to study relationships at this age. "I'm fascinated by what people are doing: Are they married, dating, on their own and happy, or do they yearn for a partner who's the opposite sex or the same sex? What is love at this stage? Why do we need to get married? It's not like we're gonna have kids. Why not just live together?"

I've been contemplating these questions myself. When the music stops, some of us are seated and coupled and some are walking independently and with every round, things can change. An unexpected meeting, death, or divorce and you're in a state in which you did not expect to be. How do you fall in love, with so many quirks and so much history to relate? How do you sustain a marriage that began in your twenties . . . on to your nineties? What if you outlive several mates? Are we hardwired to keep coupling and recoupling?

For me, what seems a fixed idea is that I'm happiest with a partner. I've been in relationships for more years than I've been solo, and looking back, I view those times when I was content with a man and my children as what Edith Wharton called "the flower of life." I've been miserable when married and elated for stretches on my own, but the belief that's stuck in place—the belief I'm determined to look into and, if necessary, blast away—is that I need a mate to be happy.

During my dinner with Joan, I ask if she thinks that coupling is a basic human need or a habit—sometimes an addiction—we need to let go of. "I don't know," she says. "My particular kind of brain finds balance and comfort in a relationship. So it's part of my self-care to be in one."

"But as you asked before, why get married?"

We carry crab cakes and salad to the table and Joan opens a bottle of Spanish rioja. She's wearing jeans, a black T-shirt, and sandals, and her finger- and toenails are freshly polished. "I want to make the commitment," she says. "This time, I would vow with my whole heart that we'll stay together till death do us part." Switching to a Yiddish accent, she adds, "The end of life is not so far, so, oy! How big a mistake could this be?"

I have not been a member of the chorus chanting "Don't" to Joan. I've come to know Gordie, who's short in stature but unusually handsome and, like Joan, playful, smart, deeply empathic, and quick to open his heart to new friends. I think they're fucking lucky. Not only do they seem well suited, but, most improbably, they live five minutes apart in Gold Hill, a rustic mountain town that has only 210 people. They met in the general store when both had just broken up with someone else.

The only possible point of tension I see is that Joan has a larger income and is more well-known, but she doesn't view this as a problem. She and Gordie decided to collaborate on a book, *Saying Yes to Change,* "and we survived without killing each other," she says.

Joan wants a marriage ceremony because "something touches me about saying, 'I will walk the rest of the way with you. I will walk into the mystery with you. We both want to become more loving and leave the world a little better place, and I vow to be your partner in that. I know there will be difficult times, and I vow to see them as grist for the mill. I don't want to leave myself an escape hatch.' "

The barrage of negative responses from others, though, began to un-nerve her, and she went to a therapist to explore whether she was in some kind of delusional state. Her friends pointed out that she's never been without a man: Her longest time between relationships was two weeks. "Am I repeating an old pattern?" Joan asked. "What am I fanta-sizing? What am I not seeing? After three tough marriages, how could I possibly make a good choice?"

She and Gordie spent many hours looking into, as they put it, "Why is this wedding different from all our other weddings?" Joan says, "We had to be able to answer that before going forward." Joan came to un-derstand that "what's different is me. When I was younger, I couldn't have articulated the vows I want to take. I didn't go into my first mar-riage thinking it would last a lifetime; I was ambivalent. My second lasted twenty-five years, we raised children together, but life pulled us in different directions." Her third marriage, she says, was "the full catastro-phe. I can never again be with somebody where I have to shrink down to a smaller part of myself. Gordie inspires me to be more."

For Gordie, what's different is a sense of sacredness. "I've never been in a relationship where we could reach such ecstasy and at the same time stay grounded and not lose ourselves," he says. "We realized that this was not an intoxication or a projection. It was a merging between two mature individuals who know who they are."

They planned to have their wedding on the summer solstice in June 2005, but six months before that, as the debate swirled around them, they drove to New Mexico and married each other—just the two of them alone. Because they were filing their license in Colorado, it wasn't necessary to have an officiator or witnesses, a policy that dates from frontier days when there weren't enough justices to travel to outlying areas and marry people. Today, you request a license, sign it, mail it back, "and you be married," Joan says. They did not tell a soul what they were doing because "we wanted a cocoon. Everyone had an opinion— marry him, don't marry him—and we didn't want their opinions at our wedding."

They began their ritual at the mineral baths at Ojo Caliente because "you need a *mikvah*!" Joan says. "We washed off the old." Then they spent three days in silent retreat at the Benedictine Monastery of Christ in the Desert, near Georgia O'Keeffe's former home, Ghost Ranch. They slept in twin beds in a simple adobe room with no electricity, taking their meals in silence with the monks. Neither had been there before. "We wanted a place that was fresh and not polluted by memories." On the morning of the fourth day—the winter solstice—they rose and began their ceremony at six forty-five, timing it so the sun would be rising and the light returning as they exchanged rings and the vows they'd written and said prayers of gratitude. They drove to a five-star resort in Taos and "promptly started to enjoy ourselves." They drank champagne, played in the waterfalls and hot tubs, and had a glorious wedding night, enhanced by the fact that they'd been chaste for three days.

That same week, not knowing what Joan and Gordie were up to, I went to a wedding of different friends who'd also been married several times before. They did it by the numbers: She wore a white gown and veil and he wore a tuxedo, kneeling in church and then proceeding through reception lines, toasts, the first dance as husband and wife, cutting the cake, and tossing the bouquet. It seemed somehow inauthentic—fifty-six-year-old bridesmaids jumping to catch the white lilies—as if they were acting in a play written for a different cast.

Joan says, "That's what we were thinking. What do you wear to your fourth wedding? On the most sacred day of my life, I didn't want to worry about where are the flowers, who's sitting with whom, and is there enough peanut butter for the satay sauce?" They did invite their friends and family to a celebration on the original date they'd picked in June, flying in their children so they could get to know one another.

Joan believes the years ahead are about expanding the capacity to love. "I'm learning to grow in compassion and kindness and patience. I'm not very patient—that's my weak suit." She continues to write and teach, but "I've already worked enough for seventeen lifetimes. If there *is* reincarnation," she says, "maybe I could apply for a lifetime as a trophy wife."

"As *if*," I say.

"Yeah, I'd make a lousy one. Although I do love to shop."

Joan says she's learned from working with people who are dying that at the end, "the only thing that matters is the quality of love. That's what we're here for, that's why we're born and go through what we do. To explore what it really means to love."

•   •   •

Whether their union proves lasting or runs its course and they move on, the connection they have at this moment causes me to come away asking, Why can't I have that? At the time Joan and Gordie went off to New Mexico, I was dating two men, neither of whom I viewed as a long-term partner. I broke off with the first and he felt bereft, and six months later, the second broke off with me and I was bereft. To my surprise—I'd grown fonder of the second than I'd expected—the pain was crushing because, like a locomotive, it pulled after it a whole train of memories of men who've left.

My pattern has been that I'm ambivalent. I've been with a different man in almost every decade, married and divorced twice, and the longest relationship I've had was ten years. The most consistently happy was with the cowboy, Zack, who'd barely finished high school, lived in a trailer in the desert when we met, and didn't read a newspaper, let alone a book. It was an impossible romance, and possibly because of this, it went on for seven years.

Each partner has been radically different from the previous ones, but my pattern is consistent. When I fall in love, I immediately spot the problem areas and reasons it might not work. I swing between adoring and finding flaws. Men say that I shower them with appreciation and I'm hard on them. Extremely giving and extremely demanding. Zack used to write little notes for me to find around the house that said, "Be nice to Zack." Then the men leave and all the negative thoughts I had go out the window and I just want them back. I only remember the good, and I lash and berate myself for screwing it up. When I was grieving after Zack left, a friend asked, "Who do you blame?"

"Who else? Me, of course."

This pattern, though disgusting, may be no worse than other patterns humans have. Sexual love is the primal mystery, the ooze where priests and gurus and wise teachers get sucked under. I remember, in my thirties, hearing a man in his sixties agonizing about the woman he loved who was pulling away, and I thought, Doesn't this end? Apparently not. Don't we become wiser? A little, maybe. Relationships don't seem to get easier, although some long-married couples say they've grown more comfortable, like worn-in shoes. Whoopi Goldberg says, "It's tough. Anyone who is *not* you . . . who is living with you . . . is a problem." Yet the hope and wish for a compatible mate are lodged like splinters in my brain.

Sally Kempton, who was a celibate yogi for almost thirty years, tells me, "You'd think, with all the experiences you've had with men, you'd be ready to let go of the illusion that a relationship with the right one will set you up for good."

"You'd think."

"What would you be like," she asks, "if you didn't have that thought?"

"I'd be sad and lonely."

"I mean . . . what would you be like if you were incapable of thinking that you need a relationship to be happy?"

"I'd feel whole and high on life," I say, but with no conviction. "I'd be excited by the adventure."

"You could be high on life and you'd rather have a boyfriend?"

Still Dating . . .

Well, yes, if truth be told. And who says I can't have both? A year after Zack left, when I thought I was ready, I tried the old-fashioned route, asking friends to introduce me to men, but most said, "We don't know anyone who's available." So I learned how to upload a photograph to a dating website, filled out the questionnaire, and promptly was swamped with e-mails.

Internet sites are the primary portals for reentering the dating pool, and people between forty-five and sixty are the fastest-growing segment moving through them. I spoke on the phone with a divorced lawyer who did volunteer work at a hospice, and we arranged to meet at a neighborhood coffee shop. He showed up looking only dimly like his picture and wearing red shorts and a fanny pack. No woman I know over fifty would go on a blind date wearing shorts, but the next three men I met through the Internet all did. With men, I suppose, the legs are often the last thing to go, and if they got 'em, they flaunt 'em. The lawyer seemed pleasant, and I wanted to give him a chance, but the contrast between this superficial and wan interaction and the intense intimacy I'd had with Zack was so extreme that tears rolled down my face.

"What's wrong?" the lawyer asked.

"I'm sorry. I didn't think I'd have to go on a date again. Start from scratch."

"That *is* sad," he said.

Others took a more jaunty attitude. Mary-Ellis Bunim, the producer who invented reality television when she and Jonathan Murray created *The Real World* for MTV, approached it like a casting call. While on location in Canada, she joined five different dating services, including JDate for single Jews, although she's a shiksa. "I've always liked Jewish men," she said. Every night in her hotel room, she ran searches and fired off e-mails, screening the men who responded and lining up fifteen to audition during one weekend—the first she was back in Los Angeles.

Using her casting instincts, she selected one and they were together for a number of years until she died of breast cancer.

I've heard other stories of people who married men and women they met online—people who're engaging, smart, emotionally mature, and ready to commit—but I didn't meet any of those. I met the wounded, the terrified, the deluded, and the attachment averse. The men who contacted me were mostly engineers who'd never read a novel or boys in their twenties with bee-stung lips. I wrote back to a twenty-two-year-old, asking why he was interested in a woman in her fifties. He answered, "Last summer I had GREAT SEX with a woman who's 50. That's why I want to meet a HOT WOMAN like you." He attached a photo of himself posed in a bikini with multiple piercings and his lips puckered for a kiss and said he was attending law school at USC. I DON'T THINK SO.

In a short time I learn to be more canny about reading profiles. The first thing I check is their relationship history. It's auspicious if the man's a widower who loved his wife, because he wants and knows how to maintain a relationship, unless, as one told me, he's still grieving and doesn't know if he can love again—a disclaimer I ignored. It's also good if he's recently divorced after a long marriage and has kids—he'll probably be more mature and giving than if he's childless. If he's over fifty and never had a wife or family, I think: Pass.

I learn not to waste time exchanging e-mails and go straight to a phone call. If you don't hit it off on the phone, it won't be better in person. But it can be sensational on the phone, you'll fill in the missing pieces in your mind and spend an hour trying on clothes and fixing your hair so it looks as if you didn't spend much effort, then walk into the café, spot him, and want to flee. Something ineffable happens when you meet in person that doesn't happen on the phone or computer or even in videos, I'm told. It's not just physical appearance, because you've seen photographs. It's something you can't know until you meet, when, like magnets that carry a positive or negative charge, you're attracted or repelled, and it happens almost instantaneously. There was a man with whom I'd had soulful and erotic phone calls that filled us with anticipation, but when we sat down at a table in Starbucks, we had trouble making small talk and our eyes caromed off each other. He sighed. "You're a nice person. . . ."

"And you're a nice person," I said. "Can we leave now?"

It's not all terrible; I've become friends with several I've met online. One took me to my first tango lesson, and another introduced me to masters ski racing. But then comes the nightmare: the man who seems so promising online and in person he's so obviously insane that you go running back to your house and eat a large amount of chocolate or walk into a store and spend money on something you'll never use. In my case, it was snowshoes.

I withdraw from the Internet service, but they keep your profile in their database, and every few months you'll find a flirtatious message in your in-box. Sometimes you weaken, because it's been a while since you've gone on a date and this gives you the illusion that you're doing something about it, but you're quickly reminded why you gave it up.

Then, on an ordinary day when you haven't washed your hair and you're wearing old clothes, you go to the store as Joan Borysenko did and run into a man you've met casually over the years and you think, Isn't he married to that blond woman who designs silver jewelry? You start a conversation and learn that he and his wife have broken up and he asks you to lunch.

The Long Marriage

In the 1970s, when the film *Scenes from a Marriage* was released, I read an interview with Ingmar Bergman in which he said: "Marriage is hell. But it's preferable to the hell of being alone." At the time I agreed with him, cut out the piece, and kept it in my purse as a kind of talisman, which did not protect me from having two marriages dissolve.

Thirty years after clipping that quote, I set out to ascertain what skill, luck, or combination enables people to sustain a long commitment. The writer Dan Wakefield says, "I have a theory: Some men are good at marriage. I'm not." I talked with dozens of couples whose relationships have lasted more than thirty years and still feel juicy and nourishing. Some asked me to change their names so they could speak without restraint. The sample is small, and there's a great variety of types: platonic, age diverse, gay, people who seem to be twins and people who're radical opposites, couples who fight constantly and those who don't raise their voices. But what's notable are the elements they share. First is a word they all use—"determination"—to keep the marriage going, even during stretches when it feels love has died. Jayne Kennedy, the first black woman to become a network sportscaster, told me, "I believe in the institution. Just because you're not in love anymore is no reason to leave." Second, they say, is their willingness to accept each other's differences, to live with "the mystery of the other," as Gordon Dveirin puts it. Third, and perhaps critical, is the ability to laugh together.

Many speak of their marriage as a spiritual practice. Jim Molloy, a computer consultant in Costa Rica, married Dery Dyer, who publishes *The Tico Times,* when both were in their fifties and had never married before. Having been on his own for fifty-four years, Jim has seen that when you're single, "it's easy to hide from your own garbage, but when you're married, it's right in your face." Before their wedding, they'd been advised: "If you look at marriage in terms of getting 'what I want,' you'll crash and burn. If you look at marriage as an opportunity for growth and companionship, you'll flourish."

A friend told me that in her twenties she asked her teacher, Chögyam Trungpa Rinpoche, "Why should anyone get married if, as you've told us, you have the capacity to love everyone and you're a fool if you think the person you love now is the last person you'll ever love?" Rinpoche fixed his gaze on her, then said, "Where else can you study passion, aggression, and ignorance in such a heightened way?"

Okay, I thought, sounds good, but how the fuck do you do that?

Most of us get married with the "determination" to adapt, grow, and learn, but ten years out we're in bloody hell. Multiple factors work against us: We live longer, we go through deep change in other parts of our lives, we're addicted to intensity and disinclined to compromise or "settle." When no-fault divorce was instituted, it became easier to walk away, and at least 50 percent of us did. I wanted to talk to the other 50 percent.

*   *   *

The first couple I spoke with, Charles and Nora Brand, have been married thirty-five years. "We've dealt with the same crap and misery that all couples of our generation have," Nora says. "We've been close to breaking up—"

Charles jumps in: "Name a subject people fight about and we've fought about it. Money, other men or women, sex, where we live, children, work, addiction . . ." He looks at Nora. "Are there others we've missed?"

I say, "Criticism? Lack of warmth?"

Charles nods but Nora says, "There, I think we've been blessed." She says they both crave affection and enjoy giving it. "I think that makes a big difference." She looks at Charles. "Don't you?"

"Yes. When we were fighting, we had sex. When we were close, we had sex."

The three of us are sitting in the sunroom of their colonial home in western Connecticut. Both Charles and Nora are letting their hair go chicly silver; he's stocky and muscular, and she's willowy and tall, wearing a lavender sweater and glasses on a pink cord around her neck. Charles is a lawyer and mediator for global corporations. Nora, also an attorney, specializes in family law.

They met at twenty-two when they were hired—along with Hillary Rodham before she married Bill Clinton—for a research project at the

Carnegie Council on Children, directed by the eminent Yale psychologist Kenneth Keniston. They worked in adjoining offices and a year after they met were married. Both were from divorced homes and swore they'd do it differently.

Nora says the gift of staying in a relationship a long time is that "you get to play all the roles. One person is usually the chaser and the other is pulling away. One is more sexually hungry and the other has a headache. I thought I was the one who was more needy and capable of intimacy and he was always running. Then there was a moment, twenty years on, when he started reaching for greater intimacy and I felt terrified!"

Charles says he thinks all women and men are afraid of intimacy because "it challenges your personality, and our personalities don't like to be messed with—by another person or by God. That's why intimacy is here. God's not. So you work with intimacy."

I ask if there's an area of tension where they haven't reversed roles.

Nora nods. "The mess Charles makes." Their place looks as if it's inhabited by a gang of college guys who've just thrown a party.

"I'm still a mess in the kitchen, and that'll never change." Charles shoots a look at Nora. "Can't beat 'em, join 'em, right?"

"I joined," she says. She tried nagging Charles to clean up, but after their twin sons were born "it was me versus Charles and the two boys who followed his example. I gave up."

Having walked through their kitchen, in which every surface was littered with dirty dishes, open jars of peanut butter and mayonnaise, and rotting food, I think this would be a deal breaker for me. But I covet the live sparks between them.

Most days, Nora's eyes light when she sees Charles walk into a room, and he seems always to have her in his thoughts. They finish each other's sentences and speak in shorthand. Nora says there are times when "things go up in flames for no apparent cause. All of a sudden we start hating each other and treating each other like shit." One time this happened, they went to a therapist who made things worse. Nora suggested to Charles that they stop trying to analyze the problem and just be kind and gentle to each other for two weeks. "It worked."

Charles believes that healing takes place in a relationship in later years that doesn't happen before, "despite all your work, all your therapy, all your efforts and insight." He wonders if people who marry again at midlife have the same kinds of breakthroughs. "Maybe you'd learn the same things with a second person." He glances at Nora and grins. "I doubt it."

• • •

After Nora and Charles, I interviewed Robert and Judith Ansara Gass, who met in 1968 when they were called Bobby and Judy. He was a senior at Harvard, organizing marches against the Vietnam War, and she was a flower child at Boston University who liked to get stoned, go out by the Charles River, and dance. They've been married for thirty-seven years, raised three kids, trained in psychotherapy, engaged in political action, and for decades have been teaching workshops for couples. I've been to their house for Passover and was struck by the sense of welcome and abundance that seems to infuse the air.

I ask how they've stayed together.

Judith says they both came from tight-knit families. "My parents were highly intelligent and had good values, but they couldn't talk about feelings. I told myself, 'I'm not doing it that way.' " She wanted an emotionally connected family where everyone could talk about their inmost thoughts. She made a decision to not go "full throttle on my career, because I knew I couldn't fulfill my vision of family if I was stressed out from work. Robert traveled a lot, and I held the fort."

Robert says they've held together because of "incredible effort, tenacity, and luck." When things threatened to fall apart, "we kept turning back to each other." The only thing he feels they've missed in a marriage of four decades is a wide range of sexual partners. They met at twenty, had had minimal experience, and stayed "pretty monogamous" while Cambridge was aflame with the sexual revolution and their unmarried friends were helping themselves to wild times.

Then, in their fifties, the Gasses took up a dance called Contact Improv. I'd first seen it at a studio, Dance Home, in Santa Monica. The principle, I was told, is that you keep contact with some part of the other person's body—arm, leg, back, shoulder—as you improvise. I watched people draping themselves like silk over each other, swinging one another in the air, and rolling around the floor—it looked like they were making love with their clothes on. I asked my friend Jodie Evans, who'd brought me there, "Does this have a name?"

She said brightly, "You mean . . . Contact Improv?"

I laughed. The words were spot-on.

Judith, who'd been a dancer growing up, had seen Contact Improv in the seventies and forgotten about it until she was at a party in Colorado and saw "a guy who was six feet two, much younger than me, and a really skillful dancer doing this sensual improvisation." When the music ended, she told him she'd enjoyed watching him, and he motioned her to come dance. She protested that she hadn't danced in thirty years. "Next thing I knew, I was flying over his shoulder, around his back, and landing on my feet. And the instant I landed, my entire concept of what's possible when you're older was gone. Just gone!"

She began taking classes and practicing three or four times a week. "It's a safe way to interact with other men and women, and at first, I was filling in some part of development I'd missed." Later, she was drawn to the art and athleticism of the form. "I grew more healthy and strong than I've ever been," she says, "and I'm in ecstasy three times a week. Ecstasy!"

I remember ecstasy.

Part of the reason Judith had quit dancing, she says, was that Robert never danced because he thought he was awkward and clumsy. One night when he was watching Judith fly through the air, a woman who teaches Contact Improv asked him to dance, assuming he knew how. He hesitated, then turned himself over to her, "and we danced for thirty minutes. It was bliss." He started coming to classes and says, "I'm a pretty good dancer now. It's fun to go places where there are thirty good women dancers and two men. The first time I noticed there was a line of women waiting for me to be free, I thought, Holy shit! Why didn't someone tell me?"

* * * *

Like the Gasses, Hal Kennedy and Wendy Chang met when they were students in 1968, but at a "big ten" college. She was a famous beauty— half Chinese, half French—and he had a reputation for being witty and outrageous—the editor of the humor magazine. They married different people, were divorced a few years later, and after a passionate courtship, they married in 1974 and moved into a fixer-upper in Chicago. He became the host of a popular radio show, and she's a master chef who runs a catering business.

I take them to dinner at Scoozi, where Wendy orders Chianti Rufina Riserva and Hal, who's been through a 12-step program, has a Coke. "We knew right away we weren't going to leave each other no matter what," Wendy says. "But we don't have what we wanted in our twenties— a soul mate. Hal and I are not soul mates."

"Why not?" I ask.

"Temperamentally we're totally different." Wendy says she craves adventure and stimulation and Hal likes to not leave the house. "We'll go someplace and be having a great time and he'll say, 'Let's go home.'

" 'Home! We're having so much fun.'

" 'Home is fun, too,' he'll say."

So what keeps you connected? I ask.

Hal says they love jousting and playing verbally with each other. They have a ritual: Every morning they stretch out on cushions in a window seat they designed for this purpose, with a ledge to hold their coffee cups and the sun—should there be sun—pouring in. They go through several newspapers, arguing and joking, and Hal tries out ideas for his show.

Wendy says the things you fell in love with have to not disappear. She fell in love with Hal's charm, warmth, and dazzling gift for expressing himself in unique ways. "We're two strong, controlling people and we constantly have to let go of things that make us crazy."

Hal believes 80 percent of the tension in marriage comes from "the friction of living together, sleeping together. It's about snoring and various appliances like mouth guards and sleep masks." Wendy has insomnia, often wakes at three A.M., and has to read to fall back asleep. When she flips on the light, Hal's sleep mask has slipped off and he's startled awake and they make muffled grumbling noises that they call "dueling mouth guards."

In the morning, they stumble down to the window seat and pick up what George Bernard Shaw defined marriage to be: "an endless conversation at the breakfast table." They brew coffee, bring in the papers, and before they've read the first page, they're laughing.

· · ·

What could I learn from these couples—and others—who've made it across the thirty-year line, bound together as in a marathon three-legged race? I still feel there's an element of luck and some innate character trait that they own and I may not. Then, a year after conducting the interviews, I receive an e-mail from Nora Brand, the attorney in Connecticut who's been married thirty-five years, saying: "We need to talk." A week later, we meet in New York for a drink, and she asks me to remind her what we spoke about before.

"Your marriage . . . what makes it strong . . ."

"Let me cut to the chase," she says. "Charles has moved out."

I suck in my breath. "Is there . . . another woman?"

"Yes."

"Oh God, Nora."

She tells me Charles has been wanting more freedom and she's been wanting deeper commitment and fidelity. "He went off to live by himself for three months—he's never been alone—and I thought it would be good for him, good for us. Then last week, he told me he's involved with another woman."

I remember Charles saying with a cocksure grin that he doubted people could learn as much with a second mate as they could by staying with one. "Maybe I should remove the interview from the book," I say. "It's not true now. . . ."

"It was true then," Nora says.

Gloria Steinem

Everything changes. I know the accepted wisdom from therapists and spiritual teachers is that you should strive to be whole and not look for someone else to fulfill your needs. The goal is to feel the love within, since the only thing in this world that's constant is your self. Even if you find the person you think is your ideal mate, that partner could be taken by illness or accident. And change cuts both ways, they say. When I was moping about the last man who'd departed, a friend, Adam Engle, who organizes meetings between the Dalai Lama and Western scientists, said this is the time when the Buddhist concept of impermanence is your friend. "You can say, Yay, impermanence! No matter how icky you're feeling, it will not last. All you've got to do is sit there and breathe and things will change. Come on, impermanence!"

He makes me laugh, realizing this could be the only time we see impermanence as a good thing.

I've never been able to swallow the accepted wisdom, but I want to look more carefully at my pattern and my belief that I'm happiest with a partner. I consult a therapist who specializes in working with couples, and he tells me his bias is that humans are social animals and have a biological need for a mate. "It takes two to make one, and we're hardwired that way." I stare at him; I'm reminded of Plato's *Symposium,* where Aristophanes relates a myth that purports to explain why humans long for another to complete us. We were once whole and round with four arms, four legs, and two faces, he said. Then Zeus split every being into two halves and compelled us to tumble our way over the earth to seek out and unite with the missing matching half. "Human nature was originally one, and we were a whole, and the desire and pursuit of the whole is called love."

The pursuit of the whole is called love. The myth resonates with me, but I know others dismiss it, and I'm interested to hear the counterargument. I want to talk with Gloria Steinem because she's never felt "hardwired that way." When I catch up with her in New York by phone, she tells me that most of her life she's been in relationships but "I never wanted to marry." When she saw couples who appeared to have been married a long time sitting in a coffee shop, not talking, "I felt sorry for them and thought, I'm glad I'm not there. I celebrated my independence." She did so publicly and famously. In a magazine interview in 1999, she criticized Jane Fonda for being a "man junkie." Gloria said she herself was finished with sex. "I'm no longer looking for a sex partner . . . I'm riveted by life, not sex." She added that at age sixty-five, "remembering something is as good as having an orgasm."

Not long after that interview, Gloria and Jane switched positions. Jane was divorced from Ted Turner and said that for the first time she was enjoying being alone. "That's a biggie for me. I thought I could never be without a man, but I am absolutely loving it."

Gloria, when she was sixty-six, astounded her constituents by getting married for the first time to David Bale, an environmental activist and father of *Batman* star Christian Bale. Her marriage was headline news, but three years later David died of brain cancer. She spoke about this at a New York conference on "Women and Power" in 2004, sponsored by the Omega Institute and Eve Ensler's V-Day group. Gloria looked regal at seventy, wearing a black sweater and slacks, a large gold belt, and her hair swept up in a twist. She said people used to stop her on the street and say, "Isn't it wonderful that after waiting so long, you finally found the right person?" She paused. "I never knew quite how to respond. It wasn't that every other man was the wrong man, nor was it that I was waiting for something external." She said she believes what we're all really waiting for is to become strong enough so that we can be "interdependent with another human being without giving up ourselves." The audience cheered.

After her talk, I asked Gloria what she means by interdependence.

"Two whole beings leaning on each other equally. Not one leaning more than the other."

But even with interdependence, I asked, why did you want to be married after you'd attacked the institution?

"That's hard to know," Gloria said. "I'd been on my own with no partner for about twelve years, which was unusual for me." She said those years of independence might have been good preparation for marriage, "given our obsession with coupling." She also put it in political terms, saying that changes in the marriage laws had allowed her to do it. "In the sixties we were giving up our civil rights. We had to go to court to get our names back." Today, she said, you can keep your own name, your own legal residence, and be approved for a loan without your husband's permission.

But that's been true for years, I said. "What prompted you to marry David—was it timing or a good fit?"

"Part of it was that he'd spent his life doing what men are not supposed to do," she said. Bale was a divorced father of four. "He raised his children and didn't pay attention to status or money. He owned two pairs of black pants and two pairs of black Converse sneakers. Men are supposed to accumulate, and he didn't." She added, "He had the greatest heart of anyone I've known."

They were planning to attend the Cherokee national reunion over

Labor Day, and just before leaving, Gloria called her friend Wilma Mankiller, the first woman to be chief of the Cherokee. Gloria asked Wilma, "Do you think it's a good idea for us to marry?" Wilma said she would call her back. "Wilma being Wilma, she went out on her property and sat under the stars and trees that night. She called early in the morning and said she'd decided it was a good thing."

I'm surprised, I tell Gloria. "You are not someone who lets other people make decisions for you."

"I am if it's Wilma!" Gloria laughed.

She and David were married at sunrise around a sage fire in Wilma's yard, with Wilma's husband conducting a ceremony in Cherokee. To ensure that it would be legal and yet kept private, Wilma had convinced a local judge to show up at six A.M. without knowing why.

Three years later, when David was diagnosed with primary brain lymphoma, Gloria was grateful they'd been legally married so she could make health care decisions and David would be covered by her insurance. The cancer had grown in multiple clusters and was inoperable, affecting his motor skills, short-term memory, and speech. "I know he recognized me and his children, but he couldn't say our names." At the end, she wasn't sure what he understood.

"I'm sorry," I told her.

"I'm sorry he went through it," she said. "I'm not sorry I went through it with him. I learned a lot, changed a lot."

When she sees long-married couples now in a coffee shop, not talking, "I see people who I assume have pledged to usher each other through the years and out of life with support and love and, dare I say, commitment?" She'd been blind, she says, "to the commitment couples make, because I'd hardly ever seen a happy marriage. Now I see there can be a rock-bottom agreement to be interdependent, regardless of whether it's exciting or interesting."

After she finished her speech in New York, 1,400 people rose and applauded. When she invited questions or comments, a young woman from Kosovo said in a thick accent, "I came here with fifty words of English and fifty dollars. I discovered your books and wanted to be like you. I became a journalist, and when my mother pushed me to get a husband, I said, 'Gloria Steinem did not marry!' " The audience laughed. "Years later," the young woman said, "my mother somehow learned on television that you got married. She told me, 'See! Even *your* Gloria Steinem finally got a husband!' "

Gloria looked at her, wondering if she had failed this young woman. Then she smiled. "So tell your mom that you have at least until you're sixty-six."

Carol Muske-Dukes

I don't know if I could have faced the tragedy Gloria did with such resilience. I might have raged at the unfairness—fate whacking me sideways. And yet, during these years, having your loved one die is a possibility.

Carol Muske-Dukes wrote a novel in 2000, *Life After Death,* about a woman who has a fiery argument with her husband, tells him she wishes he would die, and the next day learns that while playing tennis, he fell straight down like a plank and died of a heart attack. Carol imagined how the character, Boyd Schaeffer, would deal with guilt, remorse, and the shock that someone she loved no longer exists. "I still feel like he's in the house," Carol has Boyd saying. "You know, like he's going to turn on the light, climb the stairs."

Carol's own husband, David Dukes, the Broadway and motion picture actor, read the manuscript and made suggestions, as he always did. On the morning Carol sent the final draft to her publisher, David flew to Seattle, where he was shooting a miniseries, *Rose Red.* He checked into his hotel, went to play tennis, and had a heart attack, falling forward like a plank. The tennis pro called the paramedics, then picked up

David's cell phone and punched "home." Carol answered the phone, and he told her, "There's been an accident."

"What do you mean, an accident?" She called the hospital where David had been rushed and managed to get hold of an ER nurse, who asked, "Do you want me to tell you what's happening?"

"Yes!" Carol said. Her seventeen-year-old daughter was standing in front of her. "Step by step," Carol tells me, "the nurse described him dying on the table in front of her. Blood pressure dropping . . . pulse rate . . . respiration . . ." Carol stops. "This is hard. I still can't take it in."

David had been in what seemed perfect health, had never been treated for a heart condition, and had no symptoms. Was this an eerie and ghoulish coincidence, or had Carol received some foreknowledge and unknowingly written what would happen? She believes it was the latter; as she wrote in an essay: "Sometime before David's death I began to know something unconsciously—something unspoken, something gathering force about him . . . What I 'knew' became what I imagined."

Six weeks after David died, she got up in the middle of the night and started writing poems. "It was like a flood—almost like taking dictation," she recalls. Writing helped clarify her emotions, "and I could fashion the grief into something—an elegy for David, a meditation on the life of the artist." The poems, published as the collection *Sparrow,* were nominated for a National Book Award.

Four years later, in 2004, I'm visiting Carol at her home in Hancock Park, a genteel old neighborhood in Los Angeles, where she sits hugging a pillow on the living room sofa with three dogs curled at her feet. David's clothes are still in the closet and his study remains as it was the morning he left for Seattle. "I still feel like he's in the house," Carol says. He was often away for months shooting a film or performing in a play, so it was normal for her to be home alone with their daughter, as she is now. Brushing back the pale blond hair she inherited from her Minnesota ancestors, Carol says they had a rich and complex marriage, but

"I don't think I'll marry again. I think marriage is hard—between any two people, but especially with two artists. When actors aren't working, they're depressed, and when they *are* working, they're depressed if it's not going right. Not that writers are any picnic." She laughs softly.

"People respond so differently to losing a spouse," I say. "Some go right out and find a new one."

Carol shakes her head. "I enjoy the solitary life. I know a lot of poets who're given to being alone. As long as I can write and read, I'll be content. Every time I pick up a book, my world is enlarged. There's great loneliness, yes, but I wouldn't give up the solitude."

Grandchildren on Your Knee . . .

The wheel turns. People you love die and babies arrive, kindling new love. When love does appear or become reawakened at this age, I've found, it may have a richer nature and be inspired by a wider variety of sources. Beverly Kitaen-Morse and Jack Rosenberg, psychotherapists who married each other at fifty-nine and sixty-three, say they've found that younger people are seeking to be loved, but in later years the focus shifts to wanting love that arises in you: "The way your body feels when you love the ocean, you love a piece of music, you love a lover, you love a child," Beverly says.

Nowhere is the expansion in the field of love more visible than with grandchildren. My daughter is hoping to have kids before long, and I'm enchanted at the prospect of reading to them and teaching them to ski. I may need to move or become a frequent flier, but I'm not willing to see them only once or twice a year. I've met people who're resettling where their grandchildren live so they can take part in raising them. Hal and Wendy, the couple who met as students in the sixties, made a commitment to care for their four-year-old grandson, Wayne, one day a week and sometimes weekends. Their daughter, Jennifer, and her partner are gay and adopted an African American boy, but on Hal and Wendy's street in a multicultural neighborhood in Chicago, this is not unusual. There are two gay male couples and one lesbian pair with kids, and "they drive SUVs and do soccer," Hal says. "On the Fourth of July it's a Norman Rockwell scene here." They close the block to traffic and hold a daylong picnic, with sack races, egg tosses, and a parade where they march to "Stars and Stripes Forever" and read the Declaration of Independence. "It's more 'family values' than what I had growing up," Hal says. He was the only child of a divorced mom with no relatives nearby. "We're an odd, blended clan and we do a lot of things together."

I ask how he felt when he learned Jennifer was gay, because she'd had boyfriends growing up and married one at twenty-five. "That's what bothered me most—that I hadn't seen it coming," Hal says. "I felt like a father should know, particularly a sensitive liberal father who's trained to pick up cues." Jennifer had called him at the station and asked if she could come over that night and speak with him and Wendy alone. Hal said sure, but Jennifer's voice had been shaky, and he called her back and said, "Just give me the headline. It's obviously something serious. Fatal illness?"

Jennifer took a breath. "Okay. Daughter of popular radio host leaves her husband and finds out she's gay."

Hal says when Jennifer came to the house, "she gave us the version of the truth she thought we could handle. We told her whatever sexual orientation our kids have is fine." A few months later, they met her new partner, Sheila, a high school teacher who's closer to their age than to Jennifer's. When the women adopted Wayne, Hal felt a bond with the baby "immediately. Biology seems not to matter. This is the child of my child." He and Jennifer have lunch once a week and mostly talk about parenting. "I'm, like, *the guy* in Wayne's life, and we do guy things." Hal loves playing on the floor with trains and cars, and sometimes he'll be reminded with a start that Wayne is black. "To me, he's just Wayne. I'm not even aware that he looks different. I'm focusing on his body language, trying to figure if he's okay or if a tantrum is brewing."

Wendy likes being a grandma because "you can act like a kid again, jumping over cracks and making up games. It brings Hal and me closer because we get to play and be silly together."

Hal says they have ferocious tag tournaments that go on all weekend. "Then we turn Wayne over to his mother. She gets to calm him down. She does the heavy lifting. We just get love."

.   .   .

We can't know with whom, other than ourselves, we'll walk the rest of the way, but if you want to see what you're good at and predisposed toward, look at your history. Joan Borysenko has had serial marriages. Robert and Judith Gass have had one and, absent an act of God, are likely to stay with it to the last breath. Gloria Steinem rejected marriage until she was sixty-six, which shows that it's possible to get off the track you've established and set down a new one. When I look at my record, I'd say I'm not cut out for the long march. I'm not going to have a thirty-seven-year marriage like the Gasses. Either I sign on for endless rounds of love and loss, flying high and crashing, or I find a way—is there a 12-step program for relationship junkies?—to gain some detachment and release.

A judge I know in New York, whom I'll call George, had love affairs with women in his twenties and, after age thirty, with men, but he managed to keep them all at a distance. He has scores of friends who adore him and compete to have him at dinners and on vacation trips, but his preferred resting state is home alone. "I've been coming to terms with this all my life," he says. "The compromise I make is that to feel safe, I've kept people away. I get panicky when someone's too close. Intimacy is nourishing, but I'd rather go hungry and have the safety of isolation."

A psychiatrist friend told George that after decades of listening in the privacy of his consulting room, he was struck by the infinite ways humans devise to manage the hard business of getting through life. Not only are there a large number, but they differ radically from one to the other. "Which is why," George says, "the notion of perversity is fucked. Perversity is the *rule,* if you define it as varying from the norm. And it's the acceptance of your own crazy way of doing life that leads to healing." In his case, George says, "the bargain I've made involves the loss of human closeness, but that's the way I've done it, the only way I *could* do it—like a tree growing around a fence post." He often has casual sex—with young guys he meets on the Internet who troll for older gay men. "If I'm lonely at times, that's the down side of the bargain. Would I rather be living with someone?" He shuts his eyes a moment. "No."

The difference between us, I tell George, is that I want intimacy and haven't been able to sustain it for more than a decade. The question is: Do I need to learn to be content by myself or learn to commit without reservation? The answer may be: Both. If my pattern continues, there'll be alternating periods of being alone and being with a mate, and that's my own crazy way of doing life.

On a morning in June, when the Colorado hills are covered with purple columbine, opening their petals like a trumpet call—ta-da!—I come home from a walk and realize: I haven't been thinking about the architect who lives in a different city and suddenly stopped calling after months of ardent e-mails. The thought ticks by that I'm free. If I'm not hunting or worrying, if there's no constant static in my mind—will he call, does he care, do I care enough, and how come the only person I can find to care about lives thousands of miles away?—I'm free. I'm more happy and comfortable on my own than I've ever been, and I'm open and willing to risk love again. It's an odd sensation, as when you cut your hair much shorter. It feels so light. Could I continue to feel like this, or will the ease and lightness drift away like clouds, following the laws of impermanence? Probably, but having sensed this once, isn't it likely I could feel it again?

7

The Second Sexual Revolution

If he makes a sudden move in bed, his back creaks and he feels a stab of pain and has to lie still and breathe. They've been seeing each other for a month, and all afternoon they've been lounging on the couch, drinking mimosas, talking, reading the Sunday *Times,* and feeling the electricity. They slide to the floor and are matched up, chest to toe, kissing, and they agree it would be more comfortable in the bedroom, but it's tricky getting up off the floor and they help each other. They both have to use the bathroom. He's in bed with his glasses off when she comes in wearing only a T-shirt, but she's not self-conscious because without his glasses he can't see anything but a blur. Perfect! He hasn't had sex in a year, since his wife died, and for her it's been longer, so when he touches her she's dry. I need to be woken up, she says playfully, and you're the man for the job. He brightens as she stands to go find lubricant. She can't remember where she put it, and when she returns, of course, he's lost his erection and didn't bring the Cialis because he hadn't anticipated this would be the day.

The next time, he pops the pill and it not only works, it's wondrous. He laughs, she cries. "We did it." A few months later, they sign up for a tantric sex workshop, which takes them to a realm where they can't tell where one body ends and the other begins and there's not just physical ecstasy but a transfer of energy between them that fills their dry cells and makes them whole. "I never had sex like this, even in my twenties!" he says.

Six months later, he learns he has prostate cancer and if he has surgery and radiation, he'll most likely be impotent. No! Not now, when I've discovered the best sex of my entire life? They make the rounds of doctors and alternative healers, do research, and select a treatment plan that offers good prospects for survival and reasonably good prospects for retaining potency. But nothing is certain. Welcome to sex in the master years.

． ． ． ．

How can sex feel more intense and expansive at this time than when we had raging hormones and could climax without effort? I would assert that we've become more complex, richened with sorrow and joy, and that there's more to us—we bring more, release more, savor more.

We've had a sexual destiny: We were the advance guard in the first revolution, and now there's a second in attitudes about sex and aging, both movements driven in large part by chemicals—the birth control pill and drugs like Viagra. As Tom Pollock, former chairman of Universal Pictures, put it, "Boomers have always taken care of our own."

From the time I moved into the freshman dorm at college, the most important relationships I've had began as sexual. That seems to be the access point, the way I've let down the bridges across the moat to the fortress. When the body lets down, love can enter.

My fear, as years ticked by, was that I would lose my appeal, desire, and capacity to make love. I'd read in medical and popular literature that women dry up, vaginas atrophy, men can't stay hard, and lust vanishes. When I turned fifty, I was afraid the best sex was behind me. I'd been at Berkeley in the sixties—an embedded reporter, smack in the epicenter of the sexual revolution—but shortly after my fiftieth, I met Zack, and our affair remains, to this day, the gold standard. I was startled by the newness of our lovemaking and how besotted I was with lust. Was I mad, depraved? Or was I lucky? The consensus among the literary lionesses—Simone de Beauvoir, Colette, and Germaine Greer—was that the third stage of a woman's life is "triumphantly postsexual." Colette had viewed carnal love as a virus she'd barely survived, and Francine du Plessix Gray wrote, "The more fortunate among us serenely accept that we may never again be seen as objects of erotic desire." Not me, I was not going gentle down that road.

What began with Zack as a one-night stand became a long-distance romance and then a partnership. Sex was the glue that kept us tight, and as he put it, "It's a hellacious bond"—when your rhythms are the same, your fantasies, tastes, and levels of desire mesh and blend because you know this is not to be found on any corner just ahead. The affair brought other riches, which I wrote about in *Cowboy*. But when it ended, I was fifty-seven. Would I ever have sex like that again? I wasn't ready to let it go; I didn't want to be "triumphantly postsexual." Given my pattern, though, what would I do during the intervals when I was alone, and what if the interval went on and on? After Zack, casual sex was bumbling and one-dimensional and it wasn't safe, not just because of AIDS and STDs, but the emotional wear and tear. How would I avoid becoming touch-deprived? I remember being frightened when I read an interview with Hanif Kureishi, who wrote *My Beautiful Laundrette*. He described taking his mother to a restaurant, "and she fancied the waiter's hands. She said to me, 'I worry that I will never be touched again, except by the undertaker.' "

I began to do research on sexuality and age, and what I found was both reassuring and troubling. It's possible for people to have exciting and fulfilling sex as long as they're healthy, but a large number are not because they lack a partner or interest. Due to illness, stress, or other factors, they have a diminished capacity for pleasure.

In 2004, the AARP commissioned a nationwide survey of sexual behavior among people forty-five and older, a group not well studied in previous sex research. Betty Friedan, writing in *The Fountain of Age,* says she was shocked to find that in the 1,700 pages of the Kinsey reports on men and women, there were only two pages on men over sixty and half a page on women. In the Masters and Johnson studies conducted in the sixties and seventies, less than 5 percent of the subjects were over sixty-five.

The most recent AARP survey reveals the shifting landscape. A glut of sexual information—on the Internet, TV, and other media—has led men to be more savvy about female anatomy and women to be more responsive and adventurous. The majority of women questioned say they masturbate, often with a vibrator. Of the men questioned, 22 percent say they've tried erectile enhancement drugs, and the percentage is growing exponentially. But the drugs don't affect one's emotions and cannot create desire. Repeated surveys show that a third of American women of all ages report having low libido, and gynecologists I've interviewed say that based on what they hear from patients, the true number is higher. A third of the nearly 1,700 people surveyed by AARP—one in three—rate their sex life as "yawn" or "bloody awful," while the rest report being "somewhat" to "extremely satisfied."

After interviewing more than a hundred people myself, I found that, as in other areas, there's a phenomenal diversity of behavior in the bedroom, from the long-married couple who sleep in separate rooms and never have sex to the woman who's enjoying it with a man so much younger that people assume he's her grandson. But the idea that older people don't make love or, if they do, it's embarrassing or distasteful to contemplate no longer applies. Jack Rosenberg, the therapist in Los Angeles who's married to a fellow therapist, suffered a heart attack and complications from a sextuple bypass operation, but after recovering, he says, "we have good sex, and I'm seventy-two." His wife, Beverly Kitaen-Morse, adds that after the surgery "every time we'd get to the point of orgasm he'd start to say good-bye, telling me he'd watch over me. There was always the chance . . . but he took the risk every time."

Joan Hotchkis

When I heard from friends that the actress Joan Hotchkis was doing a hilarious performance piece about sex as we get older, I immediately called for a ticket. In the ad for the show, *Elements of Flesh, or Screwing Saved My Ass,* Joan is shown lying nude on her side, with a piece of flowered silk draped over her torso but baring a round, pink buttock. She's willowy and beautiful by any standard, but the ad, when it ran in the *L.A. Times,* triggered a rash of phone calls and hate mail. What infuriated people was not that Joan was naked or using words like "screwing," but that she was doing it at sixty-eight. "You are ugly, old, and through—a whore which no man wants," one letter said. When I saw the ad and read how old she was, I thought: This woman is sixty-eight? There's hope.

In the show, Joan acts out scenes from her own sexual history and, like Anna Deveare Smith, takes on the voices and mannerisms of people she's observed. To prepare for the piece, Joan sought out men and women in their sixties, seventies, and eighties, many of whom refused to talk about sex. I told her that Eve Ensler had no trouble getting women to talk about vaginas. Joan says, "It's easier to talk about your vagina than about having sex after you're sixty."

One of the men she spoke with, whom she calls "Chuck" in the show, was married at seventy-five to a woman nearing eighty. They did it in the shower, at friends' homes, on the airplane, everywhere at any hour, and she had orgasms for the first time. Chuck told Joan that most older people don't have sex because the culture makes fun of them. "But the later years are the golden age of sexuality because no one bothers you and life is not so rushed." Joan believes that humans are "made to be touched, to snuggle together like puppies, to smell each other's smells and feel each other's fluids, yet many older people haven't been held or touched in decades."

When I visit Joan in her condo in Santa Monica, which has four flights of stairs to keep her agile, I ask if she thinks boomers will stand for not being touched.

She laughs. "Not if they stay in character."

Slender and gaminlike—she could play Peter Pan—Joan wears a stylish red shirt and cowboy belt, with her ash blond hair cut smartly. "The physical body is holding up," she says, but she struggles with short-term memory loss and has Post-its on the TV, VCR, and DVD about which buttons to push. She's been acting since she was nineteen, trained in New York with Lee Strasberg, and was a member of the Actors Studio, but TV viewers know her as Jack Klugman's girlfriend in *The Odd Couple*.

"The male gaze was on me from the time I was fourteen," she says. "Apparently I was very beautiful," but in her family—the Bixby dynasty, which owned a twenty-six-thousand-acre cattle ranch in California—the word *beautiful* was used only for horses and yachts. "Look how she comes about—beautiful!" Joan says, mimicking her grandfather. Joan married at thirty, had a daughter, was divorced, and never wanted to marry again, "but I always wanted to screw," which was not a problem, she says. "I never had to flirt, never lacked a date." Then, in her early sixties, she lost the male gaze.

Joan says she hasn't had a "full-blown passionate affair for ten years. I don't have the stamina to go through the hurt and pain, the arguing and rejection—everything you go through when you fall in love." But she misses screwing and still has a drawer full of sex toys and silk lingerie. "When I did the performance, I was hit on by men," she says.

While she was rehearsing, a friend who teaches psychology told her, "Joanie, if you're willing to be a dominatrix, you could have all the lovers you wanted." Her friend said that because men are conditioned to be aggressive, "they get really turned on being a submissive." Her friend posted an ad on the Internet describing Joan as a "beautiful, very special older woman who's a dominatrix" and received more than a hundred responses. Her friend screened the applicants, and her first questions were: "Do you know where the clitoris is? Do you know what to do with it?" She narrowed the field down to five, whom Joan then spoke with on the phone. "Voice is important to me," Joan says. "I've learned not to question my instincts. We're animals, and no animal is attracted to every other animal. I like voices that are deep, but I don't care about grammar or anything like that."

The man she selected was a computer engineer, married, in his forties, who said this was his first foray into "getting my needs met."

"You didn't care that he was married?" I ask.

"I didn't want love, I wanted sex."

Her friend coached her—"she gave me the lines. I commanded this man to write me erotic letters every day, and he did pretty well." Joan went to Frederick's of Hollywood and bought the costume and props: "a black bustier that was easily unhookable, a black garter belt, a mean-looking necklace—black leather with stainless-steel prongs—a whip and dog collar." First she had the man take a walk with her in the Santa Monica Mountains. They went behind a thicket to a clearing, she put the collar on him and said, "You're my dog. Heel, dog!" As he was on all fours, preparing to lick the soles of her feet, a group of Brentwood ladies with jingling gold bracelets "went jabbering by. We were afraid they'd see us, and that got the guy really hot." Next she rented a hotel suite on the ocean and ordered him to meet her there. "I made him strip for me—he had a gorgeous chest—then lie on the bed, and I stood above him in my high heels, cracking the whip. But I ruined my own act because after each stroke I'd say, "Oh! Did I hurt you?" She laughs. "I broke character." They both had orgasms, but she decided "he wasn't interesting enough or talented enough about touching. You know how some people are tone-deaf? He was touch-deaf. And it's hard being responsible for everything: making plans, calling for reservations, deciding what we'll eat and what games to play. Orders, orders, orders! How do men do it?"

The episode found its way into her performance piece and was a show stopper. The audience howled and cheered as Joan, slight as a pixie, planted her feet apart and said, raising her arms in victory: "I refuse to go unfucked to my grave!"

Two to Tango

Right on, sister. But when sex is not available, I've found that a safe way to be sensual, to feel the contours, warmth, and softness or firmness of another's body, is dancing. Eve Babitz, who wrote *Two by Two: Tango, Two-Step, and the L.A. Night,* once told me dancing is "better than sex because it lasts longer." And there's no risk of disease or emotional entanglement. You don't care what your partner does in the world, what he looks like, what he reads, or if he votes red or blue, if you have a great time dancing you go home elated.

It's the zipless fuck or, more accurately, the fuckless fuck. In the eighties, when AIDS brought casual sex to a screeching halt, it's no coincidence that there was a resurgence of dances where couples hold each other, like swing, salsa, and two-step. Joan Hotchkis does competitive ballroom dancing. "At least three times a week I get held against the body of a man," she says, "who's usually much younger and has a girlfriend." Robert and Judith Gass do Contact Improv, and shortly after moving to Colorado I took up Argentine tango. This is not the head-snapping, rose-in-the-teeth, Rudolph Valentino–style tango, but a social walking dance that flourished in Buenos Aires and Paris in the 1940s, fell out of favor, and was revived in the 1980s and 1990s, so that today every major city in America and Europe has a booming tango community. In Argentine tango, people dance in "close embrace." One of my teachers, Tom Stermitz, says there are two modes: "close and closer."

Tom looks nondescript: a short man of fifty who teaches wearing a T-shirt, cargo shorts, and Birkenstocks with socks. His movements look understated, and he comes just to the top of my chest, but he holds me in a strong embrace and I don't have to think because I have no choice but to swivel and glide as he wants me to.

Tom says most men in postfeminist America are politically correct. "Tango is not." He urges men to "put the masculine chest in play. Unleash that macho energy!" He tells them to cast off the persona of the nice guy slumped at his computer, slaving around the clock. "Touch, flirt, and be bold!" The greatest challenge, he says, is "to convince men it's okay to hold a woman close. We're dancing in a hug." He demonstrates with me, then says, "Women take less convincing."

What's hard for women is to surrender to being led. The very notion of "following" makes me tense. "Women have been indoctrinated that to succeed in the world, they have to be assertive and take the first step," Tom says. "Tango asks them to do the opposite—wait and receive." The roles are strict: The leader indicates and the follower responds—in Spanish it's *marcar* and *responder.* The instructors tell women: Lift your chest and connect with your partner's heart. What they mean is lift your breasts, move in close, and press them to his torso, inviting him to lead you. One of my favorite dance partners, Joe Reling, a real estate salesman with a tattoo on his bicep, says the first time a woman with enormous breasts placed them on his chest as if on a shelf, he had to sit down and compose himself.

In the beginning, tango is not fun and I don't think it's for me. I find the music schmaltzy—remember "Hernando's Hideaway"? With other dances like salsa or swing, there's a basic step you learn and repeat no matter what you're asked to do. After a few lessons, you can get up and have a good time. Not with tango. There's no basic step, but a "vocabulary" of possible moves—walk, cross, pivot. Each step is unpredictable because it's improvised by the leader. When he "indicates," the follower must move first, "opening the door" by extending her leg back, and then they go.

In my first group class, I stand, nervous and worried that I won't be able to tell what the leader wants. You have to sink into a kind of trance and listen to what he's saying with his chest. You can't talk or look in your partner's eyes or you'll be distracted and miss his cues, so you stare at his shoulder or keep your eyes closed. (This appeals to inarticulate guys.) Every five minutes we change partners, and one man I dance with raises his hand and asks for help. "She's doing the steps before I lead them," he says.

The teacher cuts in to fix the problem. "You're trying to lead," he says. "You need to wait for the signal." I'm mortified. I feel as if my worst fear is being announced in neon lights: "This woman is domineering. SHE CANNOT FOLLOW!"

Tango requires you to be spontaneous and pay attention, which seems good training for life: to not anticipate what might happen and how you'll respond, but wait and see what the indications are and act. This is not simple. I'm told that it takes women a year and men several years, practicing at least twice a week, before they feel comfortable at a dance. Women progress faster than men because most have had dance lessons growing up and it's easier to follow than to lead. So they say.

After two months of classes, I shore up my nerve and drive to Denver for a dance, or *milonga,* at the Mercury Café. I'm not prepared for what I see: someone's vision of a psychedelic Hispanic fantasy ballroom with loud violin music and over-the-top sentimentality. There's a wooden floor, and in a ring around it are tiny tables, each with a winking candle and bud vase containing a dusty artificial rose. Strings of plastic flowers, iridescent stars, and planets hang from the ceiling, and the dancers look like apparitions in the dim light. The crowd of more than a hundred seems evenly split between men and women. Most are single or couples who met at tango class or took up dancing because their therapist recommended it. Unlike swing clubs, which attract people in their twenties and thirties, the Mercury skews older, perhaps because tango is slow and doesn't require strenuous exertion. A former ballerina in New York who's in her fifties tells me, "At this age you can't do ballet or modern anymore, but you can tango. The dance is intricate and challenging, so lots of former dancers become obsessed with it."

Joe, the real estate salesman, asks me to dance. He leads me into back *ochos,* or figure-eights, but I don't pick up the signal and just walk backward. Joe stops and looks up at the ceiling. "What?" I ask.

"Never mind," he says. "People get intimidated here because there are so many good dancers. But they were all beginners once." I start to relax, and for the first time it actually feels like dancing, not an exercise I'm bumbling through. Joe says, "Now that people see you can dance, you'll be fine." He goes off, and another man, Tom Frost, beckons to me. He's tall and slim—our bodies line up perfectly—and he makes it easy and fun, twisting his torso, which makes mine twist, and when he lengthens his stride, so do I. There are loops of time where it seems the music is moving us and it's thrilling.

School for Sex

Dance, chocolate, skiing, and toys from Babeland, the online pleasure store, can keep the juices flowing, but there ain't nothing like the real thing.

While I was immersed in tango, I received an ad for a workshop in tantric sex given by Charles and Caroline Muir of the Source School of Tantra in Hawaii. I'd taken the seminar with Zack and was still on the mailing list. I couldn't imagine going to such a weekend by myself, but I wanted to revisit the experience we'd had—and relate it in detail—because it offers evidence that sex is a lush mystery and there's no age at which we can't enjoy it. Some of the people taking the course with us were in their seventies, some were not conventionally attractive, and a good number were unpaired. Transcendent sex, it was revealed, is not about how thin or fat or youthful you are, it's not about staying hard for hours, and you don't need a steady partner. It's not about the body, yet the body is the instrument. It's about union, which happens on the interior.

In 1997, when Zack and I had signed up, we already were having what we considered the best sex of our lives. My sister had urged me to take the course but I'd declined, thinking it was unnecessary. Then I heard it recommended by others, including Jill Eikenberry and Michael Tucker, the actors on *L.A. Law*, who were down-to-earth and not easily gulled. "It transformed the way we think about sex," Tucker said. "It took us to states we'd never imagined, and I realized, This is what we're here for, to love like this."

What do they teach you? I asked.

"You know, the G spot? Vaginal orgasms."

"Oh, come on," I said, "vaginal orgasms don't exist. We settled that twenty-five years ago." Tucker smiled, suggesting he knew otherwise.

In 1997, the assertion that massaging the G-spot could lead women to ejaculate and have vaginal orgasms was bizarre, and tantric sex was the fringe. Now the Internet is filled with sites like seehersquirt.com and diagrams of the G-spot and how to find it. Even the conservative Right has discovered spiritual sex. Robert Irwin, who describes himself as "an average, middle-aged Christian man" who married "a lovely Christian woman," hosts a website where he sells an e-book that promises to show the Christian husband how to find his wife's G-spot, make her squirt, find his own G-spot, be able to come three times in an hour—at any age—and be able to have an orgasm without ejaculating, which he claims is the most glorious and spiritually satisfying big bang of all.

A great deal of nonsense poses as tantra, and no one knows how it was practiced when it arose in India about 3000 BC. Scholars believe it was a system for consecrating life that included exercise, breathing, meditation, music, and sexual rites designed to bring the participants into union with the divine. The Source School of Tantra still seems one of the more serious and responsible groups for exploring "conscious loving." In 1997, when I showed their brochure to Zack, he was intrigued. "How can you ever know too much about sex?" he asked.

On a Friday night, we walked into the Wilshire Room of the Sheraton Miramar in Santa Monica, pinned on name tags, and sat down in a row of chairs. Others had removed their shoes, but Zack would not take off his black boots with red lightning bolts.

"Why are we doing this?" he asked.

"You wanted to," I said.

"That was before."

"We can always leave."

There were more than a hundred participants, and the majority, to my surprise, were in their forties and older. They were accountants, doctors, sales people, and filmmakers, and twenty-three were single. Charles and Caroline made their entrance wearing turquoise shirts and black slacks. Charles, forty-nine at the time, was tall and slim with dark curly hair, and Caroline, fifty-three, was blond, big-breasted, and earthy.

Charles said the subject of the weekend was conscious sex. When he'd begun giving this workshop in the eighties, he'd asked people to name all the words they knew for the penis. Charles picked up a list. "We collected more than a hundred and fifty: cock, pecker, prick, dick, stick, dong, shlong, big bong, weeny, wiener, hot dog, sausage . . ." He paused. "That was the meat section." In tantra, he said, "we use the Sanskrit word lingam, or 'wand of light.' " He took out a puppet—actually a child's toy, a magic wand that lit up with orange sparks when he pressed a switch. "We're going to ask you to trade in your dick or prick for a wand of light."

Zack rolled his eyes.

Caroline said, in a voice that was surprisingly deep and smoky, that most names for the vagina are "so demeaning they're not worth repeating. The Sanskrit word is yoni, which means 'sacred space,' and through this space comes life itself." She picked up her puppet, a foot-high yoni made of purple velvet with red lips and a gold clitoris. Then Charles put his lingam puppet in her yoni puppet to demonstrate some of the "thousand and one varieties of movement. Keep her surprised," Charles said. "You don't always want to go straight down the fairway." By this time, people who'd been sitting tensely were laughing and lounging on the floor as if the puppets were from *Sesame Street* and it was perfectly normal to be talking about lingams and yonis in the Sheraton Miramar.

Zack and I went home and tried some of the techniques they'd taught, including "Climbing the Himalayas," which was pleasant but, as Zack put it, "underwhelming." We talked about quitting but that was impossible; we had to see how far this would go.

* * * *

On Saturday morning, Charles and Caroline began setting the stage for the "initiation" we'd do that evening—sacred spot massage. Charles talked about the area in the yoni called the sacred spot, or G-spot after the gynecologist Ernst Gräfenberg, who's credited with discovering it in 1955. It struck me as significant that this spot, which supposedly has been in women's bodies for millennia, was "discovered" by a man who named it after himself. "Every woman needs healing and awakening there," Charles said. Caroline nodded. "Most women have had traumas—infections or abortions, cancer, sexual abuse, sex you didn't want, sex that hurt." She said the traumas are stored in the yoni and cause it to shut down.

Charles said the G-spot is located on the upper inside wall of the vagina, midway between the opening and the cervix. "It's the south pole of the clitoris, the internal pole." I shook my head. I'd always thought the G-spot was hokum and that searching for it would be as much of a snipe hunt as chasing the vaginal orgasm. Zack, whispering, told me a joke he'd heard: "What's the difference between a golf ball and a G-spot?"

"What?"

"A man will spend twenty minutes searching for a golf ball."

Charles stressed that this night was for the women. "Guys, it's not about you getting off. We'll do that tomorrow. Tonight is your chance to serve." He said the sacred spot massage should last at least an hour, and during it, the woman might experience numbness, pain, strong emotions, or exquisite pleasure. "It may take a year of practice before this area is awakened."

Charles said that continued stimulation could bring on vaginal orgasms. I raised my hand. "I have a problem with this." I asked Caroline if she could describe the vaginal orgasm.

"For me, it's like night and day, the difference between clitoral and vaginal orgasms," she said. "A clitoral orgasm is like a male orgasm, a big bang. A vaginal orgasm feels like waves of pleasure through my whole body. And it's easy. You don't have to work and strain."

What bothered me about Caroline's description was its vagueness. A clitoral orgasm or, I would say, an orgasm, is a clear event. Meg Ryan could simulate one perfectly—recognizable to all—in *When Harry Met Sally.* Could she sit in the deli and simulate the other kind?

Despite the skepticism in the room, Charles went further: He said that sacred spot massage could cause the woman to ejaculate. What she ejaculates is a clear, sweet-smelling liquid called *amrita,* or "divine nectar." "It comes out of the urethra, but it's not urine," Charles said. "And it's not just moisture or lubrication. It's voluminous. We measure it in cups, sometimes quarts. It takes three or four towels to absorb it, and I've seen it shoot eight feet in the air and hit the wall."

"No!" someone cried.

I looked at Zack. "I don't know what the hell they're talking about."

*   *   *

During the lunch break, I went to a bookstore and browsed through the section on health and sex. Is it possible, I thought—is it conceivable that I've reached my fifties, had two kids, and don't know my body? Sure, I'd heard of vaginal orgasms before. The prevailing wisdom from Victorian times until the late sixties was that immature women have clitoral orgasms and mature women have vaginal orgasms. Freud had written, in "Three Essays on the Theory of Sexuality," that if girls fail to "change their leading erotogenic zone" from the clitoris to the vagina, they'll be prone to neurosis and hysteria. At Berkeley, my friends and I had read Freud's essays and were mystified. All the orgasms we'd felt were in the clitoris, no matter how they'd been achieved. But we had secret doubts: Perhaps we weren't real women, experiencing all that a woman could.

Then came the first women's liberation groups, which circulated pamphlets like Anne Koedt's "The Myth of the Vaginal Orgasm" and Susan Lydon's brilliant essay "The Politics of Orgasm." Lydon stated that the clitoris was the center of all orgasms and that men had trumped up the notion of a superior vaginal orgasm to keep women dependent on them. Lydon's assertion was backed by scientific evidence. Masters and Johnson had hooked up women to electric sensors and monitored them during orgasm, and found: "The dichotomy of vaginal and clitoral orgasms is entirely false. Anatomically, all orgasms are centered in the clitoris."

This ushered in the reign of the clitoris supreme. We were liberated from Freud, our experiences were validated, and we buried the vaginal orgasm under cement. While the clitoris ruled, the vagina was made an inferior place. It lacked the nerves and exquisite sensitivity of its cousin, and gradually this changed the way men made love. The new attitude was conveyed in the movie *Coming Home,* in which Jon Voight, paralyzed from the waist down and confined to a wheelchair, was able to give Jane Fonda such pleasure it made her breathless and ready to leave her dick-proud husband.

Around this time, college students reading *The Sun Also Rises* questioned why Jake's impotence meant he couldn't have a life with Lady Brett. A young man at the University of Oregon, where I was lecturing, asked, "Why couldn't he just go down on her?" Because, I said, in 1926, to Hemingway and the community, this was unquestioned: It takes a penis. By the late seventies, the penis was nice but expendable.

In "The Politics of Orgasm," Lydon had written that "women defer to whatever model of their sexuality is offered them by men." During the tantra workshop, though, I began to consider the possibility that for three decades we'd been deferring to the women's line. Was the vagina more potent and responsive than we'd believed? Or were we now being taken in by a New Age shill?

                                    .   .   .

After lunch, the Muirs showed a clip from a video they'd made, *Secrets of Female Sexual Ecstasy,* in which they were nude as he massaged her sacred spot with his fingers, looking in her eyes, and then clear liquid squirted out of her and drenched her legs. When the lights came on, people looked stunned. Zack broke the silence: "There's gonna be a hot time in the ol' bunkhouse tonight!" I wanted to sink into the floor. Charles said, "Remember, the only goal tonight is to try the technique and report on what you find. Women, I've warned the men not to let you start a fight. Our experience is that one out of four of you will try."

He sent the couples home and invited the singles—again, the majority were over forty—to stay for a "ritual" in preparation for sacred spot massage. Charles said the women would choose their partners. "For the men, this means taking the risk you won't be chosen. If you are chosen, you're making a commitment to serve the Goddess in whatever form She comes to you."

Eight people stood up and left the room, and those remaining were praised for their bravery by Mair Simone, who'd been introduced as a "certified dakhini"—a sexual priestess who could be called on to help couples during the "holy act." I wondered what her certification process had involved. Mair asked the six men to sit in a circle on the floor with their eyes closed. Then she asked the nine women to form a circle within the circle, facing the men. They joined hands and walked around and around. "Look for guidance," Caroline said. "Whom should I choose?"

The women were told to walk to a partner and take his hands. All the men were immediately chosen except Ralph, a divorce lawyer in his fifties who had thirty extra pounds on him and friendly, impish eyes. When Mair saw he wasn't being chosen, she sat down in front of him but, before taking his hands, looked back at the four women who hadn't picked a partner. She beckoned to them, seeing if one had felt shy and might change her mind. Julie, a redhead who had pocked skin and a large nose, walked forward and took Ralph's hands.

"Open your eyes, guys," Charles said, "and behold the gift."

Later, Ralph would tell me that when he opened his eyes, he thought: This is the gift?!

Mair came up and asked Julie if she was okay. "I'm a little uneasy. I'd feel better if you came along." Mair asked Ralph if she could join them and he agreed.

On our ride home, Zack was cranky. He'd been bored and irritated when taken aside with the other men for "coaching" by Charles. Zack said, "These guys were duds. They were complaining: You mean we have to serve and we don't get anything?"

I told him what Michael Tucker had said after the workshop. "I always thought I wanted my pleasure, but the point is to fill the woman with pleasure and then the man will get everything he wants and more."

"These guys didn't want to hear that," Zack said. "They wanted to measure the sacred spot with a slide rule. Is it an inch, two?" We walked into the house, drank some cognac, and he was still gloomy. He said he didn't belong there; nobody had talked to him and he didn't want to talk to anybody. "This happens a lot when I go places with you."

"I thought the woman was supposed to try to start the fight."

. . .

We found the G-spot. An erogenous zone that I hadn't known existed— a zone that was just as feverish and riveting as the clitoris, if not more so because of the novelty. I felt as if concrete was cracking; a political edifice was toppling.

I had a strong sense memory of being nineteen, with my first lover, and I remembered how astonishing it had felt—simple intercourse. That's what it felt like again. Then Zack and I found ourselves in a green and secret glade, shot through with a sense of the wonder and love in all things. We lay silently with our chests pressed together, breathing in unison, and there was a fusion between his skin and mine, his ribs and mine, his heart and mine.

"I've never felt so close to you," I said softly.

He smiled. "You're my wild little angel."

. . .

Sunday morning in the Sheraton Miramar, the men and women looked as if they'd taken Ecstasy, the love drug. Ralph was sitting on the floor, beaming, his arms around Mair and Julie, the redhead with pocked skin. Couples were kissing, lacing their fingers together. The women didn't sit so much as flow over the chairs, and the men looked powerful.

Charles asked people to describe their experience. Julie raised her hand. She said that Ralph was "the most giving, loving man I've known. I woke up this morning, touched my own arm, and felt I was being loved. I walked outside and felt the sun loving me."

"She got her money's worth," Zack whispered.

"Did you find the sacred spot?" Charles asked.

Julie rested her head on Ralph's chest and said dreamily, "Mm-hmm." Ralph smiled.

Later, Ralph told me that when he'd sat down to do the ritual, he'd found Julie so unattractive he had to force himself to look at her. "But as we stared into each other's eyes and synchronized our breathing, everything in the room began to melt away and we just merged. I went into a state of ecstasy."

Interesting, I thought—more evidence that age and the condition of one's body are not the determinants of sexual bliss.

In the afternoon, Charles and Caroline began instructing us in what they called "healing for men." Charles said men don't have to be erect—"lingams are usually soft"—and they don't have to come to reach the heights. The relief in the room was palpable; you could hear the guys exhale. Charles whipped off his belt and trousers and lay down in swim trunks, holding the lingam puppet in front of him. "This region in men needs healing—from all the times it was rejected, criticized, teased, from having its neck wrung in masturbation." Caroline sat down and, using the puppet, showed us "thirty-seven ways to touch a lingam." One was "the Arnold," which involved gripping the muscle at the base so it became pumped.

At the end of the workshop, it seemed the men had been given short shrift. We'd spent a day preparing for the women's night and a few hours for the men's. I asked Charles about this and he said they'd purposely made women the priority. "Women need to be healed first because they're the most scarred. If the woman of the house is happy . . ." He smiled. "Good things will flow."

*   *   *

And they did. The practice—whether it's called Christian sexuality or tantra—carried Zack and me to altered states. With no effort on his part or prior intent, Zack was so nourished after the weekend that he stopped smoking. He'd been consuming two packs a day since he was fourteen and had tried many times to quit, but after three days of "conscious loving," the addiction fell away.

We had four more years together before we found, ultimately, that sex alone could not sustain us. What we created when we were by ourselves—the laughter and deep communion—did not carry into the outside world. Friends viewed us with puzzlement, and our children reacted with hostility. Zack became increasingly dysfunctional financially, and as I lost my ability to work in TV, there were clashes and resentment that rent us apart.

So I was left with the dilemma many will face: How do you satisfy the need for sensuality as years go by? The question is not just for singles. What happens to couples when one partner shuts down and the other still wants intimacy? I talked with a man in New York who's leaving his wife of twenty-eight years because she's finished with sex and he feels, if anything, more lustful. She argues that this is no reason to break up the family; lots of their married friends have settled into cozy companionship. But he isn't willing to sneak off to liaisons, as some of his friends do, or pay an escort. He wants the whole enchilada.

A number of singles at the tantra workshop solved the problem by finding a "buddy" with whom they could "practice," just as friends. But for me, this wouldn't work. The level of trust and vulnerability required to open one's body to another is likely to trigger emotions I associate with love. I can't draw the line. "I'm that way also," Caroline Muir said when I interviewed her recently. "Most women can't draw the line. Once he's penetrating us and it's wonderful, we're in love!" She gives a deep sigh. "We decide, 'This is where I want to be,' and we overlook a lot of problems."

In the late 1990s, friction over this issue led to the breakup of her marriage with Charles. Caroline says that from the time he began studying tantra, "he's believed that for his own learning, he needs to open to love when love comes toward him." He and Caroline had many partners. "It was fabulous, fun, tremendously exciting, and I always knew that in the inmost reaches of his heart, I was the one, but there came a point when I couldn't take it anymore. I couldn't open to one more woman in our bed." She said her life is simpler and saner "if I keep my sexuality for me and my partner. That's my choice. Charles tried to do it my way, but it came down to the fact that it wasn't his way."

They still teach together, but at Charles's prompting, Caroline started teaching "the feminine mysteries," creating what she calls Divine Feminine workshops, where straight women "initiate" one another to attain "sexual wholeness."

This sounded weird to me. But an internist I met in San Francisco, Karen, a widow in her fifties who's stunningly slim and beautiful, told me she'd attended a Divine Feminine workshop when she was grieving. "The idea of doing sacred spot massage with women was totally yucky!" Karen recalls. Then Caroline Muir, whom she'd met years before, told her it was not about being sexual with other women but about healing and nurturing, "which you obviously need."

Karen agreed. "At that point I might have gone to any port for comfort." She drove to the workshop expecting to see a small number of spacey ladies bedecked with crystals and feathers. Instead, there were thirty-five professional women: lawyers, businesspeople, therapists, and college teachers. As they introduced themselves, Karen says, "the common thread was that they'd learned to be assertive, tough, and competitive with men but they have trouble being receptive, being feminine."

The women took turns working with each other—massaging backs and stomachs, doing partner yoga and dancing—"and a lot felt hokey," Karen says. They ate soft comfort foods like guacamole, macaroni and cheese, and chocolate soufflé. They were asked to hug each other with total acceptance, the way a mother comforts a child, "and when the first woman held me like that, I started to cry," Karen says. "I thought: This is not about sex, it's about love. The love in the room was so sincere and generous that I felt cared for and slept well that night for the first time since my husband died."

The following day, the women, all together in one room, were invited to remove their clothes if they felt comfortable doing so and, working in groups of three, take turns giving and receiving sacred spot massage. "I thought, I don't want to do this!" Karen recalls. Caroline told her she didn't have to. "But I felt so connected and understood by these women that I figured: You're here, you might as well go for the full Monty." Before she could change her mind, Karen asked her two partners if she could go first. The other women massaged her with oil, "and it felt soothing." One was a physical therapist, and after she helped Karen relax, the woman asked if it was all right to enter her sacred space. Karen said yes. She closed her eyes and, after a few minutes, opened them and said, "Why did I not want to do this?" The three women laughed. "It felt wonderful," Karen recalls. "Usually when we hug our women friends, there's a boundary, an invisible line we don't cross. In this gathering we could let down the barriers, give and receive warmth, and it was safe because no one was going to want a relationship or make demands."

Sex with women is not something that attracts me, but listening to Karen, I could see that just as sources for love widen in later years, so could sources for sensuality and the joy of being in a body. Joan Hotchkis had told me she's learned "how to have a moment be as fully felt and sensual as it can be. When I'm smelling something, I inhale deeply and feel the scent through the skin of my nostrils. When I'm hearing beautiful music, I stop and let it fill my whole body."

Karen says, "I would rather have sex with a man I love, but when that's absent, there are other ways of finding physical comfort so we don't become starved." Caroline Muir said during our interview, "So many women, myself included, have suffered, trying to extract or pry—just pry out tenderness and nurturing from a man. So I teach: Don't expect to get all that with the man in your life. Love him for the unique and different creature he is, and for real nourishment, go to the women."

Well, this is the fringe, the edgy version of the Red Hat Society inspired by Jenny Joseph's poem "Warning," which begins: "When I am an old woman I shall wear purple / With a red hat which doesn't go . . ." The message is, I won't give a shit, and in Red Hat clubs around the country, women over fifty adopt names like Queen Pin Head and Lady Smelly Good, wear purple clothes and red hats, and meet for uninhibited fun.

But what's pushing the envelope are groups with names that include words like "divine" or "goddess" and are aimed at cultivating feminine sexual energy. I went to a meeting of women who'd taken Caroline's workshop and were gathering once a month to keep the flame going. They were hugging full on, chest to chest, belly to belly, moving their hips together playfully in ways I've never done with even my closest friends. They would kiss each other with sweetness on the forehead or hand, and I was struck by how natural and relaxed they seemed.

The equivalent for men, I've heard, is wrestling. A friend tells me that in his men's group, they become physically close by grappling and sparring, sometimes without clothes, as in the famous scene from D. H. Lawrence's *Women in Love*. Are we surprised? Women cuddle and men fight?

Caroline Muir said of her work with women, "It's like we're weaving a web of the feminine together with male-based teachings." She's been told—though when I ask about her sources she can't be specific—that in ancient cultures, women priestesses would initiate young women. "Our sacred sexuality is the fountain of youth," she says.

I look dubious.

"Why not? That mythical source of rejuvenating water is certainly not down in Florida. What if we're all walking around with the fountain of youth inside us?"

I laugh. This concept is not, I think, ready for prime time. But neither was tantra when I first heard about it. People may turn to esoteric practices or find more traditional ways to relight the fire, but I'd wager that the majority of this cohort—and certainly this reporter—will not go without sex or sensuality into that good night.

8

Get a Job

When labor began, my first child came rocketing out so fast that a friend had to drive me straight from a lecture on Jewish humor to the hospital and my husband had to be paged at the racquetball club. Five minutes after my husband arrived, in his shorts, the baby was placed on my chest and the pediatrician on call appeared. To my dismay, it was not one of the senior doctors, but the youngest and newest to the practice, Vicky Paterno, MD. Over the years, though, Vicky was the doctor I came to request and whom my children, now in their twenties, still would prefer to see over any other doctor. Earthy and warm, with the animation of her Italian ancestors, she combines state-of-the-art medical knowledge with practical wisdom and sends us off feeling cared for and reassured.

In recent years, she's added travel medicine to her practice, so I consulted her before going to India. When I told her the subject of this book, she said, "Hurry up and finish because I need to read it. I'm only fifty, my daughter's off to college, and my job is not challenging. There's nothing I see now that I haven't seen a hundred times before. But I could have another thirty years to work. I can't just quit and die!"

Vicky wants intellectual stimulation. "Should I go back to school? I could practice in East L.A. because I speak Spanish and would be appreciated and make a difference. But I'm not sure I want to do medicine for another thirty years."

She joined a choir, she says, "and that's fun, but how much fun can you have? I'd go to Italy in a second, but then I'd be getting divorced because my husband won't go, and he's my best friend."

* * *

Vicky was grappling with the problem that had brought me to my knees: What would I do with my energy and skills for the next thirty years? When I'd left California and moved to Boulder, I had no work and was on a mission to find a new calling. I'd been told that my previous life was over. I started interviewing people who'd either walked away from jobs they'd been performing successfully for decades or who'd been unceremoniously dumped. I found that all of them had spent time in free fall, lost and in some cases paralyzed, before they found a way to pursue work they love on their own terms.

Most of us are work junkies and define ourselves and identify others by what we do. Seven out of ten in the forty-six to sixty-four age range say they expect never to stop working, according to an AARP survey. My father used to come home from his radio repair shop every night at five for a family dinner at five-thirty, which my mother cooked. No one I know today has a job they quit at five.

Thomas Moore, who started spending time in Ireland ten years ago, concluded that Americans "work too hard. The Irish know how to enjoy life more. We think we're virtuous by working hard, and then work goes away and who are you? When everything that justifies your existence disappears, you're left with your essence."

Being left alone with your essence, though, is not like being left in bed with a down comforter. "There's a lot of pain and confusion," Moore concedes. What contributes to the pain is that your essence doesn't come clear like the message on the Goodyear blimp—impossible to miss. I remember attending a fiftieth birthday party where a group of friends were ruing the fact that they're fixed in jobs they never set out to do. Lucy, a lab technician who does research on kidney disease, says, "I didn't plan to go into this field. I took a part-time job that led to a full-time job, and I ended up specializing in kidneys. But . . . it's not me."

What would you do if you could start fresh? I ask.

"I don't know," she says. "I honestly don't know."

When we were younger and asked, "What should I do with my life?" we were bent on proving we were good and having the world acknowledge our talents. I remember, at twenty-six, walking into the office of a magazine editor, pitching a story, and convincing him I was absolutely the best person to do this, then walking out on the street and stopping cold. Jesus! How the hell would I pull it off? Now we know what we're good at and have seen that the world's approbation is transitory.

The imperative at this time is not to find the right job or a replacement job, but to align yourself with your purpose, with the truth you've come to recognize about yourself. While I was still in California, what confounded me was that I felt writing was at the core of who I am. If I'm not writing, I feel off-kilter, and life is not as rich as when I'm translating event and feeling into narrative. Not knowing how to address this, I

visited a friend who gave up writing and found challenge and fulfillment in a field in which she'd had no experience.

Marcia Seligson

The actors onstage are singing the love duet from *Brigadoon,* but Marcia Seligson can't let herself slip into enchantment. With a week to go
before opening, she has to fire an actor, replace the lead dancer who just
sprained her ankle, and find a chiropractor for singer Debbie Gibson,
who hurt her back and needs treatment. "Live theater is dangerous because there are no retakes," she says, "but that also makes it thrilling. I
just wish I'd started this when I was younger."

Marcia created Reprise!, which produces three classic American musicals in Los Angeles every season, when she was fifty-seven. It was an
immediate success; Reprise! has the highest resubscription rate of any
theater in Los Angeles. But Marcia, who'd been a writer who disliked
writing, spent more than ten years fretting and circling before she came
up with the vision for the company.

On a Monday, a nonworking day for Reprise!, Marcia and I are sitting in the loft/office of her condo in Marina del Rey, looking out at the
ocean. "When I'm talking to people on the phone in New York, where
it's snowing, and I look out the window and say, 'Oh, my God! The dolphins are going by,' you know what they say? 'Fuck you.' "

We laugh. Blunt and gregarious, with blue eyes and a pleasingly zaftig
figure, Marcia speaks with comic hyperbole. During a recent bout with
the Atkins diet, she says, "I lost ten pounds, then I ate one piece of bread
and gained it back."

Marcia and I have been on and off diets since we met in the seventies,
when we were both writing for magazines. By any measure Marcia was
successful: She was constantly working and had lucrative book contracts. "But I hated the isolation. I loved doing research and learning
about things I didn't know. But after writing my brains out, I never got

much feedback," she says. "What I hated most was the drudgery—day after day, month after month, sitting alone in my room."

The crisis that forced her to quit writing came after she got married at forty-four to Tom Drucker, a psychologist and management consultant. They were offered a contract to write a book together, *Good Marriage*, about successful long-term marriages. "The arrogance! We'd been married a minute and a half and knew nothing," Marcia says. "And our writing styles were different and we didn't agree on anything." They had a friend, a therapist who lived nearby, and they'd call him and say, "We're having a conflict. Are you free?" Marcia says, "We spent more time on his couch than we did on the book." They wrote 150 pages that Marcia felt "weren't any good. Our editor left the business and nobody wanted the project. I told Tom, That's it. I've gotta do something else."

She considered going to law school and becoming an advocate for women's rights, and also thought about "becoming a shrink. But then I realized, you'll be back in a room alone with crazy people telling the same story over and over. I thought I might be good with groups or in a kind of therapy where I could say: Here's what you should do. Leave your husband, get a job, get a lover, and stop kvetching!" After pausing to laugh, she says, "That's why I love being a producer. I get to tell people what to do."

Her husband, Tom, proposed that before going back to school, she should spend a year with him as a psychological consultant. Marcia worked with him and enjoyed it but kept being lured back to writing. An editor would call with an assignment, she'd write it and complain that she hated doing it. Tom told her to just stop. "Give yourself time to do nothing. See what happens." Marcia says she tried that for three months but "I didn't come up with anything."

She loved gardening, so she called a landscaper and said, "I'm thinking of changing my life. Could I follow you around for a couple days?" She also toyed with starting a soup business. "I was going to be the Martha Stewart of soup."

The ideas came and went, but what she knew was: "I didn't want to write another fucking book." Her doctor referred her to an executive career coach, Marta Vago, who questioned her about what she was good at, what made her feel inspired, and was there a time when she couldn't wait to get up in the morning and start work?

The first thing that came to Marcia was the time she'd spent producing benefit concerts for the World Hunger Project. "I loved creating something out of nothing, surrounding myself with talented people, and doing work that made a difference." She liked running from appointment to appointment and managing a staff of three hundred volunteers.

Marta told her she was a natural producer, not a natural writer who wants to sit alone in a room with her thoughts. "It's amazing you've stayed at it this long," Marta said.

They began looking into what she might produce. "What did I know about? What did I love?" Marcia had grown up with music—playing piano, singing, and going to musical theater. She'd majored in music and sung in the collegiate chorale, and her family had invested in musical shows. "As we talked about it, I had this idea for Reprise!" Marcia called friends who were actors, and they loved the idea. "If they'd said, 'It's dumb, it'll never work in L.A.,' I wouldn't have done it," she recalls. "But there was never enough musical theater in L.A. There were only touring companies, and they didn't do the great old shows." She began inviting people out to lunch, asking for advice. "I put one foot in front of the other for six months. I had no idea how to start a theater; I didn't even know stage left from stage right. If I'd known how complex and hard it would be, I'd never have had the balls to try it."

People asked if Reprise! would be commercial or not-for-profit, and Marcia said, "I don't know." She put together a board of directors who advised her to make it not-for-profit and found a performance space—which is difficult in L.A.—the Freud (pronounced "frood") Playhouse. And then, she says, "two magical things happened. I decided I needed to have stars and approached Jason Alexander." He'd become a household word playing George Costanza on *Seinfeld,* but Marcia knew he loved to sing and dance and had won a Tony for *Jerome Robbins' Broadway.* She called him cold, told him her idea for Reprise!, and asked if she could take him to lunch. He agreed, and she said she was putting together the first show. "Is there a Broadway musical you'd like to do while you're on hiatus from *Seinfeld*?"

Jason said he'd always wanted to do *Promises, Promises,* which had been a hit in 1968 and was the only musical Hal David and Burt Bacharach had written. Marcia secured the rights, and Jason committed. "That gave me credibility," she says, "because nobody had heard of me." Jason said later that he'd assumed she was a rich West Side dilettante who was going to fund the show herself. It wasn't until they'd started rehearsals that he took her aside and said, "You haven't done this before, have you?"

The second "magical thing" happened when Marcia learned she needed a musical director. "I wasn't even sure what such a person did." A friend of hers knew Peter Matz, a legendary arranger, composer, and conductor who'd racked up Emmys and Grammys, worked in TV and film and on Broadway, and collaborated with Barbra Streisand, Marlene Dietrich, Noël Coward, and Liza Minnelli. Her friend proposed that they take Peter to lunch and ask whom he'd recommend. "I was dazzled by him," Marcia says. "I brought a little list of people who'd been recommended, none of whom I knew." Marcia described her vision of Reprise! with such passion that when she finished, Peter leaned across the table and said, "I hope you're going to ask me to be your musical director."

Marcia started to cry. "We got other stars after that because if Jason Alexander and Peter Matz were doing this, it had to be real."

I ask why people were eager to sign on, given that she had no track record and was paying minimal nonprofit fees. "Because they love musical theater," she says, "and it was a short run. We had one week of rehearsal and six performances. Now we've expanded to two weeks of rehearsal and sixteen performances, but it's still a one-month gig, and all the Broadway stars want to do it."

Marcia says it took her three years working full-time to get to opening night. She spent $50,000 of her own on lawyers and taking people to lunch. "And I never wrote again." Her board of directors helped raise funds and gave personal loans. The first season they did three shows, all of which sold out. After *Promises, Promises,* they produced *Finian's Rainbow* with Andrea Marcovicci, then *Wonderful Town* with Lucie Arnaz. The actors worked from books in the first two shows, but Lucie Arnaz refused. "She said, 'I can't act if I'm looking at a script,' and that was the end of the books," Marcia recalls. The next season the shows were fully costumed, staged, and choreographed, using a single set and a chorus who could both sing and dance.

"It's thrilling to work with top actors and singers—to watch them create," Marcia says.

Don't you ever want to get up onstage with them and sing? I ask.

"Always. Always."

Her dog, a golden retriever named Spirit, comes bounding up to the loft, followed by her assistant, who tells Marcia she has an urgent call. When Marcia returns, wearing a black T-shirt with the white Reprise! logo, I tell her I'm in awe of the life she's been able to conjure up.

"It's terrific fun, a lot of pressure, and all-consuming," she says. She works seven days a week and is at the theater till midnight for a month before each show opens. She's given up a lot, willingly. "The last ten years, I haven't had lunch with a girlfriend or played piano, and I've hardly read a book. I stopped my spiritual work and haven't been active in politics, both of which I miss."

She says Reprise! is well established now and could run on its own, but "we're always struggling for money. That's the nature of not-for-profit theater. We either lose money or make a little on every show, and if we have a bad season, we could close."

Marcia says she doesn't expect to be running the company in six or seven years.

Why not?

"I don't want to work this hard. It's still fun, but Reprise! isn't enough to satisfy me anymore. I have an appetite to do other things."

Such as . . . ?

She stretches her legs out on the couch. "I needed to create something big and successful that challenged me, and Reprise! satisfied that. But there's nothing else I really *need* to do in life."

She wants to study conducting, to become involved with piano once more, and maybe "spend a lot of time with a chamber music group." She'd like to learn about Buddhism and Jewish meditation, and she's had a fantasy of renting a house on a cliff in Big Sur and spending a year reading. But her husband, she says, "is terrified of me retiring from Reprise! He thinks I'll be okay for a week and then I'll get depressed and nag him."

She has friends, she says, "who do nothing but play golf and tennis, and that sounds horrible. I know I need to be out in the world, I need to be making something happen."

·   ·   ·

After spending the day with Marcia, I felt like the woman watching Meg Ryan in the deli in *When Harry Met Sally.* I wanted what she's having. I wanted to be running a theater company, choosing the plays, hiring the singers and dancers and giving notes and living on the ocean watching dolphins.

I decided to go to the same career coach Marcia had consulted, Marta Vago, hoping to emerge with a similarly glorious project, but that did not occur. I began to see that, unlike Marcia, I'm happiest when I'm alone in my room, writing. I'm not good at managing a staff of hundreds. A great day is when I don't have to leave the house and the phone doesn't ring. I also like the phase that precedes this: traveling to places

I've never been, doing research, and conducting interviews. I thrive on alternating between going out and retreating.

The problem was that even with Marta's coaching, I could not persuade anyone in TV, film, or publishing to hire me for the projects I wanted to create. Marta suggested, "It might be time to say, 'I lost the battle.'" But could I give up writing? If it's in your blood to tell stories, to "throw the bait of your experience into the sea of language and wait and work for the right words to attach," as Seamus Heaney expressed it, can you pack away your gear and not feel that you're refusing the call? I interviewed a therapist, Dennis Palumbo, who'd been a staff writer on *Welcome Back, Kotter* and written the movie *My Favorite Year,* starring Peter O'Toole. He'd quit the business, gone back to college for a PhD, and become a psychotherapist who specializes in working with creative people, which he finds endlessly rewarding. Marcia Seligson had also made the break from writing and not looked back, and so, I thought, must I.

Jac Holzman

For encouragement, I turned to Jac Holzman, who in his forties sold the company he'd founded, Elektra Records, left the music business, and went into retreat. Jac belongs to the generation ahead of the boomers, but he played a key role in the culture of the sixties. When we met in 1968, Elektra was hot, the music was on fire, and Jac was riding high. Tall and lean, with red hair and muttonchop sideburns, Jac lived with his wife and kids in an elegant co-op in Greenwich Village, which was furnished with cozy red velvet couches, lit by hundreds of candles, and equipped with a killer sound system that no one but he could touch. Jac's son recalls, "You had to have a pilot's license to operate my dad's sound system."

When he was nineteen, Jac had dropped out of college to start Elektra in his ratty walk-up apartment. He drove around New York on a motor scooter with a bulky tape player strapped on back to record folksingers. What was unique about Jac was that he owned three talents not often found in the same person: creative ability, technological know-how, and shrewd business sense. Making records was not a business; it was a calling. He personally scouted and signed musicians, produced albums, picked the singles, and planned the strategy for campaigns.

In 2002, when I was volunteering as a host for KCRW, the public radio station in Santa Monica, I interviewed Jac about his memoir, *Follow the Music.* "How do you know," I asked him, "when you hear a musician who hasn't hit yet whether he's going to develop and become a major star? Is it luck on your part, or instinct?"

"First of all," Jac said, "I don't give a damn whether they're gonna be stars. I care about: Are they unusual, and will they be fun to work with? Maybe if those two things ring true for me, I'll find an audience for them or they'll find an audience and it will all work out wonderfully."

It worked out wonderfully when he signed Josh White, Theodore Bikel, the Limelighters, Phil Ochs, Judy Collins, Tom Paxton and Tom Rush, Harry Chapin, the Paul Butterfield Blues Band, the Doors, Carly Simon, and Queen. The Doors had made a demo that every record company rejected, but Jac had been told to go hear them in a club on the Sunset Strip. "I was not at all impressed," Jac says, "but for some reason I kept going back, night after night. On the fourth night, suddenly I heard songs they hadn't played before: 'Light My Fire,' 'Alabama Song' . . ."

Which one is that?

"You know, 'Show me the way to the next whisky bar . . .' "

I love that song.

"I saw what happened when Morrison and the band were so *on* that they sucked all the oxygen out of the room and you couldn't breathe! They met all my criteria: They were great, fun to work with, and different from any other artist I'd heard."

He feels the same about Judy Collins. When we play a cut of her singing "Suzanne," I look up and see tears on his cheeks.

"What's going on?" I ask gently, still on the air.

"I love the song—" His voice breaks, and for a moment he can't speak. "In a nutshell," he continues with suppressed emotion, "I've been privileged to work with the artists I've worked with. They've enriched my life so much."

I ask if he regrets leaving Elektra.

"No," he says, "I was tired. And I hated what was happening to the business. Money had become the reason for doing everything. Marketing was more important than the music, and when that happens, there's no room for me anymore. I'd had my biblical seven fatted years—more than seven—and I wanted to spend time in my own interior." He'd been divorced by then and moved by himself to Hawaii.

What do you do, I ask, "after holding a job where everyone calls you El Supremo, where you single-handedly decide what music the world will hear and what gets sent to the trash heap, have a limo and private plane at your disposal and rock stars waiting nervously for you to hear their work—to give it what they call 'the Big Listen'?"

Jac smiles. "I wanted to get back to basics: think about who I was and what I wanted to do." He lived in a one-room condo on the ocean in Maui, which he refurbished with the spare beauty of a ship's cabin. "I had some books, a music system, a tiny TV, and a small hot tub. I had what I needed." He traded his Porsche for a rickety old Valiant and his leather jackets and custom suits for shorts, T-shirts, and flip-flops. He did his own housekeeping, took up scuba diving and underwater photography, "and I spent time smoking strange herbs and tasting mushrooms." He also continued working on technology projects for Warner Communications Inc., shuttling between Japan and California to keep the company abreast if not ahead of electronic advances.

After eight years on the beach, he was ready to move back to the mainland and work full-time for Warner. "I went back because I wanted to be fully used," he says. "I found I'm happiest when I'm operating with everything I've got—the entire tool kit." He was at Atari, which he'd been instrumental in purchasing for Warner, when he received a call that Robert Gottschalk, the chairman of Panavision, another Warner company, had just been murdered. "There was chaos, rumors, nobody knew what had happened, and the phones in Gottschalk's office were tied up," Jac recalls. "But I knew the private number for Gottschalk's executive assistant. I got through, and he confirmed the murder." Jac told the assistant, "Please stay off the phone for five minutes. I'll call you right back." Jac hung up and paced his office. "I thought: Here's a company that's shell-shocked and needs a CEO. It's a business you know nothing about—the world's largest manufacturer of motion picture equipment. Do you want a line job again? If the company does well, you could take some of the credit, and if it fails, you could take all the blame." He says he realized "this was not something you could decide rationally. So I thought I'd call the guy and see what blurted out of my mouth." Jac called the assistant and said, "I'm taking over the company as of now. I'll be in at ten tomorrow morning." Then he called Steve Ross, CEO of Warner Communications, and said, "It's true that Gottschalk's been killed. Don't worry, I've taken over the company."

"How can we help?" Ross asked.

"Cash my checks, and don't call me for six months. I promise that if I get in trouble, you'll be the first person to hear. And please send me a first-rate CFO [chief financial officer]."

Jac proceeded, he says, "to have some of the best and most instructive years of my life." Being a classic control freak, he'd always studied and made meticulous preparations before acting, "but I couldn't prepare because I'd parachuted in." He arranged for tutors to help him learn the business and showed up every morning at seven to shake the machinists' hands as they came to work. "I walked the floor," Jac says. "I realized the machinists were the heart of the company, and I needed to build them into a team. The company was losing five million a year when I took over, and we had it *making* five million within twelve months."

In 2005, when I interviewed Jac in Santa Monica, he'd been retired again for five years, then gone back to Warner to create a company, Cordless Recordings, that releases original music on the Internet. "I've worked and not worked," Jac says. "When I'm not pulling down a paycheck, I still want to do things that are meaningful. What I've come up with is: You don't have to figure it all out. Pick something and do it. Take a look at what's out there and see what you'd like to stand next to. Or if you don't see anything . . ." He shrugs. "Wait till lightning strikes." He gives a mischievous grin. "Because it always does."

* * *

Not for this reporter. I've tried standing next to something I like—radio. From my first days in journalism, I've had a zest for conducting interviews, for creating a sense of instant intimacy that leads to gold: when the guest is reaching for thoughts, laughing and expressing ideas that he or she hasn't articulated before. When this happens the air seems to change—it's charged, alive—and if you're driving while listening, you don't want to leave your car.

I became a guest host and commentator on public radio stations, made a demo, and was asked to be an interviewer on a new show that never made it to the air. I found that, as in other competitive fields, it's tough to land a paying job. Cathy Goodwin, a career consultant whom I contacted after reading one of her reviews on Amazon.com, suggested a different approach. A former marketing professor in Canada, Cathy had moved to New Mexico and set up a consulting firm. Like Dr. Ruth, whose prescription for every sexual problem is "Put ze voman on ze top," Cathy has a universal fix for job problems: Start your own business. According to a recent poll, people fifty-five and over make up 16 percent of the workforce, but they account for 30 percent of self-employed consultants and entrepreneurs.

"My clients tell me, 'I don't want to start a business. I'm not an entrepreneur. I want another job,' " Cathy says. "Most clients want to take a test that will tell them what to do with the rest of their life." Cathy tells them tests are a waste of time. "By midlife, any aptitude or personality test will show that you're good at what you've been doing and suggest you do that. But what if nobody wants to hire you? You might have to start a business whether you like it or not." She suggests that you start small, and anything that interests you can be a business. "Exotic trees can be a business. Knitting can be a business. You don't need much except a computer."

You need more than that to start a radio station, I say, unless you're going to broadcast online.

"Why not do that?" Cathy says.

I don't have the technical skills; I like having a professional engineer at the controls, and I've seen that starting a company is fraught with risk. You need the constellations to line up: the great idea, the will and resources to plow through obstacles, and luck.

The Future of Money

The elements came together for Marcia Seligson, but Bernard Lietaer, who designed the system to convert twelve separate currencies into the euro, started his own business and nearly lost all he had.

A bearlike figure with dark hair, a beard, and gold-rimmed glasses, Bernard writes books in five languages, consults for multinational corporations, and promotes ideas not often heard in the public discourse. He wants to redesign the world's monetary system to relieve suffering and believes money is the strongest leverage point—"and the greatest blockage place"—for change.

Born in Belgium, Bernard came to the United States to do advanced studies because "you don't live in the Roman Empire and not go to Rome." In 1967, he enrolled at the MIT Sloan School of Management, which, he says, "was the most square place in Cambridge." While other students were smoking pot, wearing tie-dyed shirts, and marching against the war in Vietnam, "at the business school we were wearing suits. I missed the whole thing." His politics and values, though, have always been liberal. "I think the government should do things to help people who've been less lucky in life, and I also believe that bureaucracy is not the way to do it."

After MIT he worked in Latin America, taught international finance at the University of Louvain in Brussels, and was recruited by a head-hunter for a job with the central bank in Belgium, the equivalent of the U.S. Federal Reserve. "I thought it was the finger of destiny," Bernard says. "The first problem that landed on my desk was the euro."

It was a formidable and heady project. He and his team designed the system by which "twelve countries with different inflation rates, different budget deficits, different governments, and currencies that fluctuated daily had to align their economies so they could use a single unit. Good luck!"

After five years of effort, the plan Bernard devised was "nicely under way," he says. While he was in Switzerland at meetings, a bank president came up to Bernard and said, "I've read your books. What are you doing at the central bank?"

Bernard laughed. "Nobody had ever asked me that. I told him I'm here to see if we can improve the monetary system, to make it more stable and inflation-proof." The president shook his head. "He told me the job of the central bank is to keep the system exactly as it is." In a short time, Bernard saw that this was correct—"the euro was exactly the same as the currencies it replaced."

He left the central bank, feeling that innovation was more likely to occur in the private sector. He helped found the Gaia Hedge Funds, which raise money for the Gaia Trust, a nonprofit group that supports environmental projects. Bernard did all the trading and in three and a half years turned an initial pool of $100,000 into $22 million. At that point, he wanted to participate in deciding how the money would be spent, but the leaders of Gaia wouldn't permit that.

"I quit to start my own fund," Bernard recalls. He was in his fifties, living on Grand Cayman in the Caribbean with a woman from Belgium, and for the first time he was ready to be an entrepreneur, to take on the risk and distribute the profits himself. He worked harder than he'd ever worked, building models of currencies that would allow him to take option positions in twenty simultaneously and reap profits from fluctuations in their prices. But when he made his first trade, "I ran into a wall. Boom—50 percent of my capital was gone! How could that happen? I lost complete confidence in myself. I thought, I can make millions for others, but when I try to do it for myself, it doesn't work."

He'd had failures before, Bernard says, "but only when I wasn't paying attention or it was not a priority. If I worked hard and focused all my energy, it never failed. That was my philosophy, okay? But in this case, I had paid attention, I had put in all the effort. It was the best work I'd done. And with the first trade, I walked into a wall." Years later, he discovered that at the time he'd made that trade, George Soros was unloading his entire position in British pounds—15 billion—on the market, "which screwed up everything. When one market goes haywire, all the others are affected." At the time, though, he had no idea that his failure was due to bad luck. This is the unseen risk of starting a business: You can be smart, make all the right moves, and a factor that's totally out of your hands can blow you out of the water.

Bernard blamed himself—which is the Buddhists' second arrow. "I gave up. I stopped doing everything because when you lose your nerve, you can't trade." He sank into a despair so profound that "I wanted to check out of life. I sent my girlfriend back to Belgium. I told her, I don't know what I'm going to do, and I don't want you or anyone else to be involved."

He left the Caribbean and drifted to California, thinking he'd live out his days on what was left of his funds. A friend, Willis Harman, an engineering professor who'd been a regent of the University of California, told Bernard, "You've studied monetary systems for twenty-five years. You know more about them than anyone and you've got to write it down." Not knowing what else to do, Bernard agreed to write a book if Willis would edit it and help find a publisher. They shook hands, but Willis said he didn't want to see fragments, he wanted to wait for the whole manuscript.

Bernard moved into a house in Mill Valley, California, started doing research, and after five years he had a manuscript, *The Future of Money.* "I gave it to Willis on a Friday," Bernard recalls. "On Saturday he was diagnosed with brain cancer and given a few months to live."

Bernard lost his editor and friend, but *The Future of Money* was eventually published in eighteen languages. Writing it showed Bernard "I still have a contribution to make."

His theme in *The Future of Money* is that complementary currencies—used as a supplement to national currencies—can create bonds between people and solve social problems. He cites the example of Japan, which has the fastest-growing population of people over sixty-five of any country and not enough money to care for them in special homes. Japan devised a currency for elderly care: The unit is one hour of service to an older person. If a teenage girl shops and cooks for a bedridden neighbor, she can use her elder care notes to pay tuition at a university or send them to a grandparent in another part of Japan who can use them to purchase care from someone nearby. "With elder care notes," Bernard says, "money is created by work itself, not by a bank."

Another example of a complementary currency is frequent flier miles—"a currency created by an airline," Bernard says. Complementary currencies work well in communities where there's a shortage of money and a surplus of time, such as low-income neighborhoods or student enclaves. When Bernard began studying these currencies, there were fewer than fifty in different parts of the world. Ten years later, he says, there are more than five thousand, including "time dollar" systems in cities like Ithaca, New York, where you can work an hour for someone in the city, receive an Ithaca dollar, and spend it at the movies or a restaurant. "The wave is starting," he says.

If he hadn't failed at creating his own hedge fund, he might not have written *The Future of Money.* "I have more humility," Bernard says, and he's come to understand his purpose in the coming years: "Doing everything I can to mutate the money system."

Barry Meyers-Lewis

Like Jac Holzman, Bernard had found the best way he could be "fully used," but I was still clueless as to what that would be for me. After a stint teaching at the journalism school, I found that I could inspire students and help them write more powerfully, but teaching was not enough for me to build a life around. Dipping a foot in other waters, I volunteered to read and discuss literature with people dying in hospice care and worked with Hispanic kids in an after-school program. But none of these endeavors gave me the unshakable sense that I'm running with the tide, doing what I'm meant to do.

On a visit to New York, I have dinner with an old friend, Barry Meyers-Lewis, who recently retired while his wife took a job, which freed him to devote his days to poetry. Although we haven't seen each other in thirty years, I spot Barry immediately, sitting at a table in Joe Allen's, drinking single-malt Scotch. I remember him as bespectacled and funny, garrulous, impassioned, and sweet. For thirty-two years he taught literature at one of the most rigorous schools in Manhattan, where he inspired and mentored not only the gifted young, but the ones who'd fallen behind. His wife, Hallie, after staying home to raise their four children, went out and found her first paying job—running a science program for young people at the American Museum of Natural History. When she leaves the house at seven A.M., Barry walks upstairs to his study to write poetry that may or may not be published.

I've come to think of Barry as one of the *lamed vavnick,* the thirty-six righteous ones in Jewish legend whose identity is hidden and whose goodness holds up the world. Barry asks that I not use his real name. "I keep a low profile."

Setting up my voice recorder, I ask how he's handling the role switch with his wife, but he ignores my question and runs off on other topics. I'm skilled at wrangling people, but Barry can't be wrangled. He talks about what interests him and as we finish our steaks, I give up, asking for the check, concluding that this was fun but, for my purposes, a bust.

We walk up Broadway to the subway so Barry can take the train to Brooklyn, but just before descending the steps, he hits the mother lode—the material I want to hear. There's no way to set up the recorder, so I fish my notebook out of my bag and scribble to get his words down while we stand by the subway and trains rumble under us.

Barry says he's come to believe the two big changes we have to make are in our understanding of time and creativity. "The point of these years is to develop our creativity with no concern for reward. In our younger years we were hustling to build a career and earn enough to put the kids through college. Now, he says, "virtually everyone should be thinking: What would you do if you could do *anything*?"

I'd be a musician, I say. I love to sing, but . . . I don't have a great voice. . . .

"What would you do if you had no buts?" Barry asks. "No worries about money? No judgments about how good the product is? Your goal is to express what you've learned and fuck the world."

Is that what you're doing in your study every day? I ask.

"Trying."

This reminds me, I tell Barry, of a talk I had with a performance artist, Nina Wise, who asserts that humans are the only animals who create art, and we need to sing, paint, compose, or dance—whether we do it brilliantly or as amateurs—for our well-being. "Think about it," I say. "We allow ourselves to play sports knowing we don't perform on the same level as the pros. I can ski with the masters without having to win races or carve turns like Bode Miller. But we don't easily allow ourselves to draw or write a play if we're not professionals. We're embarrassed at our efforts. . . ."

"There's no time for that anymore," Barry says. "Creativity better be its own reward."

A homeless man pushing a shopping cart yells, "Excuse me!" and we jump out of the way as if a train were speeding toward us.

"The sidewalk's wide," I say, "and there's nobody else on it. Why didn't he go around us?"

"He's too attached to his straight path," Barry says.

We laugh.

"Serving people is another way of being creative," he says. "You want to feed the hungry? Better get busy." He's always wanted to set up a soup kitchen, but when his parents turned ninety and moved to an assisted living facility, he decided he had to take care of them first. When his father told Barry that his hands were shaking and he didn't know how he could cut his nails, Barry volunteered. "I clip my father's finger- and toenails and get a tremendous sense of satisfaction. I have to give it my full attention or I make mistakes, I clip too close—oy vey! It becomes a creative act. What could be more Buddhist?"

He says the first time he clipped his father's nails, "I had a sudden memory of being little, sitting on his lap as he did that for me. I saw his nails, and then, like an overlay, I saw my own nails as a child. It was like Proust and the madeleine."

Ten years ago, Barry says, he never could have spent an hour cutting his father's nails, he would have paid someone to do it. "I believed my time was money, but that's no longer true, if it ever was. My time is not money. I'll give you another example." He says last month the software on his computer became corrupted, and he called a friend in Providence, Rhode Island, Jake, a computer engineer, to ask who could fix it. Jake offered to fix it himself. Barry mailed him the computer, but when he called to make sure it had arrived, he couldn't reach Jake. He told Hallie, "He's not returning my calls or e-mails, and he's compulsive about e-mail. It's been four days—he's disappeared from the fucking planet."

Hallie told him he was overreacting, maybe Jake was busy or had to go out of town. . . .

"You don't understand," Barry said. "He'd still check his e-mail." He puts his hand over his heart as we stand on Broadway by the subway. "A man and his computer . . . all my data, my files . . ."

Barry became hell-bent on tracking the engineer down and called Jake's father, a tax attorney in his eighties who goes to the office every day. "He doesn't remember what happened ten minutes ago, but he remembers the entire tax code. This guy will die at his desk, but I call and he doesn't answer."

Hallie thinks it might be too early—nine A.M.

Barry tells her, "He's there at five in the morning. By nine he's eating lunch!" He keeps calling and at ten reaches the attorney's assistant, who informs Barry that Jake had a heart attack and a quintuple bypass.

"So we drop everything and drive four hours to the hospital in Rhode Island," Barry says. "I kiss the computer good-bye—and the freedom I feel! We've been hit with the reality of getting older, sick, and dying. The hell with the software and the data. Nothing goes with us. Everything is shed."

Barry and Hallie spent the day at the hospital with Jake, his father, and relatives. "Jake almost cried when we walked through the door—he couldn't believe we'd driven all that way," Barry says. "I thought I had retired, but real retirement is from the bullshit of conference calls, power breakfasts, and thinking your time is money. Hallie lost a day's work and I didn't complete the verses I was working on, but at this point the only thing that matters is bucking this guy up. A friend has been cut open, and we are here."

. . .

In the weeks that followed my dinner with Barry, whether it was his influence or the cumulative force of talks and reflection, I began to understand that I did not have to go on a desperate hunt—as I'd felt I must when my screenwriting career collapsed—for a new job or vocation that would be the spine of my life. My spine was in place; I simply needed to change the angle of perception. Like Marcia Seligson, I kept being drawn back to reporting and writing, but unlike her, I felt exhilarated by the work. I was haunted by Barry's question: "What would you do if you could do *anything*?" He had added, "If you knew the world was going to end in two days, what would you do?"

"Take notes," I said, not hesitating.

What was imperative for me was to make the shift Barry and others had proposed: from creating for a purpose to creating for the joy and challenge of the undertaking. I began to accept—and it's a daily struggle—that whether I'm writing for *The New York Times* or publishing the piece on my website, whether I'm recording an interview with J. Lo and being paid handsomely or volunteering at a small radio station that hardly anybody listens to, the creative work itself is what I need, as I need air.

This does not come easy, for as Ray Manzarek said, we're competitive animals. But the ax fell for me in the spring of 2003. I'd spent two months writing an article for a prestigious magazine, and I'd worked hard, completing what I felt was a strong piece. The night after I sent it to my editor, I awoke from what could only be a writer's premonitory nightmare: The article had been rewritten by Gay Talese to the point where it was unrecognizable and was being published in a kids' throwaway rag.

A few days later, I received a call from my editor saying the article was being killed. He could not tell me why, he'd thought the piece was excellent and could only conclude that the editor in chief "doesn't like you."

"He's never met me."

"I understand, but he thinks you're a *Village Voice* type . . . ."

"I never wrote for *The Village Voice*."

The editor sighed. "I'm afraid it's not going to be fruitful for you to submit anything else here."

I drove to a beach I knew would be deserted and started walking. I felt humiliated. They were not just killing the piece, they were killing me, locking the door, now and forever—a magazine for which I'd written countless pieces in the past, some of which have been reprinted in anthologies. Then something snapped, and I thought, What does it matter? If they'd printed the article, people would have sent me e-mails or called saying they liked it and had learned something, and in a brief time it would be off the stands and I'd have to start up the hill again. I've been hot and cold, made money and lost it, succeeded and flopped, and I could do either or both again and probably would.

I felt depressed in the days that followed (although the piece was accepted by a different magazine), but in that moment by the ocean, I realized I'd had a terrific time reporting and writing the article and knew I'd done it well. That's the only reason to continue—for the periods when your mind is humming, working on the case even when you're taking a shower or sleeping and everything you see, hear, and read feeds into the narrative that's unspooling.

There's a story I've always liked about Tennessee Williams. Someone asked what he wanted for his birthday, and he said, "What every writer wants: a day when the muse is with you and you're hot."

On such days, I may walk into my office with low dread because I don't know how I'm going to breathe life into a story. I'll sit there scribbling phrases, crossing them out, twirling my hair, and then . . . characters will begin to say things I hadn't expected, or sentences will roll out that startle me with their rightness. I lose the sense of time as I'm carried to that place John Fowles describes in *Daniel Martin* as "the sacred combe" or sacred wood—where you feel you're walking through a lush and fertile grove where no human has set foot before and every animal, every plant, seems both "tamer and more magical here than outside." No critic's review or disappointing sales figures can take away that time in the sacred combe.

Jon Carroll, whom I met when we worked on the *Daily Cal* at Berkeley, has been writing a column for the *San Francisco Chronicle* for decades. He intends to continue as long as he's physically able, he says, partly because "you write to find out what you think." He describes how he'll see or read something that gives him an idea for a column, "and I know intuitively if it has heft, if I can bite into it. Then I start writing, beginning to make arguments, and I'm sometimes shocked by where the damn thing goes. I had *no idea* it was going that way, *no idea* that's what I thought. And I'll find humor or a joke that I set up four paragraphs earlier without being aware of it." He laughs with delight. "It makes you believe in God."

9

School's Out

We are told that retirement is the time of freedom and leisure:
poets have sung "the delights of reaching port."

These are shameless lies.

—Simone de Beauvoir, *The Coming of Age*

Ten years ago, walking down Main Street in Sun Valley, Idaho, on Labor Day, I ran into a man who'd been a college classmate, Bruce Kaplan.

"What brings you here?" I asked Bruce.

"I'm retired. I live here."

Retired—at fifty-one? He was the first person my age I knew who'd retired, and I was envious.

"I worked hard," Bruce said a little defensively; he'd been a plastic surgeon in Palm Springs, California.

"I've worked hard, too." At the time, I was writing and producing *Dr. Quinn, Medicine Woman* and raising two teens, and I was fried. It occurred to me that there would be a new division within our age group: between those who can afford to retire and those who have to keep earning, just as there's a division between those who bought houses when they were affordable and those who didn't. I envied Bruce because I wanted to retire from stress, sleep deprivation, and a load that felt too heavy, but I did not want to stop working.

More than 75 percent of boomers plan to work beyond age sixty-five, according to the Merrill Lynch New Retirement Survey. When I meet people who tell me they've retired, I notice that I lose interest and assume they've quit the game and are leading a diminished life. But Robert Atchley, PhD, who's spent his life studying aging and was director of the Scripps Gerontology Center at Miami University, says retirement is like a breakout because "you get to follow an inner gyroscope—that's where direction comes from in these years. It doesn't depend on what the outside world thinks."

Atchley, sixty-four, leans across the table where we're having tea. "I do not give a flying fuck what anyone thinks about what I do with my time."

I laugh.

"You can quote me on that," he says.

Wearing jeans and a button-down shirt, he looks at home in the teahouse near the University of Colorado. When he began his teaching career, he says, radical professors were beginning to wear jeans and flak jackets. His boss called him in and said, "If you want to be a nonconformist in the parts of your life that matter, it's a lot easier if you're a conformist in the other parts." Bob considered this and decided, "I didn't give a damn about the dress thing. I adopted the Lands' End look and have dressed that way ever since."

"What's the Lands' End look?"

"Traditional: chinos, button-down shirts . . ."

"You're wearing jeans," I say.

"This is Boulder. I blend in." After retiring from teaching, he and his wife searched the country for a new place to live and picked Colorado. "Right now I'm being paid thirty-five dollars an hour to just be here."

"Who's paying you?"

"The Ohio State Teachers Retirement System. I put in my thirty years. I'd studied retirement, and when I made choices about jobs, I always asked: What kind of retirement program do they have?"

I'm surprised; when I was in my twenties in the sixties—the time he began studying gerontology—"the *last thing* I wanted to think or hear about was retirement," I say. At Berkeley, one of the qualities we saw as separating us from the previous "silent generation" was that we did not aspire to work for corporations that offered stability and good benefits. We'd heard stories of people who saved, planned, and sacrificed for retirement only to get sick or die before they were able to enjoy it. We rejected the notion of delaying pleasure and adventure, of toiling at an unfulfilling job so you could retire in thirty years. Our ideal was to seize the day and take off for the high road. As one of my roommates, Tasha, recalls, "We were going to make life interesting and were willing to suffer pain and end up poor in a garret if necessary."

Bob Atchley says he took a class in gerontology because he was working for his PhD in sociology at American University. "They didn't offer a lot of courses, so I took everything they gave." The class was taught by Clark Tibbitts, "the granddaddy of gerontology," who was director of aging in the Department of Health, Education and Welfare. Atchley was assigned to read a text that stated, he recalls, that "women don't have the same problem as men with retirement because they have the housewife role to fall back on. But my mother and her friends were all professional women and that statement didn't apply to them." With a laugh,

Atchley says, "I set out to prove that retirement was just as damaging to women's self-image as to men's."

He interviewed retired women at the Institute of Lifetime Learning in Washington. "I fell in love with those ladies!" he says. "I went in with the idea that retirement was nasty and caused people to lose self-esteem and get sick. But these ladies knew who they were, what was satisfying in life, and how to go out and get it." At the end of the second session he conducted, the woman being interviewed said, "Is that it? When are you going to ask me about the good stuff?"

Atchley revised his questionnaire and in his thesis argued that retirement for these woman was "like a grand hall pass." As people get older, he explains, they become increasingly uncomfortable "living a life that meets other people's ideas of what's good, true, and beautiful." Retirement offers an opening "to leave all that behind."

He did a larger study of four thousand people—both men and women—and came up with the same findings. For most people, he says, "the dominant effect of retirement is release."

Bob Baxt, DDS

The concept of retirement as "a grand hall pass" was not one held by me or most of those I interviewed, who tend to view retirement as a precursor to boredom and death. I was in accord with Simone de Beauvoir that assertions about the delights of retirement are "shameless lies." Intrigued by Atchley's view, I set out to find people who were eagerly planning or enjoying a retirement they viewed as liberating.

All roads led to Dr. Bob Baxt, DDS, who for years has been voted the best dentist in Boulder. I arrange to meet Bob, fifty-seven, at Vic's coffee shop, a poor choice because he's continually accosted by patients. He's easy to spot: tall and boyishly attractive with dark curly hair, wearing a skintight biking shirt and black spandex shorts. He's cut back working to two days a week and has just ridden his bike forty miles in the mountains. After buying a latte and chai to go, we drive to his office and shut ourselves in his consulting room.

"It's time for me to play. I'm dying to play," Bob says.

Raised in Brooklyn, he still speaks with a street accent and likes to quote his Jewish mother. He became a dentist, he says, because "literally my father told me to." His father worked for the Federation of Jewish Philanthropies and gave Bob and his two brothers a choice: medicine or dentistry. Bob didn't have the grades for the first so he picked dentistry, "and I've been in the field ever since. The only way I can talk with people is if they're lying down in a chair."

But they can't talk back, I say.

"Oh yes, they can. I've gotten to know so many wonderful people, but it's taken a toll." His wife, Cindy, who's worked with him for twenty-five years and whom I spoke to separately, says, "You try doing it from eight to five—running, running from chair to chair, one patient to the next without a break." Bob says what makes it draining is that it's so intimate.

"You're in people's mouths?"

"Right there—it's very Freudian. Women who've been abused or raped might get triggered, because as the patient you have no control. You're lying down. A man is hurting you, and you can't push him away."

"But the patient agrees to get in the chair, it's voluntary."

"It's not!" Bob says. "If you're having tooth pain, you have to do it. You're vulnerable, and you have no idea what I'm doing to you technically. We had a woman last week who started crying in the chair. All kinds of emotions came up, and I had to be there for her." For this reason, he makes a point of talking with new patients before working on them. "I enjoy getting to know each one, but at this point in my life, I want solitude. My philosophy is . . ."

The most popular dentist in town tips back his chair. "Leave me the hell alone! And I'll leave you alone." He says this with such merriment it's hard to take him seriously.

He's had fantasies about retiring almost since he started practicing. Cindy says, "In our forties, our goal was to pay off our debts. We didn't take expensive vacations in Europe." They decided that when their daughter, now sixteen, leaves for college, they'll leave, too. They bought a town home outside Phoenix and started spending weekends and holidays there. "I want to be where it's warm," Bob says. "After dental school I moved to Vermont, and my mother said, 'A Jewish boy is not supposed to be cold!' We wandered in the desert for forty years and got waylaid in Miami, but we don't belong there. We come from desert."

He settled in Boulder in the seventies because he had friends there, liked the mountains and easy outdoor life. "I wanted to get strong." He did construction work, ran and biked, and in 1978 opened a dental office. "I did what I was trained to do, but for twenty-seven years I haven't had a chance to play."

He says that simple things please him most: "walking the dog, taking a drawing class and learning how to sketch a shadow. It doesn't take much to make people happy."

"Are you kidding? It takes a lot for some."

Bob says there are days at the office when "nothing fits, nothing goes right, and I'm angry and frustrated. On a bad day of cycling, when it rains or people pass me and I can't keep up, I'm still loving it."

The Baxts recently sold the town home and decided to build a house not far from there in Tonto Verde, a community for people over fifty-five that will eventually have eight hundred homes, two golf courses, multiple pools, gyms, and clubhouses. "You can look out at national forest, but it's not trees, it's cactus," Bob says. Most of the people moving there are in their sixties or older, live in the Midwest, and spend winters in Arizona. "There's a lot of goyim," Bob jokes. "Republican goyim. I don't know how we'll fit in." Cindy wonders if they'll be bored, and Bob says he might do pro bono dental work with Indian families.

I ask if any of their friends are moving to a retirement community. No, Bob says.

Could that be because there's a stigma?

"Stigma, shmigma! That's what my mother would say. Get over stigmas. The question is: Will it be fun?" He's always wanted to build a house, and "you know what? If it doesn't work out, you sell the house. Bad things could happen in your life. In my practice, I've had ten women in one year diagnosed with breast cancer, and a number have died. So if a house doesn't work out . . ." He shrugs. "It's not terrible."

I ask why, given his stated desire for solitude, he chose to build in a planned community. Bob says Cindy likes the idea of having others nearby, and he's come to think of those in Tonto Verde as "the real chosen people."

"Excuse me?"

"How many men get to retire with their wives? How many marriages last that long? And you're both healthy and have the money to build a house in a beautiful place and play together? It's so rare. I think God put all these lucky couples in a little community so that other people . . . wouldn't hate them!"

We laugh. In a quieter tone, he says, "I think it's gonna be a ball. Will I like not being stressed out and exhausted from giving, giving, and giving emotionally?" His voice drops to a whisper. "You bet."

Jane Fyrberg

Since meeting Bob Baxt, I've found that doctors, dentists, and others who've been tethered to a time clock tend to be attracted to a leisure-based retirement. Jane Fyrberg, an emergency room doctor in Honolulu for twenty-five years, retired at fifty-eight and says, "It's delicious!" She compares it with what happens when you're in elementary school, it's May, and you're tired of sitting in class all day and long to be let out for the summer. "I feel the working career is like that, and when you finally finish the required part, it's recess! It's vacation! It's the glorious stuff that comes after school's out. That's how I saw retirement, and I couldn't wait to get there."

She says she loved medicine and her patients but "it narrows your life to focus on one area for so long. There're wonderful things you can't experience when you're immersed in medicine or law."

Such as?

"Playing violin in a symphony, or studying hula—not the tourist hula, but the traditional hula that's serious and sacred."

Jane is tall and athletic, with bangs and straight fair hair that falls to the middle of her back. Always cheerful, with acute powers of perception, she moves at a pace none of her friends can keep up with. Raised in Georgia, she came to Hawaii on vacation after college, said, "I am never leaving this place," and never did. She met a navy pilot, Bob, while surfing, they fell in love and married, became doctors, and worked in the ER at Kaiser Foundation Hospital. They had four daughters and, at Jane's insistence, adopted a baby boy when the first four kids hit their teens. Jane's passion for babies and children is legendary and reminds me of that of Mia Farrow.

As Jane and Bob were about to retire, intending to dance, play bridge, and, in Bob's case, build a house for their daughter, "another baby landed on our doorstep," Jane says. "Staring at that baby, we had to ask, What was the most joyful part of life so far? What made us happiest? The clear answer was: Having and raising kids. So why not do that in retirement?" She says the decision was "enormous, because I was also caring for an Alzheimer's mother."

The unexpected child came when Jane got a call from a foster mother who was about to pick up a baby but was suffering chest pains and had to be hospitalized. She asked Jane—or Dr. Jane, as many call her—if she and Bob would take the baby for a few days until the adoptive parents arrived from Pennsylvania. Of course, Jane said. She and Bob signed papers to be temporary foster parents, picked up the baby, whom they called Makua after the surfing beach where they'd met, and stopped at Long's Drugs to buy diapers, bottles, and supplies for a few days. But after a week the baby was still with them. The adoptive parents had backed out, and the Fyrbergs were asked to keep Makua for two more weeks while the agency offered him to the next three couples on the list. All three declined when they learned that Makua's mother, who came from a tiny Pacific island, Majuro, had tested positive for syphilis. "People would look it up online and freak out, thinking the baby would go blind and have facial deformities," Jane says. "But that didn't scare us because Makua had been given IV penicillin from the moment he was born and had no effects. He'd been cured."

When the agency called to say it would take still longer to find adoptive parents, Jane said, "You better take him out of our house right now, or when you come to get him, we're gonna be out the back door to South America because we can't give him up. We're not seasoned foster parents who can just hand back a child." Jane describes the baby as having "enormous brown eyes that were dear and curious and the sweetest cupid's-bow mouth. We fell in love with him on day one."

"Both of you?" I ask.

"Both of us—this time."

The previous time Jane had brought home a baby—a preemie whose teenage mother had begged Jane to raise him because she couldn't—Bob had said, "No way!" He refused to look at or touch the child. "It's me or the baby," he told Jane. "We have enough children, we're stretched far enough financially. We're just not doing this."

For two years, Jane kept the baby out of Bob's sight and prayed that he wouldn't walk out. They never discussed the child, whom Jane named Beau. She and Bob barely spoke those years, until one morning when Bob was working in the yard, Beau picked up a shovel and tried to help. After a time, Bob leaned down and showed him how to hold the shovel. Jane sat inside watching, holding her breath. After an hour, Bob walked back inside, trailed by Beau, and said to Jane, "The kid's a natural with a shovel." She started to cry.

Jane doesn't know what caused the difference in Bob's attitude when Makua arrived. "It might have been his age or the fact that he'd retired, but he couldn't keep his hands off the baby, and Makua's first word was 'Daddy.'" After they'd kept him a month, Jane asked the agency if they could adopt him. "We know we're older, past the age you accept, but would you consider us?"

"Are you serious?" the representative asked. "We're pricey."

"How pricey are you?" Jane asked.

"Twenty thousand dollars."

"What!" I say. "They should have paid you. This was a child no one else wanted."

"Isn't that the truth?" Jane says. "But they didn't. We forked over the twenty grand. Gladly! We would have sold our house at that point because we loved the baby so much."

"When he's twenty, you'll be . . ."

"Eighty," she says. The Fyrbergs made arrangements for one of their married daughters to take Makua if something happens to them. And Jane found that the baby triggered a reversal in her mother's condition. Jane had brought her mother from Georgia to Hawaii after she was diagnosed with Alzheimer's. She eventually lost all memory and also lost the motor responses for holding a spoon, brushing her teeth, and walking. Jane says that when her mother was a young schoolteacher with an encyclopedic knowledge of history, politics, music, theology, and poetry, she'd begged Jane never to put her in a hospital or home. She had a phobia about hospitals, and Jane said, "Don't worry, I won't."

What puzzles Jane is that her mother possessed "a phenomenal body of knowledge. Where has it all gone?" At times, Jane feels heartsick and helpless, but when Makua arrived, she brought him into her mother's room and started caring for him there. "From the first day, my mother held out her arms to hold the baby, and other motor responses returned. I'd been feeding her baby foods, and she began to take the spoon from me and feed herself, then progressed to adult food." Her mother still doesn't know who Jane is, and "she can't remember from day to day that we have a baby, but her face lights up each time I bring him in."

I tell Jane I don't think I could care for someone with advanced Alzheimer's. "I couldn't do it," Jane says, "if I didn't have wonderful things like the baby, music, and dance." She's wanted to study hula for twenty years. "The hula I'm learning is not 'Little Grass Shack' or 'Lovely Hula Hands.' It's traditional hula done only to Hawaiian chant, and you're not allowed to dance until you've studied the language and learned the many meanings to the song. You peel away the layers and take it into your soul, so when you begin to dance, the meaning comes through your face, your body, your hands and feet—from everywhere." When she was working at Kaiser, she had twelve-hour shifts and a constantly changing schedule. "You couldn't plan more than two weeks ahead, so a hula class that meets every Wednesday at seven—you could never commit. But now . . ." She shoots her arm in the air. "I can say, Yes! I can be at your class. I don't have to report to anybody anymore. I don't have to stay in that building for twelve hours."

She asks if I've felt the same eagerness to retire and do other "wonderful things."

No, I tell her. I think the difference is that I've worked mostly freelance and set my own hours. I never felt shackled; I didn't have to ask anyone's permission to take a month off. But the few times I worked for someone else on a TV series, I did feel exhausted at the end of the season and dreaded going back.

"I suspect, Jane, that if you didn't have this baby, there'd come a point when taking hula lessons and playing bridge wouldn't feel like enough."

"You're right," she says, "because that doesn't fill the hole. If I didn't love children, I might be looking for a third world medical clinic. I think babies are *my* creative work—my canvas. They're a blank sheet, and you have to look into their soul to see what calls to them and where their passions lie. It's thrilling to see what emerges—like the image developing in a photograph."

She thinks a moment, then laughs. "Maybe I better plan on getting another baby at seventy." She says older people who're healthy and energetic "have so much to give a child. They have the time, the home, the experience, and the love . . . so why not?"

Tracy Newman

Consider Tracy Newman: In 2004, at age sixty-one, she's an executive producer and creator of the ABC hit comedy *According to Jim*. She retires from TV, turning her back on money and power to revive her passion for folksinging. Small and wiry, with spiky blond hair and black harlequin glasses, she does not look, dress, or move like she's in her sixties but in her forties. She's taken a class in songwriting and decided to work in the country genre. "Country is forgiving," Tracy says. "They won't criticize your voice if they like what the song's about. And they don't care how old you are. I mean, what is Willie Nelson—a hundred?"

On a spring evening shortly after retiring, she makes her way to a high school in Los Angeles to play one of her songs for two "evaluators" from the music business. She hasn't performed since her twenties, when she used to sing at the Bitter End in New York and McCabe's in Santa Monica. Her guitar chops are rusty, her heart's pounding, and her hands are shaking so badly she's afraid she won't be able to hit the notes. After the evaluators listen to the first two people and rip their songs apart, Tracy stands, clutching her guitar. "I have to do this right now or I'm scared I won't do it," she says.

Two months before, Tracy was one of the bosses—the evaluators of everything—on *According to Jim*. She was one of the few women show runners and perhaps the oldest in television, which made her a phenomenon. The star, Jim Belushi, did a double take when she announced she was leaving to try to sell country songs. It was like giving up being a star to become a waitress.

Tracy and I had met during college, when we were spending our junior year in Italy. She always carried a guitar, wore a floppy green hat and no makeup, and quit before graduating to sing in coffeehouses and clubs. After hustling for ten years, she concluded she couldn't earn a living as a singer, left the business, and became a nursery school teacher.

A few years later she took an improv class at night and joined a fledgling comedy group, the Groundlings. "I fell in love with it," Tracy says. "We thought we were the future of comedy." She brought in her younger sister, Laraine Newman, who was discovered there by Lily Tomlin and Lorne Michaels and spirited off to *Saturday Night Live*.

Tracy herself was "deathly afraid of performing," so she gravitated toward teaching, directing, and writing. The Groundlings became a breeding ground for comics, including Will Ferrell, Lisa Kudrow, Phil Hartman, Jon Lovitz, Julia Sweeney, and Pee-wee Herman. For Tracy, it turned out to be natural training for writing sitcoms because she was constantly reworking sketches. One of the actors, Jonathan Stark, asked her to collaborate on a spec script for *Cheers*. "We were a good team because he's ten years younger, a man, and flat-out funny—which is the coin of the realm—but he needs to be corralled to get work done and can barely type or spell." They were hired to go on staff at *Cheers*, and "our bosses were guys from Princeton and Harvard in their twenties," Tracy recalls. "Jon fit in pretty well but I was like their mom. I was forty-six, had a kid, and was having hot flashes and marital problems."

Cheers, then in its tenth season, was run like a beautiful machine. The staff writers were the best in the business and worked so fast "we were out by six P.M. I learned so much." She and Jon would turn in a good script, she says, and the staff of thirteen would sit around the table and rewrite it completely. "By shooting time it was magical, and not a line of mine was left."

After *Cheers*, Tracy and Jon worked on other comedies and for four years on *Ellen*. They and three others wrote the "coming out" episode for which they won an Emmy. But Tracy paid a price; the other shows were not run like *Cheers*. The staff worked from ten A.M. to midnight, and the pressure of turning out a new episode every week led to friction, rage, infighting, and crack-ups. Tracy got divorced and didn't see much of her daughter. "I'd get home at midnight and have to get up at six to fix her breakfast and take her to school. I just wasn't there—that's her overall memory. She has a lot of anger and I have a lot of guilt."

Tracy found herself staying in TV for the money. She and Jon tried to get their own show on the air, and wrote eight pilots that were rejected before getting a green light for *According to Jim*. During the first season, Belushi made it clear he did not want a woman running the show, Tracy says. "He went on *The View* and said, 'Men make good leaders and women make good managers. That's why on my show, the executive producer is a man and his partner is a woman.'" When Tracy heard Belushi say that, she thought, Okay, if I'm not gonna be the leader here, maybe I won't work as much and I'll have less stress. She let Jon run the writing room and deal with Belushi, and she began to pull back emotionally.

By the third season of *According to Jim*, Tracy saw that she was no longer needed and retired. She told the actors, "At this time in my life, I don't want to work eighteen-hour days." The minute she left, she says, "I stopped thinking about the show. I don't even watch it now! I jumped back into writing songs, and boy, what a treat it is that I don't have to earn a living." After years of making large sums, saving, and investing cautiously, she felt like the street musician who could play real good, for free.

Tracy's boyfriend, Reni Santoni, the actor who was Clint Eastwood's partner in *Dirty Harry*, thought that when she quit her job she'd have more time to hang out with him and travel. But the opposite occurred. "On the TV job," she says, "any free time I had I wanted to escape—drink wine, cook steaks, hang out by the pool, and fuck. Now that I have all the time and no schedule, I don't want to escape. I'm always writing. On a nine-to-five job, or in my case nine-to-midnight, the weekend comes and it means something. Now it doesn't mean anything. Saturday is just another day I can get something done."

• • •

One year after her retirement, I meet Tracy for open mike night at Kulak's Woodshed, a storefront in the low-rent district of North Holly-

wood. Tracy stands on a green carpet surrounded by about twenty people sprawled on secondhand couches and mismatched chairs. Some
have brought their dogs. The owner, Paul Kulak, set up the place to pro-
vide "great, free, live music from singer-songwriters." There are six
videocameras and everything is streamed live on the Internet.

Tracy sings a number about her relationship with her sister, Laraine,
and a song about when she and Reni fought and broke up and he sent
her an e-mail saying, "I have to come over there because I left some
kisses inside you. I need them, and I know where they are."

When she finishes, we walk next door for a drink.

"You didn't look scared about performing," I say.

"I'm not now. The thing I've been afraid of is that I'm gonna fuck up,
play the wrong chords or forget the words. But if I own the stuff, if I've
practiced it to within an inch of its life, I'm okay."

"I had no idea you'd get over your fear this fast," I say.

Tracy nods. "When I'm up onstage with *my songs,* I love it." Her goal
has changed as well. When she retired from TV, "I just wanted to sell
songs. Now I'm feeling that somebody my age will break through as a
performer. And it might be a woman. And it might be me."

That's intriguing, I say, because the pros—Joni Mitchell, Carly
Simon, Carole King—have problems getting record contracts and think
a mainstream hit is an extreme long shot.

They're right, Tracy says. "But I'm not gonna go to a record company
and try to get a deal." What she might do is buy ads on local TV late at
night and play snippets of songs that have "a great melodic hook. If people hear a song on TV or the Internet and can't get it out of their heads,
maybe they'll buy it, and you could get a hit record that way."

"I love your confidence," I say.

"I have confidence in my songwriting." She recently won second
place in the Unisong International Songwriting Contest for a Christmas
song she wrote with a friend, Lynne Stewart. "We won five hundred
dollars!" Tracy said.

She's recording a CD of her songs at her own expense and says she'll be happy "doing small gigs and selling the CDs myself. Do I want to be a star? No. But if I become a star, am I gonna kick it out of bed?" She laughs. "You never know what could happen."

· · ·

Retiring from TV certainly gave Tracy a grand hall pass, greased by the fact that she'll be receiving residuals for decades. But creative people—even if they don't have Tracy's income stream—are used to setting their own agenda and dealing with erratic earnings. Most will continue to practice their craft indefinitely. Picasso is said to have asked, on the morning he died, if there was a canvas stretched and ready to paint.

In other fields, people who retire often change their direction. Robert Atchley turned from teaching to service work. The strongest appeal of retirement, he says, is that it's "a blank slate. There's no big plan or blueprint for it in the culture. It's a vague, do-it-yourself life stage that turns out to be a tremendous advantage."

"How is it an advantage if people are forced to retire?" I ask.

"They respond in different ways. Some become determined that they'll never retire. Others may go through some stock taking and decide it's better than they thought." Atchley says people misperceive what retirement will be like. "They don't know how it feels to relax into a life that fits your own body rhythms. You have to be willing to run fairly fast to keep in step with the world today." Tracy found this when she quit TV and could write songs without having to hurry. The song is done when it's done, she says, instead of being slammed to a finish at midnight because the episode shoots in the morning.

Even after hearing Atchley's spin and talking with people who've retired, I don't relish the prospect unless there's fire at the center of what follows, even the quiet fire of introspection and learning. But I can see that a mix 'n' match, create-your-own way of living with no blueprint or expectations may appeal. Woody Wickham, who retired as vice president of the John D. and Catherine T. MacArthur Foundation, where he distributed $25 million a year in grants, spends a third of his time volunteering, a third doing consulting work, and a third fishing in Montana. "I'm concerned about having enough money," Woody says, "and absolutely convinced I should spend what I have."

Atchley says that the majority who retire, even if forced, "adapt very well. The data—the indicators of whether they find life meaningful and enjoyable—are higher than for people in their twenties."

"What about people in their forties who are hitting their stride?" I ask.

"They may be hitting their stride, but how big a load are they bearing?"

Big.

Atchley smiles as he lifts my cup and pours more tea. "Elders tend to run lighter. And that has value."

We'll see.

10

Our House

Caramba, what rain. It lashes the windows of the bus as we bump over potholes and careen around muddy mountain roads. We're crammed into seats built for tiny Costa Ricans, so our knees smack against the seats in front of us. All is gray, nothing visible but clouds and fog. It's day one of Christopher Howard's beach tour for people who're thinking of moving to Costa Rica, and the eight other gringos who've come here in October, euphemistically called the "green season," are grumbling. Chris had encouraged us to come, saying it would rain in the afternoons but mornings would be sunny. Then, a few days before we flew in from Toronto, New Jersey, Michigan, Maine, and Texas, the rains turned fierce, washing out roads and bridges and forcing Chris to reroute our trip. The nine of us are all in our fifties and sixties, some have retired, others are ready to quit working, and we've come to see if this could be our next home.

Costa Rica! The country has buzz, it's the relocation destination of the moment because—as the magazine articles tell you—it has no army, no enemies, no terrorists, and it may be the most advanced nation in the world for environmental awareness. The beaches are pristine, the ocean and rivers are unpolluted, the rain forest and wildlife are protected, and you can drink the water from the tap. Health care is provided from cradle to grave, labor is cheap, the government is stable, and the local population, called Ticos, are sweet, nonconfrontational, and celebrate *pura vida,* which means, literally, "pure life."

After leaving the capital, San José, in the central valley, we drive to the crest of the coastal mountain range. Chris points off to the west. "There's a beautiful view of the ocean out there—if it weren't cloudy."

So you say. That's how Ali G responds when guests on his TV show make claims.

Rosa Materson, who was born in Puerto Rico, moved to Houston, and married a doctor, says, "I sure hope the weather improves, because I haven't seen one thing that would make me want to move here."

Chris puts his hands to his face. Tall, with unruly black hair, he fell in love with all things Hispanic and moved to Costa Rica in his twenties, married a Tica, and has a teenage son. "I feel bad, you people came all this way. . . ."

Rosa's husband, Dick, a physician who walks with a cane due to acute respiratory distress syndrome, shrugs at Chris. "If you can't control something, like the weather, you might as well accept it. Life is short."

"But with the rain, you can't appreciate the place," Chris says. "This is not typical."

We stop at a roadside restaurant to use the bathrooms, but every toilet in the women's room is full of excrement and won't flush.

Pura vida.

Back on the bus, I try to stretch out my legs in the aisle. Why the hell didn't I pay more attention to the weather? I should have rescheduled this trip, come during the dry season, or gone to Mexico, where there are large colonies of expats. I know a New York publicist who quit her job after her kids left for college, moved to Zihuatanejo, and loves it. She offered to show me the beaches and introduce me to her friends, but I'd thought that Mexico did not have as much buzz.

Costa Rica! Another hour on the bumpy road and we arrive, stiff and weary, at the Pacific, shrouded in gray mist. We pass Dominical, a surfing village, then pull into La Cusinga Lodge, perched on a cliff overlooking what we're told is a magnificent beach. Sitting on the terrace, encircled by clouds, we find lunch cheering: fresh hot pancakes made from crushed plantains, mango juice that's just been squeezed, rice with chicken and the addictive Costa Rican salsa, Lizano, which is sweet and mildly spicy with hints of curry and rich vinegar. Absorbed in eating, we don't notice that the clouds are dispersing. After a few bites of coconut cake, I look up and see the ocean—not gray but sparkling turquoise—with waves rolling onto a half-moon bay of floury sand. A rocky island rises in the distance, and oh . . . my . . . God! Just to the right, six feet from us, there's a tree in which are perched about twenty birds whose ultrabright colors make them seem unreal: toucans with chartreuse-and-apricot bills, a fiery-beak aricari, red-footed honeycreeper, and scarlet macaw. I remember, in another tropical country, walking for hours with binoculars and finally spotting, barely visible through the leaves, one toucan. Here there are twenty, close enough to reach. I'm embarrassed to tell you how quickly my mood reverses. I love this place.

Chris introduces us to a loquacious blonde, Annie Drake, an expat who says she's a descendant of Sir Francis Drake and carries a green parrot in her arms wherever she goes. "Her name's Buffy," Annie says, stroking the parrot. "She was born with a deformed foot and can't walk or fly." Annie founded South Pacific Real Estate Services with a young Tico, and she'll be our guide for the next two days. "I've been all over Costa Rica, and I think this is the most wuuun-der-ful spot," she says. "I can't wait to show it to you all."

"This beach is extraordinary," I say.

"Well, guess what? There's a lot next door that just came on the market."

"Really? Does it have the same view?"

"Exactly."

Be still, my heart. I want these birds, those waves, the orchid trees that cover the hillside, and the view of Ballena Island, where they say that whales and dolphins come to breed. Will my friends want to live here, too?

* * *

Six months earlier, I was standing in the kitchen of Andy Weil's house in Tucson, chopping ginger and peeling shrimp to make pad thai. The four of us who are cooking together go back decades. Andy and Woody Wickham were roommates at Harvard; Kathy Komaroff Goodman and I lived together at Berkeley. We currently live in Chicago, Tucson, Manhattan, and Boulder, and it's rare that we're all together unless we plan a date and ramrod it into our schedules.

We've called this meeting for a purpose. We want to have *the conversation*—on the subject that's being discussed in other gatherings in almost every city I visit: How can we arrange to grow older with our friends? How do we find or build a place where we can live in some kind of cluster so that we're independent but connected? And how can this cluster morph into an alternative to a nursing home?

In New York, Sharon Salzberg, author of *Loving Kindness,* says she and her colleagues "have this conversation again and again. Where are we going to go when we get older, and why aren't we living in communities now so we can take care of each other or have people take care of us?" She adds, "It's hard to imagine how we'll pull this off, but it's bound to happen because so many people are thinking on it."

No one wants to be parked in a nursing home, surrounded by others with whom one has nothing in common. Tracy Kidder, who spent a year observing a Massachusetts nursing home to write *Old Friends,* says, "Imagine: You're in your last place on earth, and you can't choose the people you hang out with?" About a third of people over sixty-five are expected to do the endgame in nursing homes; the rest will stay in their communities. Marion Woodman, the author and analyst who's seventy-eight, is determined to do the latter. She says she's made arrangements to be cared for in her home, but this may mean she'll pass her days in the company of an immigrant who speaks minimal English.

Looking ahead, sniffing the wind, entrepreneurs in the senior housing business are setting up homes for Asians, or academics, or gays. Paul Krassner says he wants to be in a home for humorists, "where there are really good drugs and lots of laughs." Woody Wickham asks, "If you're going to a home based on affinity, which part of your persona will be your guiding star? Your politics, sexual orientation?" He thinks a moment. "Is there a cynicism and satire group I could join?"

At our meeting in Tucson, we sit around the fire after dinner, not sure how to begin. After a silence, Woody says: "Where are we going to live?"

We agree that if we don't make plans, our kids or the government might end up making them for us. It's time to set things in motion, acquire a site. Andy wants to look in British Columbia, where the dollar goes further, or Costa Rica. I tell them I'd like a place that's warm and close to an airport so our kids can visit. Kathy thinks it's important to be near a major medical facility. "What about Tucson?" Andy says. "It's warm and has good hospitals." He says he has enough land for us to build our own places, along with a house for guests and caretakers. But if we do that, I point out, it'll be Andy's place and he'll inevitably be responsible and in charge. "Unless," Kathy says, thinking aloud, "we buy shares of his land or a piece of it so we own the place together." But that becomes complicated. Andy's owned the ranch for twenty years; could we afford to buy in at current prices? I ask what happens if we marry, divorce, or take a partner nobody else likes. "What if one of us dies or wants to leave?"

Blank looks.

Then there's the question of who else will live in the community. Twelve seems like a good number. We throw out names of friends, a sister, a brother. Do we all have to approve, or is anyone welcome? Woody suggests we could invite prospective residents to go on a raft or hiking trip for a week and see how we get along. I try to picture this: some geezer version of fraternity and sorority rush?

I remember that when my parents were in their seventies, they bought a condo in the building where my aunt and uncle lived. "Every time a unit came up for sale," I say, "they alerted their friends, until there were eight or ten of them there. They ate meals together, went square dancing . . ." I can't finish the sentence, thinking of my white-haired mother and aunt dressed like little girls in their flouncy square-dance skirts and Mary Janes.

Woody turns to Andy. "Do you have any chocolate?"

"Yes!" He cracks out the dark, 80 percent cacao organic chocolate, which he says is good for your health, and we decide to watch a movie.

The next morning, Woody says that after sleeping on it, he thinks we shouldn't try to plan the whole operation but "start with the four of us." Talk to others. Check out why and where people are moving. Visit communities. Figure out how, as another friend puts it, "we can crack the code."

• • •

What's behind this wish to grow old with like-minded peers? Is it a reaction to the specter of nursing homes, or a late-blooming tropism to connect with our familiars? Joan Borysenko says, "It's in our genes. We were the generation in the communes, remember?"

"Did you live in one?"

"No, but I felt I was a step away," she says.

Only a small percentage lived in communes, but those people set a tone, conducting an experiment we could follow vicariously. They learned—and taught us—it was workable not for everyone to live under the same roof, but to have separate dwellings. They practiced "voluntary primitivism," rejecting materialist culture and vowing to live "in harmony with the earth."

The communes being set up today are not about primitivism but companionship, in lodgings that are attractive, comfortable, and ecologically correct. The most successful and fast-growing model is the cohousing project (there are more than 160 in the United States), in which people buy their own homes in a neighborhood that's laid out to encourage interaction. They share spaces like a garden, a kids' play area, and a common house where they eat together regularly. I'm intrigued by the concept, because it attempts to meet the deep-seated and twinned needs I have for solitude and belonging.

A journalist I meet, Dan Glick, invites me to a party he's throwing at Nyland, the first cohousing development that was built in Colorado. Dan is head-turning handsome, with blue eyes and dark hair. A single father, he's lived at Nyland twelve years, during one of which he took his two kids out of school and traveled with them around the world, seeking out endangered species and writing about the trip in *Monkey Dancing*.

I pull into the parking area where residents must leave their cars and walk up curving lanes to their homes. Dan had told me, "It's designed so you might actually talk to people, instead of pulling into your garage and entering your house from there." He said the lanes encourage " 'coho moments'—where you see somebody, have coffee, maybe go for a bike ride or take home some vegetable soup they just cooked."

The houses are modest in size but inviting, with clean, contemporary lines and cheerful colors like teal, barn red, and yellow. I watch people returning from shopping, unloading their cars, and piling their groceries into red wagons, which they pull down the lanes. It reminds me of Fire Island, only it's Family Island. On the lawns, which merge into one another, there are wading pools, barbecues, kids running in packs, and mothers tending patches of irises and giant red poppies with petals like paper fans.

I hear guitars and voices singing the Beatles, "I've Just Seen a Face." I make for them like a heat-seeking missile and find a group of about thirty gathered on Dan's back porch. He's mixed up a bucket of margaritas, and others have brought food. The age range is wide, and to my surprise, there are numerous singles. Dan says with a dimpled smile, "We have every type of American family dysfunction: divorced, blended, single parents, gay couples . . ." Fred, an electrical engineer, offers to show me around Nyland. It has forty-two homes; none is for sale now, but they run about $400,000 for a three-bedroom, two-story house with money views of the Rockies. I ask how new members are accepted. Fred laughs. "There's no admissions committee. People visit, and it's their choice if they want to move here, not ours."

I'm reminded of young people who started rural communes in the sixties and declared them "open land"—free to anyone who wanted to set up a tent or build a dome. Hardly any of those communes are still standing. With cohousing, the critical difference is that people have their own incomes, buy their homes, and tend to be more organized. Visitors learn they'll be expected to contribute time. Residents at Nyland eat together four nights a week, although it's not required, but each adult must cook and clean up for the group once every two months. "The advantage is that except for that one night, you show up and get a home-cooked meal, while your kids can play and you can have adult conversation," Fred says. "For a single working dad, it's awesome."

But for those who don't have kids at home, it may become grating to have two-year-olds screaming and running around the dining hall. Susan, a librarian, says she and her partner want to move to Silver Sage

Village, the first cohousing for people over fifty being built in the state. "I'd like to come home from a busy day and have a glass of wine and a quiet meal," Susan says. "It's not like that here."

When the party at Dan's winds down, he settles back on the couch with his feet up. He threw the party to boost morale, he says. "We're going through a tough time. In the early years, people were gung ho and idealistic, but now, if we call a meeting, we're lucky if twelve people show up." Dan says one family doesn't get along with the others, which causes discord.

I groan.

"That would happen even if you did this with your friends," Dan says. "You'd end up fighting in ways you didn't anticipate. Conflict is inevitable, but most of the time we can resolve it." He picks up a mandolin and fingers chords. "Am I ready to move anywhere else?" He shakes his head no. "I really like interacting with other people's kids, watching them grow up, and knowing my own kids have other adults to turn to. I come down positive on cohousing."

When I drive away from Nyland, I'm intrigued and racked with questions. Is there enough privacy? Would I want to eat with a hundred people four nights a week? Is it too removed—in the countryside east of Boulder—from shops, restaurants, and the library? I'd enjoy the closeness with kids—I miss having them at home—but I'm also curious about Silver Sage, the cohousing being constructed for people over fifty.

The following week, I meet with the builder, Jim Leach, who's president of Wonderland Hill Development Company. Jim had been a conventional developer for thirty years, known for using green building techniques, when he was hired by the founders of Nyland. "I started reading about cohousing, which began in Denmark in the eighties, and got real excited," Jim says. He became a convert, built fifteen cohousing projects in four states, and he and his wife, Brownie, are planning to move to Silver Sage.

"We're not just building a place to live," Jim says. "We hope to attract people who want to age with purpose, who're interested in giving back and spiritual growth instead of living in a recreation-based complex around a golf course." He works with the architect, Charles Durrett, known as the guru of cohousing because he coined the term and has designed more than thirty-eight. They're planning Silver Sage so "members will never have to move," Jim says. Although the people buying in now are healthy and walking, "everything is wheelchair accessible, we're building rooms for physical therapy, special tubs with ledges, and space for caregivers." The units will sell from $110,000 to $685,000, because Boulder requires that 20 percent be "affordable."

Annie Russell, who's in charge of "community building," leads the meetings for new members while cohousing is being built. In her sixties, Annie has the sunny, rallying nature of a den mother and wears lush colors, dangling earrings, and her white hair cropped short. Annie helps the members set ground rules and procedures for resolving conflicts, but once they move in, they're on their own. Jim Leach says, "We create living organisms, and they're unpredictable. It's amazing to see what character they take on."

I find it noteworthy that Jim, Annie, Charles Durrett, and most of the development staff live in cohousing themselves. Annie has a home in the same cohousing village as her grown son. "Not everyone there is my friend," she says. "You develop bonds of various strengths. It's a slow process, and we like it slow." When prospective members come to a meeting, she tells them: "We're not asking you to get married today. Come back for a second date. Down the road, maybe we'll get engaged."

　　　　•　•　•

I attend one of the first group dates for Silver Sage. I drive down Easy Rider Lane to the meeting place, where I find ten women and thirteen men sitting in a circle with Annie Russell. Some have taken the first step, put a deposit on a home, and as Annie tells them, "You people are going to set the tone for the community." Most have graying hair and are dressed from casual outdoorsy to a suit with a pager. Several are moving from multigenerational communities. Tom (I'm changing names except for the leaders) lived in cohousing in California and says, "I lost my wife three years ago, and the support that was given to her and to me was . . . it was just phenomenal. But it's a slow, complex process. . . ."

Jim Leach nods. "That's what they say about cohousing: It's the longest, most expensive personal growth workshop you'll ever take."

Everyone laughs.

Myra, a heavyset woman with a buzz cut, says, "Living close together will bring up your stuff. What happens when you get taken over by a two-year-old who wants to throw a tantrum? Because somebody is going to push your buttons."

Myra is pushing mine. She talks more than anyone, says nothing of interest, and I find myself getting irritated every time she raises her hand.

Tom says, "You talk things through. You spend a huge amount of time and energy doing this, but that's when bonding takes place. For some people it's laborious, but for others it's life-giving."

I think I'm in the first camp.

They talk about how the community will make decisions. Tom says, "One fellow in our group was an Israeli attorney, and he thought consensus means that everybody gets exactly what he wants and we don't go forward unless we're in complete agreement."

People hoot and laugh.

"The way we learned to do it," Tom says, "is like this: If I oppose Plan A, I ask myself, 'Can I live with Plan A?' If I can, I yield, in service to the community moving forward. If not, I communicate that and we process it further."

I'm beginning to remember why I never joined SDS or one of the early women's groups.

Annie reports on a conference she just attended, where she met Dene Peterson, a former nun who founded the first senior cohousing in America, ElderSpirit in Virginia. Annie passes out a sheet that states their aims: mutual support, late-life spirituality, and helping each other die at home. Annie says, "They're explicit about facing aging and dying. We haven't gone down that road. We're trying to emphasize life and joy—"

People rise up in dissent; they *do* want to talk about how they'll age and die. Linda, who's lived at Nyland, says, "We all have to face death, and none of us has done it before."

"Maybe not," someone says. They laugh.

Another member, Gilbert, says, "If we have to end this life, I want to go out with grace."

Linda nods. "That's the main reason I'm here. It's important work, and this is an opportunity to do it with like-minded people."

•   •   •

Social chemistry is hard to define. You can walk into a party, look around, and feel uncomfortable—something in the way people are dressed, laughing, eating potato chips, makes you withdraw into yourself and want to flee. Then you can walk into another gathering where you know nobody and feel at home. Whatever the cues are that make you feel at ease and game to jump in, they weren't happening for me at this meeting. I think the reason many I know are saying we want a community with friends is that, at the point when we're more restricted and can't get around easily, we'd like to have intellectual companionship, with people who're interested in the books we read and share humor and references and maybe have a similar background or spiritual goals.

When I tell this to Charles Durrett, he points out that if all the people in your current neighborhood ate dinner together every week, "you'd find at least two or three to bond with." Charles is skeptical of trying to build a community with friends. "At least a dozen groups have come to our offices and asked us to design a project for them. They say, 'We love each other, we were roommates in college . . .' but when push comes to shove, six months later, one family isn't ready, one loses a job, one gets divorced, one wants to live on the other side of town . . ." He says it's never worked out. "But if you start the project and put out the word in a large enough area, you'll get twenty-five people who're ready to do it now, in this location, at this cost."

· · ·

Stephan Rechtschaffen, MD, followed his own approach in Costa Rica. A cofounder of the Omega Institute in New York, Stephan had been visiting Costa Rica for fifteen years, looking for property. In 2002, he and a business partner bought sixty acres on the ocean in Nosara, near the beach where giant sea turtles lumber over the sand in the moonlight to lay their eggs.

"I'm setting up a community for friends," Stephan says. He's developed fifty home sites and sold half by word of mouth. When his youngest son finishes high school, Stephan plans to move to Nosara full-time, although most of his friends will be there only part-time. "Down the line," he says, "who knows?" He's writing the bylaws for an association of owners, then he'll withdraw and let the group run the community. "I don't want to be the mayor," he says.

I ask why he picked Costa Rica.

"I like living in a country whose values are consistent with mine. The direction of the U.S. is abominable to me."

Don't you think it's important, I ask, to be part of the opposition, to stay and fight?

Stephan sighs. "Certain people didn't want to leave the *Titanic.* They thought, If we're here paddling, it will help. I *do* think it's important to try to help, but we're past that point. It's important not to be stupid."

To reach Nosara, on the Nicoya peninsula, you have to fly into a local airport or drive five hours from San José. I ask Stephan, who's nearing sixty, if he's thought about access to medical care or wheelchair accessibility. . . .

"Quite honestly," he says, "I don't focus on that. I'm healthy, I do whatever I did at twenty-five."

Unforeseen things can happen. . . .

"I'll deal with them when they happen," he says. "If people are squeamish about this issue, they won't come. I may say this with arrogance, but I like it that the friends who're being drawn here are risk takers in life."

"It's not about being squeamish," I suggest. "If you know it's going to rain, you pack an umbrella."

Stephan laughs. "I never have an umbrella. I just get wet."

• • •

Nosara is not on Christopher Howard's beach tour. He thinks it's too "Californiaized. There's a yoga center, massage places, even sushi," he says. "If you go farther south, you get better value, and I think it's more authentic and beautiful, like a tropical Big Sur, where the mountains drop down to the sea."

On day two of the tour, in the Cristal Ballena hotel, I awaken to sunshine pouring into a lavish room with a canopy bed and private garden looking out on the ocean. It's remarkable how luxury and sun can put you in the mood to buy real estate. "Parrot Annie," as she's called by the Ticos ("Everyone here has a nickname," she says), takes Rosa and me in her Jeep to look at property. "I'll tell you the good and the bad," Annie says. "We have nineteen wuuun-der-ful restaurants here, and the most expensive meal costs ten dollars. Lots of French and French Canadians settled here, so there's a bakery where a guy makes baguettes just like the ones you find in Paris." We hit a bump that throws us into the air. The dirt road is crosshatched with ruts and potholes, so it's Mr. Toad's Wild Ride.

"Are the roads always this bad?" Rosa, a motherly figure, asks.

"It's worse because of the rains," Annie says, "but you need four-wheel drive, that's for sure."

We pass through Ojochal, which is only a few blocks long with a hardware store, market, liquor store, badminton club, and a funky bull-ring where Annie says they have a rodeo once a month. "They put inner tubes around the bulls, and the men try to ride them." Do badminton and bull riding suggest the character of the place?

Annie stops at a restaurant by the river to confirm that we'll be there for dinner. "There are no phones yet, so you have to go in person."

No phones—in the whole town?

Annie says she's been waiting nine years for phone service to arrive. "They keep telling us, Next week. They say the lines are installed, all they have to do is pull the switch."

"Why don't they, then?" Rosa asks.

Annie shrugs. "You get used to it. Actually, it helps you get to know everyone better because you're always stopping by. The people here are wuuun-derful."

It reminds me of Victorian times, when people would call on one another and leave cards.

But how do you do business? I ask.

"You can get satellite TV, which gives you high-speed Internet," she says. "But if you're in a rush . . ." She smiles. "You're in the wrong country."

We pull off the road by the land I want to see, not far from the tree with the twenty toucans and the view across turquoise water to Ballena Island. Rosa and I follow Annie and her partner, Moises, through the jungle growth to the top of a rise. We can hear the gathering, rising—*shoof!*—of waves on the sand, but we can't see the ocean.

"What about the view?" I ask.

Moises says the environmental laws forbid cutting down many of the trees, because it would destroy the habitat for animals and birds. "But local workers can trim the branches and clear away shrubs and vines.

You'll have a beautiful vista." He parts some branches, and I see a sliver of water.

What's the price? I ask.

"We don't know yet," Moises says, "but I think it should go for between six and seven hundred thousand."

"That's a lot."

Annie shrugs. "Prices have doubled in the last two years. It's still way less than you'd pay in the States for five acres of oceanfront land."

"No more houses on the beach for fifty thousand?"

They laugh. "If you go to Nicaragua, you can find that," Moises says.

I do the math. If the four of us buy this piece, it's $150,000 each, and it's hard to imagine the price won't rise.

On the way back for lunch, I ask Parrot Annie, who's forty-eight, what it's like being a woman on your own here. "I have five dogs, and I feel pretty safe," she says. "There're a lot of men here to date, but most are looking for young Ticas with no brains." Annie covers her mouth. "That didn't come out right."

Chris Howard had told me that Ticas are "slim, beautiful, adoring, and sexually liberated, but unless the guy speaks Spanish they can barely communicate." Annie says it doesn't seem to bother them. "The women don't care how old or attractive the man is, as long as he treats her with kindness. A lot of women have been abused or abandoned with their kids. If one marries an American, she's upgrading her life."

I look at Annie's blond hair and ask, "Is there a place to get your hair colored?"

"Sure is, in San Isidro. They do foils and everything."

She pulls into her office, where she spots a colleague, Julie Ann, talking with another friend, Shirley. Annie says I should ask them about living here. The three women range from forty-eight to fifty-nine, and they've gone native, dressed in halters and tiny miniskirts. Shirley is tall and toned, with long hair going gray and a small gold stud in her nose. She's a widow, she says, and "the toughest thing is that if a pipe breaks, you can't go to the phone and call a service person." She says you have to drive around, asking people, 'Who knows how to do plumbing?' then track the guy down and plead and bargain with him to do the job. In San José there's a handyman service, Maridos para Alquilar (Husbands for Rent), but the concept hasn't reached Ojochal yet.

Julie Ann, who moved here from Atlanta with her husband in their late fifties, says, "Every morning you wake up and think, What's gonna go wrong today?"

Annie agrees. One day she was attacked by an anteater near her pool, and on another she got into her car, started driving, and felt something pawing her shoulder. "It was a sloth." There's a jaguar living by her house whom she named Mick Jaguar.

Julie Ann laughs. "I like being a pioneer. We circle the wagons, and *anything* is an excuse for a party."

Annie says they throw a full moon party on the beach every month; it's potluck, and "everybody comes. Americans, Ticos, internationals. They all mix."

Do they? I'd heard the opposite.

"Maybe in other parts, but we don't have class divisions." When she first arrived, Annie says, she missed having women friends, "but now there's a group of women who meet every week. We call it the Garden and Gun Club."

Julie Ann says, "It's like the Wild West." Annie explains that a few years back, there was a rash of crime. "Outsiders came and were robbing people on the road, breaking into homes and raping women." The community raised money to bring in special police, Annie says. The women bought guns and went to target practice with two Vietnam vets who taught them to shoot. "It took four months for the police to arrest everyone in that gang, but they're gone."

After a lunch of fresh-caught snapper, fried plantains, and rice, we drive into the mountains to look at homes with ocean views. The places are sold "turnkey"—completely furnished from beds to pots and pans—

and range from $300,000 to $500,000. Again, it seems not cheap, but the upkeep is low. They have open-air kitchens because the climate is mild and the breezes keep away bugs. One of the owners shows us his bills: $125 for property tax, $17 for electricity, $40 for water—*for the year.* And the gardens! There are birds of paradise as tall as palm trees; local blackberries, or *moros;* lime, mango, banana, and papaya trees; and go-to-sleep plants whose leaves curl up when you touch them. The flowers are hallucinatory: pink lobster claws, monkey eggs, and the handkerchief plant with red cones that sprout gauzy white flowers like a handkerchief. "Everything grows fast and huge," the owner says. "You never have to water."

Jerry, who retired from a job at the phone company in Michigan, tells his wife, Judy, "You'd be out here all the time, moving plants around. Wouldn't you love it?"

Judy shakes her head no. "I want to be able to walk to a small, small town and to the beach."

This area is not for me, either, having to drive up and down the mountains on wet roads with potholes—called *huecos*—hairpin turns, and steep drop-offs. If a bridge floods and you don't make it over by nightfall, you have to sleep in your car. As author Bruce Jay Friedman once said, "You're either on the beach or you're not. The fellow who's 'a short drive away' might as well have to be flown in by Concorde."

We gather for dinner at a pizza restaurant, which begins with platters of local shrimp, fresh-made tortillas, and pork cooked with green chilis and tomatoes, followed by lasagna and three kinds of pizza. Chris jokes that this is "an eating tour disguised as a relocation trip." Tim, a Nordic-looking developer who grew up in Zimbabwe, tells us why buying land here is smart. "With ninety million North Americans retiring in the next ten years, Costa Rican real estate can only go up." Moises says the government has allocated funds to pave the road (the one that's currently washed out) from the northern beaches down to Ojochal and to build a hospital and international airport just south of here. "We know they're going to get built," Moises says, "because politicians are snatching up land nearby."

"Right now it's the frontier," Tim says, "but when the phones are hooked up, when the new road is paved, the airport and hospital constructed, this place will boom!"

I feel adrenaline pumping; I'd better move fast or I'll miss the train. It reminds me of the fever that gripped people during the dot-com boom of the nineties, but I don't want to repeat what I did then: I bought tech stocks in 2000, one month before they crashed.

Rudy Matthews, one of our group, who fought with the marines in Vietnam, then taught PE in public school in Tampa, Florida, says he might buy land and just hold it. "It's hard to lose money if you've got an ocean view, unless you get hoodwinked into buying in the maritime zone."

What's that? I ask.

An engineer who's come to give us a talk explains: "The first two hundred meters from the mean high tide is the maritime zone, which belongs to the government. No one can build in the first fifty meters, and in the next hundred and fifty you need to get a concession from the government, which is good for only twenty years, then apply for a building permit, which they don't easily grant. You could pay a fortune and later find out you can't even put up a lean-to."

I shoot Annie a look. "The land we saw this morning?"

"It's just outside the zone," she says. "That's the beauty—you'll have clear title and won't be regulated by the government."

The engineer warns us, though, that we still have to get soil samples and do a tree survey before we buy, because "you can't cut down protected trees, and they keep adding new ones to the list. Also, the land may not be stable, or you'll have to drill down forty feet and install footings."

Reality sets in. We'll be far away, and who's going to supervise this? Who'll walk us through all the tests, red tape, and hurdles, who'll grease palms and show us how to avoid quicksand?

· · ·

During the night, I'm jarred awake by what sounds like an avalanche of rocks on the roof—rain that's part of a hurricane winding up over Central America. It's impossible to sleep. The garden outside is black, but when lightning cracks, the flowers and trees light up like an acid flash. In the morning, as we make our way through sheets of water to the bus, Chris tells us that in twenty years in Costa Rica, "I've never seen it rain this hard."

So you say.

Because the road up the coast is impassable, we have to drive all the way back through the mountains to San José, then down to Jaco on the Pacific farther north. If we'd been able to use the coast road, it would have taken three hours, but the detour costs us eight. We stop for lunch at La Fiesta del Mais, the Corn Party, for "typical food": fried pork rinds, rice with chopped chicken and vegetables, and corn on the cob with kernels so tough they taste like animal-grade feed.

The next morning, the rain stops and we tour condos for sale—ranging from $200,000 to $500,000—in Jaco, the closest beach town to San José. "That's it," Chris says after we've finished, "I've shot my last arrow." Only two of the group now seem keen to move here, but they're all going to attend a seminar on the logistics of relocation: residency cards, medical care, taxes, and how to bring in your goods and car.

I leave the group and fly north to check out Nosara, which is the "it" spot among Europeans and Americans. The plane lands in a field right beside the town, on a dirt strip that's surrounded by billboards advertising real estate. It quickly becomes apparent that foreigners are on a feeding frenzy: buying, selling, subdividing, building, and flipping. I take a taxi to the office of Nosara Development, with whom Stephan Rechtschaffen is developing his community of friends. One of the employees, Olivier, a tall, buff Tico with a black ponytail, drives me to the site in his Jeep. The land feels primeval, enchanted, as in a fable where all the trees and flowers have been placed under a spell. The grass is lime green, the ocean is Popsicle blue, and swarms of hummingbirds dart like flying jewels among the exotic flowers and trees.

On the road back to town, we bump over the ever-present potholes. "Instead of *pura vida,* it's *puros huecos,*" Olivier says. I ask how he feels about foreigners buying up property while many Ticos work for $1 an hour and will never be able to own a piece. Olivier says it's complicated. He's happy that money and jobs are pouring into town, but . . . "We lose our country, and another culture comes. Next week, for example, we celebrate La Fiesta de Halloween, but it's not ours." He frowns. When he was little, he says, he rode a horse to school. "My father had horses, and we rode everywhere. Now my children don't even know how. They go on bike. But the foreigners make money renting horses to tourists. Why aren't we doing that?"

I ask if he thinks resentment among Ticos could lead to a revolt.

Olivier shakes his head. "That's not our character."

A number of Americans, I learn later, are involved in projects to support the Tico community. I have dinner with Beverly Kitson, who's the doyenne of expats and used to dance with the Costa Rican ballet. On the day we meet, she's playing tennis at eight A.M., then going kayaking on the flooded Nosara River, which she hopes will be "really fast." She and her husband, David, bought their land in 1970 for less than $3,000. They'd joined the Peace Corps as teachers and were working in San José when a volunteer told them about the spot. They had to ride horses up a cliff to reach it, looked at the view of river and ocean—the most spectacular view in Nosara—and said yes. They retired at fifty-eight, intending to live full-time in the cabin they'd built and enlarged over the years, but David died of cancer shortly after retiring.

A group of their friends conferred with Beverly about creating a memorial and decided to build a library for the Ticos. At the time, Nosara did not have a high school; most children quit after sixth grade or had to go board in another city. The government requires that a town have a library before it will build a high school, so creating the Biblioteca David Kitson also brought a high school to Nosara.

Taking charge, Beverly spent ten years raising money from individuals and foundations so she could build and stock the library and hire a librarian—a Tica whom she sent to the States for library studies. Beverly recruited gringo volunteers to tutor children and read with them after school, to teach English and computer skills to people of all ages and run book groups. "You have to understand," Beverly says. "In towns like this, Ticos don't know what a library is. They've never held a book in their hands, even in school. So for them to come in and read a book is . . . life-changing."

Sitting on her terrace, watching the river spill into the Pacific as the sky turns salmon and gold with the setting sun, I wonder if I have the temperament to be an expat: self-contained, patient, adaptable. Beverly does; she has deep friendships with Ticos, and the library has become the passion that animates her days. "It's replaced dance."

On Sunday morning, I start my transit from Nosara back to my home. I'm the first to arrive at the dirt airstrip and sit on a bench under the bamboo shed. I feel peaceful, sorry to leave. I listen to the howler monkeys making *ruff-ruff* sounds like dogs and watch Ticos pass by on foot, bike, and horseback. They all wave. The airline agent arrives on a scooter, carrying a portable scale that she hangs from a pole in the shed to weigh luggage. Families gather to watch the plane land, and before I can see it they cry out, "*Ya viene el avión!*"

The trip takes seventeen hours door-to-door. There's only a morning flight to San José, then I wait five hours for a plane to Miami, then have a two-hour layover for the flight to Denver and the shuttle to my house. When my friends ask, "Are we moving to Costa Rica?" I say, "I don't think so." I'm drawn to the slow pace, learning to speak Spanish fluently, and, as Beverly Kitson puts it, "living in a zoo" with toucans, monkeys, and jaguars. But it's hard getting there and back, and if I'm writing, I need to be wired, with dependable phones, roads, and mail service. I'd like to spend two months in Ojochal, but as a home base for a community? The search goes on.

What I've come to understand is that, once again, people will take different steps to build community or go solo, to choose where and with whom they live and how they're cared for if that's needed. New models are constantly arising, like Beacon Hill Village in Boston, a concierge service that supplies everything from help with shopping to home repair to twenty-four-hour nursing care, so that residents of Beacon Hill can grow older in the homes they love.

Some communities will arise spontaneously; some will be built by developers. Some friends will decide to share a house or take units in the same building, and some will leave it to the fates.

At this writing, Andy has just built a house on the ocean in British Columbia, Woody's splitting his time between Chicago and Montana, Kathy bought land in Canada and keeps an apartment in Manhattan, and I've just adopted a cat in Colorado. We're probably a decade away from living in the community we envision; I hope we get there.

11

Revolution No. 9

It will be different this time—not the way it was when we were young and in the foxholes, during that rare spike in history when, as Hunter Thompson put it, "the energy of a whole generation comes to a head in a long fine flash." In San Francisco, he wrote, he could drive across the Bay Bridge at any hour and wherever he traveled, there was "a fantastic universal sense that whatever we were doing was *right*, that we were winning." We helped integrate schools and hotels, put women and people of color in jobs they'd never been allowed to do, shut down Harvard and Columbia, drove President Johnson out of office, and stopped the war in Vietnam.

Now we live in a country where we're losing. The pendulum has swung so far to the other side that I'm sometimes in dumb shock. If you've ridden the wave, been part of that long fine flash, it's crushing to live through this reversal of what we visualized and worked for. While I was never at the forefront of political action in college, I showed up for demonstrations. Then, in my thirties, I remember the moment when I became too busy to drive to Delano to picket with the striking grape workers and was relieved to be able to write a check instead. As decades passed, I wrote checks with less frequency. Every four years I'd become impassioned during the presidential election, and if the candidate I had supported lost, I had sink back into disheartenment.

When I embarked on this book, I wanted to find out what it would take to revive that spirit. What had happened to the hundreds of thousands who'd put their bodies on the line in what was then called the Movement for a New America? I wanted to see if they still have hope, still are fighting the good fight, and it turns out many are. A significant number are teaching, serving in government or in the nonprofit world. What intrigues me is that many who gave up their involvement— whether large or small—to focus on careers and kids are feeling the itch to engage again.

Read My Tits

In September 2005, I was in New York on business, staying with Kathy Goodman, when she said, "There's a march in Washington tomorrow against the war in Iraq. I think we should go."

How could we do that?

"Jump on the Amtrak and we're there in three hours. I've done it before—no problem."

I protested that I didn't have time. I was in New York for only a few days, and the march would exhaust me: six hours on trains, endless walking, noise, and crowds. More important, I thought it would be meaningless. "This administration doesn't pay attention to demonstrations," I said. "There are more people protesting the war in Iraq than ever marched against the war in Vietnam, and the story isn't being covered. Truckloads of money have been raised on the Internet for candidates, floods of e-mails and petitions have been sent to the White House and Congress, and they haven't made a dent."

Kathy shrugged. "I'm tired of being angry and not doing anything. Let's get our bodies there and be counted."

I'd learned that when Kathy makes proposals like this, it's best to abandon all resistance and pack a bag. At seven the next morning, we took the subway to Penn Station, waited in a long line, and then heard an announcement: "All southbound trains have been canceled until further notice. They're having mechanical problems on the tracks, and there's no estimate as to when service will resume."

What! Hundreds of people were milling about the station and they were loaded for bear—wearing protest T-shirts and carrying placards and leaflets. But there was no way to get to the demonstration.

"Thank you, Karl Rove!" one man shouted. People laughed briefly, then got on their cell phones and relayed information. The special buses chartered to take people to the march had already departed. The only options were to rent a car, but not many were available, or fly, which would be pricey if we could even get seats.

Now that we were being thwarted, I was determined to get to Washington at any cost. Kathy and I took a cab to LaGuardia and bought seats on the next shuttle flight. The plane was filled with people we recognized from Penn Station, and they were all in our age group, probably because younger activists couldn't afford tickets. "I'll be damned," the woman across from me said, "if they're going to stop me from exercising my rights."

Landing in Washington, we closed ranks and took the Metro to the staging area near the White House. Most of the people we saw on the train, in the stations, and on the streets were carrying antiwar signs and banners as they moved inexorably toward the Ellipse between the White House and the Washington Monument, converging like rivers running to the sea. And oh, to join that sea! It had been at least thirty years since I'd marched, and I'd forgotten how good it feels to be part of a great common effort and feel the lift, the power, of seeing you're not alone.

Hurricane Katrina had just wreaked devastation on New Orleans, and people carried signs: MAKE LEVEES, NOT WAR. There were life-size puppets and street theater: One group were dressed as wealthy socialites, wearing tuxedos and gowns and toasting one another as they hoisted a banner that read, "It's a class war, and we're winning!" Everywhere I looked, the majority were over forty—the same people who'd marched in the Vietnam era. I thought, Where are the masses of young? An Episcopal priest, Jim Lewis, said, "Young people are not as angry as we were about Vietnam. There's no draft, they're not being forced to kill, and if they're middle class, they don't know anyone who's died or been crippled in the war."

I went looking for Jodie Evans, a founder of CODEPINK, one of the sponsors of the march. She was easy to spot near the stage, wearing a shocking pink hat with enormous pink feathers over her long red hair, a pink T-shirt, and what looked like a pink tutu. Jodie was escorting one of the speakers, Cindy Sheehan, who'd lost a son in Iraq and camped out near President Bush's ranch in Texas, requesting a meeting. Jodie, fifty-two, has been an activist all her life and moves at a hundred miles a minute. She's a spectacular fund-raiser, organizes fact-finding missions to troubled regions, ran Jerry Brown's office when he was governor of California, and became the first female campaign manager when Brown ran for president.

She and several friends had started CODEPINK on the run. Jodie and Medea Benjamin, founder of Global Exchange, were in Washington in October 2002 when they heard that President Bush was about to ask

Congress to approve a preemptive strike on Iraq. "I thought, My God! We have to try and stop it," Jodie recalls. She and seven other women decided to protest outside the White House the next morning, expecting to find "all these people who don't want war. But when we got there, we were shocked. There was no one—no one but us."

Four of the women took off their shirts, which caused the news cameramen to scurry toward them. The women had sewn doves of peace on their bras and written on their stomachs with black marker: "Read My Tits: No War in Iraq."

What bra, I wondered, do you wear for the action? A Wonderbra, a chaste cotton number, or a hooker's bra with tassels from Frederick's of Hollywood? Jodie said she wore what she had with her—blue lace. The idea had come from two young college women who'd heard that in some Native American tribes, when the braves returned from war, their wives would stand on the edge of the village and bare their breasts to pacify their husbands—turn their thoughts from killing to nurturing and love. Jodie, then forty-eight, wasn't eager to expose her chest. "But when I saw the college girls about to do it, I joined."

After putting their shirts back on, they walked to the Capitol and stood in line for seats at a hearing of the House International Relations Committee. "We were at the front of the line, so we got in, and all the cameras were trained on us because they thought we'd take off our shirts again," Jodie says. They did not undress but started yelling, "No war in Iraq!" Committee chairman Henry Hyde ordered Medea Benjamin arrested for clapping, and the others were escorted out of the building.

They returned to the White House the next morning, taking the name CODEPINK to counteract the terrorist warnings coming from the White House—code red, code orange. Every day the women took turns standing vigil, dressed in pink, and others joined them. Within two years, CODEPINK had 250 chapters and 100,000 members, known for their fearlessness and in-your-face tactics.

The women traveled to Iraq, taking buses on the treacherous road from Jordan to Baghdad to observe the conflict firsthand, brought Iraqi women to the United States to speak with members of Congress, and worked with military families grieving children who'd been killed. Jodie knows what it is to lose a child. When she was twenty-nine, on vacation in Mexico, she waded into the ocean carrying her two-year-old daughter, Lala. A powerful wave arose with no warning and tossed Jodie over and over, wresting the baby out of her arms. When Jodie stood up, gasping for breath and screaming, there was no sign of Lala. Jodie never saw her daughter alive again.

"After losing Lala," Jodie says, "I can't be intimidated or frightened. What can anybody do to me?"

Jodie met Cindy Sheehan when Cindy came to a CODEPINK rally, and partly because they'd both lost children, they bonded quickly. In August 2005, Cindy called Jodie on her cell phone and said she was in Texas for a conference and had just decided to drive to Bush's ranch to knock on his door and say, "Please speak with me." An hour later, Cindy called and said the police had forced her and a friend off the road into a ditch. "I'm not leaving," Cindy said.

"I'm on my way," Jodie said.

She put out an Internet bulletin to CODEPINK members to come join Cindy, canceled all her meetings, went to an army surplus store, and bought tents, sleeping bags, Porta Pottis, bug repellent, water, and food. She packed the gear in duffel bags, got on a plane for Texas, and stayed for a month in what the women would name "Camp Casey" after the son Cindy had lost, Casey Sheehan.

The protest in Texas moved CODEPINK from the fringe to the front pages of mainstream media. Cindy, a working mother, became the face of the antiwar movement, encouraging others to speak out. Jodie had dropped all her appointments and left her teenage son in California to support Cindy because, she says, "I know what it's like to be in the depths of grief." She also knows that "action takes you out of the darkness. It gives you your life back." CODEPINK's members are predominantly middle-aged women, and when they meet to talk, Jodie says, the theme is: "Activism got me out of my chair."

When your actions don't produce results, though, I asked, how do you keep going?

"The only thing you *can* do is keep going. I mean, we ask ourselves, Why couldn't we stop the war? Where did we fail? But what we've done *has* had an impact. More people know the truth. . . ." She falls quiet a minute. "I don't understand why everyone *doesn't* do what I do. Then at least you can say, I tried."

Danny Goldberg

The march, instead of exhausting me, had been energizing, and when I returned to New York, I met with a friend who uses different channels for political action. Danny Goldberg, who calls himself "a rock 'n' roll guy," started in the music business when he was nineteen, eventually served as chairman of several record companies, and in 2005 became CEO of Air America Radio. He's also "an activist by avocation." A long-time officer of the ACLU, he debated Tipper Gore when she wanted to censor rock lyrics and took on Democrats and the entire American Left in his book, *How the Left Lost Teen Spirit.*

Tall and rangy, with a boyish smile and rumpled brown hair, Danny escorts me into his office at Air America on Sixth Avenue. "I'm on the couch!" he calls out to his assistant. The couch? Am I supposed to be his shrink? He drops onto a beige couch, and I realize he's just signaled that if there's an urgent call, he's at the phone extension by the couch.

In your book, I say, there's a chapter called "To My Fellow Former Hippies," where you write that we still have to "complete our destiny." How would that happen?

Danny takes a breath. "First, we have to accept that progress takes a long time. The sixties were an anomaly—in terms of the speed at which things changed. For example: Rosa Parks sits down in the front of a bus, a few years later there's a march on Washington where Martin Luther King says, "I have a dream," and Congress passes the civil rights bill. Betty Friedan writes a book, a women's liberation movement is born, the Supreme Court rules, and suddenly women have the right to choose. Rachel Carson writes *Silent Spring,* and a few years later there's an environmental movement. Lenny Bruce goes to jail for using foul language, and a few years later Richard Pryor can say anything he wants."

Danny laughs. "We got used to change happening quickly. But the reality is that it takes a lifetime of work. You don't do it in a few years and live in Utopia. If you have that expectation, you'll get despondent and say, 'What happened to us? We suck. We're a shitty generation. We tried to change the world and it didn't work, so why try anything else?' " He sits forward on the couch. "But if you look at the arc of a hundred years, there's been amazing progress. When my grandmother was born, women couldn't even vote!"

After Bush was reelected, Danny himself fell into a slump and toyed with moving to Canada. But he recovered his taste for political work and believes that progressives now are "where conservatives were in the sixties. We're building a base, it's growing, and we probably have another twenty or thirty years before we'll see the fruits. We'll be really old!"

"If we're still here."

Danny asks, "You know that Jewish saying about doing your part?"

"Tikkun olam?" Repair the world?

"Right. We don't have to fix the world completely, but we're compelled to do our part in repairing it. That's it! Do our part."

Danny grew up in a liberal family and organized protests in his high school, but when he arrived at UC Berkeley in 1967, he says, "I didn't get involved with SDS or any political groups."

"Neither did I."

"They seemed humorless and creepy," Danny says.

"And those meetings! Arguing for hours over minutiae . . ."

Danny says, "I was more a rock/drug type. The way I connected emotionally was with the music. I've got a short attention span, which is one of the reasons I love rock. You get to the hook within one minute!"

We laugh, lounging on the couches as if we're back in New York in the seventies when we met. I hadn't known Danny at Berkeley because he'd arrived after I graduated. "I dropped out the first week," he says. "Why would I go to class if my parents weren't around? All I wanted to do was buy and sell drugs, and by May I'd been arrested."

For what?

He looks up at the ceiling. "Possession of needles, hashish, Seconals, and methedrine. And a .38 Derringer."

"Danny!"

"I was hanging out with bikers, doing what I thought was cool. I clearly wanted to get arrested because I walked up to a cop when I was stoned and asked for directions." Because he was seventeen, he was released to his parents' custody after a week in juvenile hall. "I wasn't raped or beaten, but it scared the shit out of me. I went to therapy and was never a druggie after that. I wasn't really addicted, I was meshuggeneh."

By the fall of 1968, he had a clerical job with a music company. He wrote reviews for rock journals, started his own PR firm, founded and sold a record company, became a personal manager for Bonnie Raitt, the Allman Brothers, and Nirvana, and later was president of Atlantic and chairman of Warner Brothers Records.

He didn't become active in politics until 1979, when he produced the *No Nukes* concerts, album, and film, starring Bruce Springsteen, James Taylor, and other superstars, to raise public awareness about the dangers of nuclear arms. The concert was a turning point. "I learned that people in the music business could play a role in public life, and I never looked back." He went on to become chairman of the Southern California ACLU, testified at congressional hearings, and raised money for progressive causes. Danny believes music can be more influential than speeches or demonstrations, because "you play songs again and again. You ask kids today about Abbie Hoffman or Eldridge Cleaver, and they've never heard of them. But ask about Bob Dylan and John Lennon, and every kid knows their music."

When Air America was searching for a CEO, the investors met with Danny. "They were such an odd company that there was no obvious candidate," Danny says. "People with a pure radio background didn't understand the culture, and lots of people who understood the culture had never run a business. A rock 'n' roll background seemed sort of right—it was both business and unorthodox."

For Danny, the job was a rare opportunity. He'd long believed that the media were deteriorating—becoming less rigorous and independent and moving to the right—and here was a chance to play a role in shaping the country's political conversation. "I thought, A door like this might not open again, so let me run through it."

A year later, he was out the door. He'd spent most of his time raising funds, hoping to expand the company into television, books, and the Internet so it would become a national brand, a counterweight to Fox News. But after he'd raised about $15 million, the directors decided to downsize the company and cut costs, and Danny felt he wasn't right for that job. "It's not my strong suit. I'm, like, the flamboyant, create excitement, nurture the talent guy. I'm not, How do we get a cheaper phone system?" He still supports Air America and feels some sadness that he's not staying.

"I've been married now seventeen years," he says, "and I'm about to have my eighth business card." He attributes this partly to his nature and partly to corporate mergers and acquisitions in the media. "Companies I worked for were bought and sold, my own company was sold. I can't tell you what my next business card will say."

"This doesn't bother you—the uncertainty?"

"I'm not crazy about it," Danny says. "But it's been my MO. I've never done anything longer than five years in my whole career, since age nineteen. A lot of jobs were two or three years, and this is not the only one that was one year. I'd love to stay somewhere for ten years, like grown-ups used to do, but that's not been my path."

He says there's a part of him "that gets combative and turned on when this happens. I didn't know if that chip was still in me, but it is." After Air America, he immediately jumped back into managing artists, including Steve Earle, and writing a book about the music business. "I've never had an idle day."

What about doing your part? I ask. *Tikkun olam.*

Danny smiles. "I still believe that progressive and liberal ideas are better for most people in society, and we've done a *terrible* job of explaining why. My contribution is trying to address that, whether it's with books, records, or movies. That's what I love about Air America, and what I'll keep working on."

What about people who don't have your resources and access to media? I ask. What can they do?

"There are a million other important things to do," he says. "The biggest challenge is to realize you can't fix problems overnight, but you *can* make a difference. Once you've realized that, set aside some time to be a citizen. See what calls to you, try a bunch of things, and if you support a candidate who turns out to be a jerk, do something else. The only way you can lose is by not trying."

Ed Wayne

Okay, I thought, it's time to find a way to plug in, do my part, but what would that be? While I admired the efforts of Jodie Evans and Danny Goldberg, I'd never felt drawn to politics. I disliked the maneuvering, strategizing, and spinning of information and had concluded that my contribution is reporting and writing the truth as best I can. But I also wanted to help people who're suffering—especially children—and I found that there's another stream of activists giving direct aid to victims of poverty, war, or natural disaster.

During the brief time I floated about in the Internet dating pool, I received an e-mail from Ed Wayne in Bosnia, who described himself as a "humanitarian." In his JDate profile, he said he was five feet six. I'm five feet ten. "Can you imagine finding everything you want in a five-foot-six-inch package?" he wrote, and added, "In Bosnia, there's a saying: 'Poison comes in small bottles.' "

Two weeks later, after he'd flown back to the home he keeps in Colorado, we made an eccentric pair when we met at Trios restaurant. Ed looked even shorter than advertised, with a runner's body and gray hair pulled back in a ponytail. No earring, thank God. Over dinner, he told me how he'd gone from being a Texas good ol' boy making money in the oil business to a lone-wolf humanitarian.

Born in Houston, Ed founded a company that manufactures valves for oil companies, and after working aggressively to make it the most successful company in the field, sold it when he was fifty-four. "I had two children, and neither wanted to go into the business," he says. "The industry was changing, and I thought: Sell it while you're healthy." It was sold in less than a month. "The good news was, I sold my company." Ed laughs. "The bad news was, I sold my company. For years I operated with one rule: At the end of the day, I wanted to have more money than I'd had at the beginning. Simple. But now I had no vehicle. What in the world was I going to do?"

He was sitting one night with a woman, drinking wine, watching CNN, when he saw footage of refugees in Kosovo being loaded onto trains. "As an American Jew, I was taught, 'Never again,' and my interpretation of that was 'Never again' for anybody." The newscaster spoke about massacres that had precipitated a "refugee crisis," with no agencies in place to help.

Ed turned to his friend and said, "I'm going there."

She looked puzzled. "Why? What will you do?"

Ed shrugged. "Whatever I can. Hand out blankets. . . ."

She said, "When?"

"Immediately," he said.

The next morning, Ed called the director of the American Refugee Committee (ARC), who asked what he wanted to do. "Make a difference. You don't have to pay me, and if I do a bad job, you can fire me."

Three days later Ed was in Skopje, Macedonia, where three thousand refugees had streamed over the border from Kosovo in one night. "The camps were a real education," Ed says. "The atrocities, the wretchedness . . . it was off the charts. If you didn't make a difference in somebody's life every day, it was because you stayed in bed."

Ed and a team from ARC drove into the mountains to conduct a survey of refugees who were afraid to come down to the camp. Ed felt miserable seeing families crammed into huts with little food and not being able to help them. He came up with the idea of buying a thousand red buckets and filling them with basic necessities like soap, towels, toothbrushes, and sanitary napkins. He told an acquaintance in Skopje, "I need to go see the bad guys."

Who were the bad guys? I ask.

"Wealthy refugees from Kosovo, living in hotels and doing business." Ed was taken to a bar "filled with guys wearing black shirts and gold chains." He asked for the head man.

"Who are you?" the man asked.

"Nobody, but I need to buy supplies for refugees just like you except they don't have money." Ed handed him a list, and the next day the man delivered one thousand red buckets and all the supplies, for which Ed paid $8,000. He found a Muslim relief worker to help with distribution. Ed told his Muslim cohort, "I want these to go to the people who need them. If I see one red bucket in a store window . . . someone is going to *die*."

The Muslim laughed. "We understand each other very well."

The Muslim leader gave Ed lists of refugees in the mountain towns, who responded emotionally when he showed up with helpers. "Every family wanted to serve us chai. We became the red bucket guys," Ed recalls. "It wasn't much—buckets and soap—but giving concrete things to people who had nothing . . ." He grins. "It was satisfying."

Ed felt like the free man in Paris—"unfettered and alive." He was letting go of what had been his prime directive: How can I make money here? At the end of the day, he had less money than at the beginning, but he was on what Joseph Campbell called "the pollen path"—pollen to the right, pollen to the left. Pollen is a source of life, and when you're on the pollen path, things flow. Ed founded a nonprofit company, Bridge of Life, and did projects in Albania, Cambodia, and Serbia and Montenegro. He questioned himself—and still does—about his motives. "I thrive on drama and I like being the little guy who saves the day. But why am I really doing this? To impress women when they ask, 'What do you do?' Because I have a huge ego from being a CEO? Because I want to get my name and picture in the news?' " He says the answer has always been: "I do it because it makes me feel good."

The down side is that he's always chasing disasters, and he's usually far from his two grown kids. The day after we met, Ed took me for a motorcycle ride and made it clear he wouldn't be sticking around. Then why, I asked, are you on JDate, advertising for a "woman to share it all with"?

"I *am* looking for that woman, but I know I'll never find her."

"Why?"

"Because of my MO. Freeze or flee."

"I don't understand. . . ."

"Neither do I." He grinned. "But I'm real good at it."

A month later, as promised, he left for Belgrade, where he was building a park in a Gypsy enclave. He sent an e-mail ahead to his contacts: "The curse returns, board your windows, hide your children!" His methods are irregular. He arrives like a stealth bomber, looks for the hardest problem, decides what he can afford to do, and spends his own money to do it. He ignores red tape and doesn't ask permission. He has one rule: The local people must work on the project, digging trenches or putting up buildings. "I pay for materials, not labor." He wears a T-shirt and jeans and drives a motorcycle or van fitted out like a police car with a siren and flashing blue lights. "We made every vehicle look like a police car so when we go to the border, they wave us through," Ed says. "I went to the garage where they put lights on cop cars and said, 'Do it.' They figure if you ask for it, you have the right."

His priority is helping children. "With adults, you can't tell who's good and who's bad, but with kids, they're all good." In Belgrade, he says, the children who're "at the bottom of the barrel" are in the Gypsy camps, where about 1,200 people live in flimsy shacks, have no water or latrines, and scavenge food from dumpsters. Ed told me, "These are not the dancing, happy, bullshit Johnny Depp Gypsies. These people are malnourished, and less than 1 percent live past sixty."

On a Sunday, Ed and two helpers broke into the Belgrade water supply and diverted a line to the Gypsy camp. When the mayor found out, he asked, "Who gave you permission to do that?"

Ed said, "God."

He built a park in the enclave—in what had been a garbage dump—because "parks do great things. If you put in swings, a soccer field or basketball court, you get kids and they learn social skills and motor skills. If you put in benches, you get older people watching the kids. If you put in tables, you get families having picnics, and later you get lovers who have no place to go."

Ed bought materials like cement and steel poles that couldn't be destroyed or carried off. Everyone in the Gypsy camp helped clear the site and assemble and paint equipment in red-and-white candy stripes. "Once they put a brushstroke on something, it belongs to them," Ed says. "I can't feed them all, house them all, or clothe them all, and I've learned from bitter experience that if you can't do it for everyone, don't do it for a few, because it'll bring out the worst—jealousy and fighting."

What he concluded he could do was go around Serbia and build a park in every major Gypsy enclave. "At least they'll have that."

Six months later, Ed flew back to the United States to see his family. He promptly had his right ear pierced, and I could no longer thank God that Ed had no earring. "You'll get used to it," he said. He was about to undertake the largest project he's done: building a state-of-the-art pediatric oncology center in a hospital in Belgrade. He'd learned that 20 percent of the children were dying not from cancer but from unsanitary conditions—no toilets or showers. "Kids were getting bone marrow transplants and not being isolated from germs." When he determined what it would cost—$150,000—he balked. This was more than he'd ever invested in an unstable country. "Okay, Ed," he thought, "it's time to be honest. Is this a game you've been playing or something important that has to be fixed?" He knew the cancer hospital had to be fixed, and it wouldn't get done without him. "I have to do it."

"Do you worry about running out of money?" I ask.

"I always worry about money." When he headed the oil valve company, he created what he called the "Ed Sanity Sheet." Every month "my accountants produced a sheet that told me, If I had to liquidate everything, how much money would I have?" Now his accountants tell him how much he can give away. "If I keep spending at this level, I won't run out of money," he says. "I can do this the rest of my life."

Why concentrate on Serbia? I ask.

"I can move fast. I don't submit plans and wait for permits, or it would take five times as long and twenty kids might die before the hospital got built. I just charge ahead. What are they gonna do—arrest me? Take me to court for building a pediatric cancer hospital? Their attitude is: You want to spend your money? Go."

What about working on problems in this country?

"Think of the bureaucracy and red tape," Ed says, and "I couldn't afford to build a hospital here." He says the United States already has more volunteers and philanthropists than any other country. "The concept does not exist in Serbia. When I tell them what I'm doing, they think I'm stealing because nobody they know spends their money on other people." Besides, he says, "it's more fun living in a foreign culture where I'm the novelty." He rents a flat, drives a motorcycle, and has a "great social life. I know more people in Belgrade than I've known anywhere." He goes to homes where "the dining table is in the kitchen and you eat and drink with writers, artists, and politicians and have great talks—in English, for my benefit."

"How do you deal with the contrast between the way you live and and the Gypsies eating out of dumpsters?" I ask.

"I have to take care of me," he says, "so I can help them. Nobody says I have to suffer."

He adds, though, that there are nights in winter when he'll be walking alone on a dreary street and think, What the hell am I doing building a hospital in Serbia?

He says what spurs him is that "our time is limited. This is the moment when you take your best shot. Look at your funds, see what you can afford to do, and find what makes you happy. If it's golf in Phoenix, get your ass to Phoenix."

Ed says that "even in deepest redneck Texas, people have done things for their fellow men and had some taste of how good it feels." In his office in Colorado, he has pictures of the children he's come to know building the cancer ward in Belgrade. He points to each by name. "He's gone. She's gone. But she's doing great!" He says if you help a child have a safe operation and that child "is alive because of what you did . . . you feel like God." He beams. "God!" He stretches out his arms. "That's way bigger than CEO."

CharlesandTorkin.com

Dr. Charles Steinberg and Torkin Wakefield did as a couple what Ed Wayne did alone: improvised a way to help. When their youngest child left for Dartmouth, Charles and Torkin flew to Africa, which to them meant, as Torkin wrote in her journal, "Earth energy, drum beats, and lions and elephants roaming the savannah." It also meant AIDS, TB, malnutrition, unemployment, incest, and rape.

Married twenty-three years, the couple have always done service work. Charles was a family doctor who specialized in treating AIDS patients. Torkin, a psychotherapist, helped found a holistic clinic. They'd taken their children with them on two-week service missions to Nepal, Peru, and Romania, but when the youngest was due to leave home, they wanted a bigger commitment. "We have skills the world can use."

On Google, Charles typed: "volunteer—Africa—AIDS." He found that the Infectious Diseases Society of America was sending Western doctors to Kampala, Uganda, to train African doctors how to administer the antiretroviral drugs (ARVs) that were just being "rolled out." It was a two-month program, but Charles and Torkin leased their house in Colorado for a year, trusting that once they were in Kampala, they'd find opportunities to work there longer.

How, I ask them, do you extricate yourself from your lives for that long—from your clients and businesses, mail, bills, house, cars, and pets? Charles says they started planning two years ahead, finding people to do their work and manage their affairs. "How many years do we have left—years when we're healthy, strong, and can take on adventures?"

Torkin says, "Whatever that number is, it gets smaller every year by one. And just consuming more and 'working on ourselves' doesn't feed us."

When they arrived in Uganda, all their senses, which had been lulled to half-sleep by the familiarity of home, started firing. On the streets they heard people drumming, chanting, yelling. And the smells! "It was a constant jumble of things burning, flowering, cooking, and rotting." In the morning they were awakened by the muezzin calling people to prayer and the cries of more than eight hundred species of birds. Charles couldn't take his eyes off the marabou, "huge, ugly storks with a six-foot wingspan who build enormous nests in the trees of the city. They look like something from a Spielberg movie, but after a few weeks you get used to them and walk by without noticing."

Charles, who has a wry wit, a brown beard going gray, and rimless glasses, started work at Mulago hospital, teaching doctors who'd never seen a laptop how to use one to determine the correct dose of ARVs for a patient. One morning, a scream of anguish split the air—a woman keening for a child who'd just died in the pediatric ward next to the classroom. Charles froze, not knowing what to do as the woman let out shriek after shriek. He resumed his lesson, but the next time this happened, he asked the Ugandan doctors how they cope. About ten children die in the hospital every week, and so many adults have died of AIDS throughout Africa that there are 24 million orphans—"the same as the number of kids under five in the U.S.," Charles says. "Imagine if every child under five were an orphan."

Torkin started doing AIDS outreach, visiting the Acholi quarter where refugees from the civil war in the north live in mud slums with no water or electricity. With her auburn hair and blue eyes, Torkin stood out as a *muzungu*—white—but the first woman she met, Millie Grace, gave her a gap-toothed smile and said, "You are most welcome. Please be at home." Millie Grace was sitting against a mud wall making colorful paper beads out of old magazine pages, then stringing them into unique necklaces that carry the flavor and color of Africa. She and other Acholi women were making necklaces but keeping them in garbage bags because they had no place to sell them. Torkin bought three, and when she wore the beads, people stopped to ask where to buy them.

An idea came to her: Start a crafts co-op, BeadforLife, to sell the necklaces in American stores and at "beadware parties" that could be run like hip Tupperware parties. Torkin flew back to the United States with samples, and after I wrote a story about the beaders in *O*, they were flooded with orders. For the first time, the Acholi refugees could buy milk, send their children to school, patch their roofs, and buy medicine they'd never been able to afford.

"The rewards are so immediate," Torkin says. "This is the best time of our lives."

I ask Charles if he agrees. He nods, adding: "Some of our friends picture us living in a mud shack with a fire in the center." He laughs. "The truth is we rent a lovely home with a garden" and they take breaks from work to go on safari in the game parks.

Torkin says, "Anyone can do this. No matter what skills you have, you can go to a city in the developing world, and if you walk around and introduce yourself, you'll find a job." She thinks everyone in the West should do this, even if just for two weeks. "If you still have kids at home, don't wait," she says. "Go with your children. It will change them."

· · ·

Inspired by Charles and Torkin and by Ed Wayne, I signed up for a two-week volunteer program in India, teaching English to orphans of low caste in Mumbai. The trip took place in November 2004, just before the tsunami hit Southeast Asia. Although I missed the tidal wave by days, the trip turned out to be an emotional tsunami, carrying the obliterating force of Shiva the destroyer—the god who's ruthless and implacable, reducing things to rubble to clear the way for rebirth.

12

We Are the World

Six minutes. That's all it should take but it seems endless because I'm dodging pools of dirty water, honking cars, trash, and shit. Keep walking, I tell myself, smile at the men in their *lunghis,* or loincloths, tied at the waist and the women in saris who stare at me with bafflement. I look absurd in my safari hat and Air Max running shoes, carrying the totem water bottle that marks me as a foreigner. Most of the Indians walk barefoot with no head covering in the rain. There are no sidewalks, no trash cans. People throw their garbage on the dirt road, where it decomposes along with cow dung and human excrement.

A car honks from behind—*blatt-blatt.* I freeze. Should I jump to the side and risk landing in shit or stop in my tracks so they'll know where I am? I choose the latter—possible death over stepping in shit—as a car barrels past me with only inches to spare.

The Indian women walk serene through it all, looking regal in their saris of shocking pink or emerald green and their blue black hair braided with jasmine. "The garbage and the flowers"—the phrase from Leonard Cohen's "Suzanne" comes to mind. How do the women look so fresh, unwrinkled, and clean? I am not fresh or clean. The "flat" where I'm staying has no hot water, and the toilet is a hole in the floor.

Why am I here? I've chosen India for my service trip because of the same instinctual pull that Ed Wayne felt for the Balkans and Charles and Torkin for Africa. I'd been to India before, and during the years when it seemed my life was crumbling, I thought I might spend six months in an ashram. I also thought I might join the Peace Corps and had fantasies of teaching English in a small school in Asia, being the eccentric foreign woman.

I checked the Peace Corps online and learned they have a program for "older Americans." Their website asks, "Always wanted to travel when you retire? See the world and give something back while you're at it?" Only 7 percent of the corps, however, are over fifty, and it requires a two-year commitment plus months of training.

A different concept had emerged in the seventies and eighties: the shorter service mission or "vacation with purpose." Bud Philbrook and Michele Gran founded Global Volunteers after they spent part of their honeymoon in Guatemala, helping a small village apply for a grant to build a drip irrigation system. Unlike tourists, the Philbrooks lived and worked with local people, which was so rewarding that they organized other trips. Today they send teams to twenty countries, and more than half the volunteers are over fifty-five.

Many groups such as Cross-Cultural Solutions, Cosmic Volunteers, and Global Crossroad send people to communities in need, but the largest and most popular is Habitat for Humanity, whose teams build simple houses for families who lack shelter. Habitat appeals to all ages from college students to seniors, partly because of the publicity that attends the involvement of former president Jimmy Carter and his wife, Rosalynn. The annual Jimmy Carter Work Project—in which thousands of volunteers build 150 houses in five days—is swamped with applicants and must cut off registration months ahead of the "build."

Since I'm a desk potato, sitting at my computer most of the day, I felt nervous about doing construction work and signed up to tutor children in India with a group I'll call the World Service Corps (WSC). My experience was "challenging" and, I was assured, not typical, so it was agreed that I would change the names of the organization and volunteers.

· · ·

I fly into Mumbai, formerly Bombay, at one A.M., where Stephen, the Indian leader of the team, is holding up a sign with my name. In the hot, steamy night, we get into a taxi, which plunges into the free-for-all on the road. Bumper stickers on the backs of trucks say, HORN, PLEASE. Honking constantly, our driver darts around trucks, motorbikes, and wagons pulled by oxen to avoid hitting cows and elephants that are walking loose on the road with seemingly no human in charge.

I'll be joining six other Americans who're donating their time and paying $1,600 to teach at the Grace and Flower Home for low-caste children. The team has already worked one week of a three-week program and is staying in an overcrowded and chaotic neighborhood on the outskirts of the city.

Stephen shows me the room in a flat I'll be sharing with him and Roger, a fifty-year-old accountant who's on his fourth WSC trip. The bed is a thin piece of foam on a wooden platform. Most Indians sleep on the floor, which Stephen prefers to a bed. "Better for the spine." This proves accurate; during my two weeks in Mumbai my back will feel better than it has in years.

By the time I awaken, Stephen and Roger have gone, leaving me a map and directions to the guesthouse where the team meets for breakfast. Because it rained most of the night, the dirt roads have turned to slippery mud, but that doesn't slow the honking cars, motorcycles, buses with people hanging out the windows, and yellow rickshaws coming straight at me. Stephen had told me to walk at a constant pace, "so people can calculate where you're going and avoid a crash. Don't start to run or you'll have to run all the way."

When I find the guesthouse, the team members are sitting around a long table, passing bowls of porridge, boiled eggs, white bread, and a basket of pineapples, oranges, and bananas. What strikes me is how polite and kind they are—mindful of sharing food and seeing that everyone has what he or she needs.

"Those mosquito bites look bad. Want some antihistamine?"

"Thanks."

In addition to Roger, there are two women volunteers who are veterans of previous WSC trips, a retired pediatrician and his wife, and a curvaceous blond sales manager in her forties who's never been outside the United States before. After breakfast we pile into two cars and are driven to the Grace and Flower Home, run by an Indian couple, Mohan and Sita Rau, who take in children whose parents have died or abandoned them. The home is under construction, with raw concrete walls, dirt floors, and one large room where 105 children aged one to eighteen eat, play, sleep, and have their lessons. They're dressed in green-and-white uniforms—shorts for the boys and skirts for the girls. The younger girls have buzz cuts to protect against lice, but they look adorable with big green ribbons tied in bows around their heads.

"Good morning!" they cry, jumping to their feet when they catch sight of us. They run up and pull on our arms. "Excuse me! Excuse me! My name is Punita." "My name is Kavita." Their dark eyes are playful, eager to love. For the first hour, I teach social studies in English from an Indian textbook. I've been told to read a phrase and have them repeat it, but they don't understand what they're saying. When I mention this to one of the veterans, Libby, who's a retired teacher from Virginia, she says, "That's how the school wants us to teach." She lowers her glasses to peer at me. "You clearly haven't volunteered before."

"Not like this."

She tells me the mission of WSC is to do "what they ask you to do, not what you *think* they need."

Sita Rau, the statuesque Indian woman who heads the school, asks me to teach songs and games also, since kids will remember anything set to music. They already know—from previous teams—standards like "Old MacDonald," but when I sing, "And on his farm he had a—" they cry out, "Tiger!" or "Elephant!" Their favorite song is "Ten Little Indians," which has a different connotation here.

I teach them a clapping game, which they take up with alacrity. "Who stole the cookies from the cookie jar?" we chant and clap together. I ask one of the Indian teachers to translate the words into Hindi so they'll understand what follows. Facing each other in pairs, they recite in their clipped accents, pointing their small fingers at each other:

"Kumar stole the cookies—"

"Who, me?"

"Yes, you."

"Coo-dunt be."

"Then who?"

Kumar looks around with glee before picking the next culprit.

"Naga Raj stole the cookies from the cookie jar!"

At midday, the volunteers meet upstairs for lunch: yellow rice with chilis, three kinds of curried vegetables, chapatis, and fruit. Pam, the blond sales manager from St. Louis, has been struggling with diarrhea and eats only plain boiled rice. Libby tells her it's disrespectful to refuse the Indian food. I tell Pam she needs to take care of herself.

I feel weighed down with depression at the squalor, dirt, mosquitoes, and heat these children live with, particularly when contrasted with the comfort and sheer excess of stuff—toys, clothes, electronics—my kids took for granted. The children at Grace and Flower sleep together on the concrete floor, use the field next door for a toilet, and bathe at the outdoor water pump. They have one uniform, which they wash every night, and they're not permitted to keep personal items or artwork they do in class, so that no one will have anything special. They implore us to learn their names because that's the one thing they own. In two weeks I will not see a child throw a tantrum or yell, "No!" when asked to perform a job.

When I tell the team I'm struggling with guilt and frustration, the veterans exchange looks. "We've already worked through that," says Roger, who's never married and lives alone in Cleveland.

Libby gives a dismissive wave. "It's the grain of sand approach. You fix one grain at a time."

* * *

At every chance, I sit and talk with Stephen, who changed his name four years ago from Raja to Stephen in hopes of faring better in business. Whether the strategy worked or by coincidence, he hooked up with WSC shortly after becoming Stephen. "To be very frank," he says, "these have been the best years of my life."

Stephen is twenty-seven, tall for an Indian and slim, despite the fact that he eats double what we do. He wears bottle-thick glasses and needs to hold a paper right up to his eyes in order to read it. The glasses make his eyes look small, and when he removes them, it's a shock—almost like coming upon someone with his clothes off—to see how large his uncovered eyes are. Stephen is always smiling, always warm and helpful to everyone, and loved by all.

For most of his life, though, he says, "I was not favored." Few children in India wear glasses, and Stephen was teased and ostracized. He could not play sports. If his glasses broke, he had to stay home because he couldn't read street signs or see cars coming. Money was scarce, so Stephen had to wait until the family could borrow enough rupees to buy a new pair. "I couldn't read, go to school, or watch television." Friendless and miserable, he articulated a philosophy: "Life is a torture to live in this cruel world."

After college, he worked for a travel agency but couldn't make a single booking. He was about to be fired when he was asked, because no one else was available, to lead a team of WSC volunteers on a weekend trip. He found it easy to make friends with the Americans. "For the first time I thought, Oh, there's something called joy," Stephen recalls. When the leader came back with another team, she called Stephen for help. They needed a bus to take the kids from Grace and Flower on a picnic; they needed hotel rooms on the beach for a weekend break. Stephen arranged everything and in the process came to know the Raus, who built the orphanage. When the founder of WSC, Mark Welch, came to Mumbai to check on the orphanage, the Raus called Stephen to translate.

As a result of that encounter, Stephen's fortunes reversed. Welch hired him as a consultant, and the following year, after 9/11, the American team leader quit and Stephen was asked to step in. "I didn't apply for this job. I never expected to be a team leader. It just fell into my lap." He revised his philosophy: "Life is a torture in a cruel world, but it's made beautiful by the grace of God."

Stephen is about to fly in a plane for the first time—to Dallas, headquarters of WSC, for three weeks of training. When he returns to India he's going to be married to Sheeba, a woman he met for five minutes when their parents shook hands on the deal.

Stephen's family comes from a low caste—landless peasants and shepherds. His grandparents lived in a mud hut and converted to Christianity because the missionaries taught that all people are equal in God's eyes. Although the Indian government has tried to abolish the caste system, it still dominates business and social relations. In Mumbai, Stephen says, no one knows what caste he is, and if they ask, he responds, "I'm a Christian." In the villages, though, "people know." Lower castes are not allowed to walk on public roads or draw water from wells. They can't own property, enter a temple, or marry into a higher caste.

Because Stephen has a college degree and a job with an American company, his parents were able to arrange a marriage with a family from a higher caste. When the two clans met, the girl's father said he'd just married his eldest daughter and had no money for a dowry for Sheeba, who was working as a nurse. Fortunately Stephen had told his parents he would not accept a dowry. "Then you marry the money, not the girl," he says. But Stephen insisted that he have the right to approve the woman they chose.

Stephen's mother selected Sheeba because her older sister lived nearby and was a Christian with a sweet temperament. As Stephen put it, "Normally her sister should be a good one, too." Sheeba's family lived in the north of India, so they had to take a bus for sixteen hours to reach Mumbai. When the families met at the home of the older sister, Stephen was flanked by nine relatives. "They arranged all the details without consulting me," he says, "and finally, as a formality, they asked, 'Do you accept?'" Stephen said yes. They asked Sheeba and she said yes. "And that was it," Stephen says. The only words he exchanged with his bride-to-be were: "See you later."

Stephen's grandmother was furious that the girl was not bringing property to the marriage. Others told Stephen's mother, "She should at least bring a car." Then there was the matter of who pays for the wedding, an all-day ritual and feast with six hundred guests expected. Traditionally the bride's family pays, but Stephen says, "We are paying."

"You're being generous," I say.

His eyes grow moist with feeling. "She's coming to live with me for the rest of her life!"

The next day, the cars don't show up to take us to the orphanage, so Stephen flags down rickshaws—three-wheeled vehicles powered by what sounds like a lawn mower engine. The sides are open, so dust flies into your eyes and nose. I'm riding with Bob and Trudy, the pediatrician and his wife who live in Boston and have trekked all over the world but never done a volunteer trip. Trudy is a hospital educator, sunny and game for adventure. Bob is white haired and fit; he retired at sixty-one after his first wife developed brain cancer and died three months later. "That was it," he says. "I realized I could die suddenly and there were lots of things I wanted to do."

Like what?

"Travel. Sit and read nonmedical stuff. Paint." Bob has the warmth and antic personality of many who go into pediatrics. He and Trudy, I find, are the only ones on the team I can laugh with.

The rickshaw swerves around a dog who's dying in the road. He's been hit and his legs are turning black, but he's still alive, looking at us with piteous eyes. Across the street at a shrine to Ram, men chant, ring gongs, and light fires on the altar.

"Why doesn't someone kill that dog—end his suffering?" Bob asks.

The rickshaw driver wags his head from side to side—the Indian form of nodding. "Someone will do that, sir," he says.

Bob looks dubious. What we don't understand yet is that many Hindus will not kill an animal or "interfere with karma," even if it might be a merciful act.

Trudy says they signed up for this trip because they wanted to help kids and live among Indians. "We had a friend from Bombay who told us, If you stay in hotels, you'll never get a sense of the real India." A cloud of dust blows through the rickshaw, making us cough. "I assume this qualifies as the real India?" I say, and we start to laugh.

Trudy says, "We'd been to Africa, South America, and Tibet and thought: We won't have culture shock. We've experienced third world countries." She shakes her head. "But we hadn't." On other trips, no matter how rough conditions were, they would check into a hotel, take a hot shower, and sleep in a good bed. "Here, there's no sanctuary. No relief from the onslaught of traffic, noise, dung, and garbage." When they first saw their room in the guesthouse with a lumpy bed, mosquitoes, and no way to escape the humidity and heat, Trudy started to cry. Bob told her, "We're not in prison, we can leave." But they wanted to honor their commitment and adapted with grace.

I was unprepared as well. I'd thought that volunteers or people who do relief work after hurricanes would get decent if spartan accommodations. Bob shakes his head no. "The docs I've met who volunteer say you work grueling hours, sleep on cots, and eat poor food. Everyone gets sick. You live with the same conditions the victims are facing." On this trip, he says, "I think the idea is that you live as the people around you do."

I tell them I'd thought I might join the Peace Corps.

"So did we!" Trudy says. "And they drop you off by yourself in the bush with nothing but a water bottle."

What were we thinking?

· · ·

In the afternoon we tutor children who are lagging. I have Wilson, who's puppylike and mischievous and the only one in first grade who can't write his name in English. When I ask him to try, he writes a jumble of letters bearing no relation to his name. So we start with W; I have him write a page of W's. We move on to I, and when I ask for W again, he grins and covers his mouth. He can't write W.

For days we work our way through the six letters in his name, but he can't write them in the proper order on his own. When I say S, he writes N. If he writes the correct letter, I clap and cheer, and he's so proud and happy that he bounces in his red plastic chair.

After dinner that night I ask Stephen if he can call me a taxi so I can buy some clothes at a tailor shop I used on my previous trip to India. He asks if he can come along because he needs to use the ATM and Internet in Mumbai. He drops me at Le Royal Meridien Hotel, where I'd bought clothes before, and says he'll pick me up when he's done. There's a health club in the hotel, and I realize with a start: I can treat myself to a hot shower; wash my hair! It's long and I haven't tried cleaning it with cold water but just pulled it back in a tight bun. Ahhhhhh, the warm water—rinsing away the dust and sweat and enveloping me with the sweet steamy vapors of soap and shampoo—it's orgiastic. I fairly float back to the guesthouse and sing out to Trudy and Bob, "I have clean hair!"

The next morning after breakfast, Stephen points to a board on which people have written team goals. He wants us to evaluate if we're meeting them.

"Number one. We are open and flexible," he says.

Trudy says, "We could use a little work there."

Stephen continues: "We accept our differences."

Libby raises her hand. "Some of us feel that having a writer come into our group a week after we started has not been beneficial. We were meshing as a team, and now we have to go back and work through the first steps again." She keeps her eyes on Stephen.

"You're speaking about me," I say.

Libby nods. "It's not personal, it's something we feel WSC should know."

Pam and Trudy disagree with her. "I've enjoyed having someone new join us," Trudy says. "It makes me feel good to share what I've learned, to realize I've come a ways."

Roger and Kathleen, the two other veterans, join Libby on the attack. They say they can't talk freely with me because I'm writing a book.

I look at Kathleen. "I don't think this is about my coming late or being a writer. I think it *is* personal."

Silence. Libby says, "Well, every time the team decides on something, you have to argue and try to change it."

Pam's mouth drops open. "I haven't seen that."

Kathleen, who has spiky blond hair at sixty and wears hoop earrings, says, "We're here because we've already made a commitment to service and we're willing to give up our creature comforts for a few weeks. You're here for your own fulfillment—that's what you told us."

"I said I wanted to find my purpose in the years ahead."

Roger says, "You're a person who's needy, and that doesn't help the team. You have a lot of needs. . . ."

"Like what?" I ask.

"Like . . . making Stephen drive you into Mumbai so you could wash your hair."

Stephen stands up. "That's not the way it was. I had business, and she was helping me by giving me a ride."

The three veterans shrug. *Whatever.*

I tell them I can leave, I don't want to stay where I'm not welcome or comfortable.

Bob tries to break the tension with a joke. "Okay, how many people think Sara should be voted off the island?"

Stephen says to me, "Don't leave." Turning to the others, he says, "WSC would like her to write about our program so other people can learn about it and become involved."

When Roger and I walk back to the apartment we're sharing, I tell him I was blindsided by what just happened. He's been helpful, and I've admired the inventive ways he teaches science to the kids. "I thought you and I were getting along well. Maybe we should talk about this more. . . ."

"Only if it will make you feel better," he says. "I didn't come here to make lifelong friends. I came to help the kids. If we focus on that, things will probably work out."

But they don't. Kathleen makes a point of looking the other way when we pass in the hall. The three veterans take offense at whatever I say or do. When I try to engage them in conversation at the table, they roll their eyes and go silent.

I've adjusted to the heat and dirt now; I think of it as camping, and the cold shower in the morning is like plunging into the ocean. But the shunning, the constant hostility from the gang of three, makes it hellish. I keep trying to form connections with them, to make things better, but Pam, who's also being attacked by the trio, tells me it's useless. "They took a dislike to you on sight," she says.

Every meal is an ordeal, with false politeness masking the tension. It's hard to chew and swallow with arrows coming at you. Pam starts taking her plate of boiled rice to her room to eat alone.

Bob and Trudy depart at the end of my first week, leaving me undefended with the veterans. I decide I have to leave also and pack my bags, but before I walk out the door, it occurs to me that somehow it's important to tough it out, to complete my work with the children. Wilson is making slow but observable progress, and I've become attached to the second graders I teach in the morning.

As I walk back alone to the flat, I stop in a storefront with public phones. I've learned you can call the United States and speak for twenty minutes for about $2. I call friends, the man I'm seeing, and my longtime teacher, Nina, because I need to talk with people who actually like me. As I'm dialing, I see little red lights winking on and off around plastic statues of the Hindu gods. "The people here hate me, I can't connect with them. . . ." I start to cry.

My friends are astounded—they expected me to be floating on clouds of bliss. "Why would they hate you?" Nina asks.

"They think I'm spoiled, needy, demanding, and condescending. I'm triggering something in them, and they're not interested in working it out." I tell Nina I like interacting with the children, but why did I put myself in this wretched situation? Since moving to Colorado, I love my home, my friends, the work I'm doing . . .

Nina says quietly, "Because you asked to grow."

I consider this. Before leaving for India I'd set an intention: I wanted to have a direct experience of who I am, beneath the personality, emotions, and mind. Not what I've read in books about the nature of the self or what various masters teach, but what arises authentically and rings true in me.

"India doesn't always give you what you want," Nina says. "It gives you what you need." She suggests I practice surrender and acceptance. "When things become difficult, say: 'I can accept this.' Even if you think you can't."

. . .

The next morning Stephen takes me aside. "I'm very sorry about what happened," he says. "I was shocked. Believe me, this is not normal. With other teams there may be some disagreement but they can usually laugh about it." I ask if he's been able to get along with all the volunteers. He smiles. "Yes. I have no partiality." This is what spiritual traditions teach—impartial love for all. Tony Hendra in his memoir, *Father Joe,* quotes his mentor, a Benedictine monk: "True courage is not to hate our enemy. To love him, to love in the teeth of hate—that is real bravery."

I resolve to cultivate love for my critics this week—love in the teeth of their disdain.

. . .

The children in the lower grades at Grace and Flower are dressed for an outing when our bus pulls up. The boys wear polo shirts and tweed pants, the girls wear gaudy nylon dresses, and all are barefoot. We're taking them on a picnic to a park and snake zoo. Each volunteer is assigned four children. I grab the hands of four boys from second grade and we move awkwardly, like a ten-legged creature, onto the bus, where we squeeze together on one seat that has no belt.

I lift a boy named Saranivas onto my lap. He's one of the brightest and most ambitious: He wants to score 100 on every test and win every game. He asks me to show him something new. I take out my notebook and draw a tic-tac-toe grid, then wonder how I'll get the concept across in limited English. Saranivas picks up the goal of getting three X's in a row, and then he picks up strategy. Before we've arrived at the park, he beats me, and I've been playing to win! I have thoughts of bringing him and another boy, Kumar, back to the United States with me, enrolling them in school, where in a short time they'll excel. It's a safe fantasy because the orphanage is not licensed for adoptions. When the boys are eighteen they'll go out on their own and find jobs, and the girls will live at the orphanage until a marriage can be arranged.

We tour the glass cages containing the snakes of India, then set the kids loose on the playground to swing and climb. At noon, they sit on the grass in a large circle while two girls bring them plates with huge portions of rice and curried vegetables. They don't touch the food until all fifty have been served. A teacher leads a prayer, and only then do they begin eating with the fingers of the right hand. I'm struck by their self-control: They're hungry but sit motionless for ten minutes with food piled in front of them and aromas drifting up from their plates. The portions they consume are bigger than what we eat, and no child leaves a grain of rice. Stephen says, "They will not leave any food because they remember having none."

After the outing I develop a painful sore throat and say I won't be coming to dinner. Libby turns to me. "Is this a play for attention?"

"Excuse me?"

"Some people get sick because they want attention."

"How perceptive," I say with sarcasm. "Thank you, but all I want is a good night's rest."

I curse her as I walk home.

I can accept this.

Right.

· · ·

I wake up in the middle of the night protesting, "No!" I've had a terrible dream. My son, age ten, is being falsely accused by a neighbor of molesting his children. I plead with the neighbor to drop the charges—my son is innocent. But the neighbor is determined to punish him.

I go to comfort my son.

"I didn't do it," he says.

"I know you didn't."

His small face contorts with pain. "But when people say bad things about me . . ." He starts to cry, looking straight in my eyes. "It makes me feel bad about myself."

"Oh Jesus," I say, flipping on the light in Mumbai. This dream will hang over me like a bad attitude. My son is twenty-two now, studying in Siena, Italy, but since he was a baby we've been close, and whenever he's been hurt I've felt wretched. I start to think about him and what the dream might suggest, and it's not until late in the day that I realize: It's me that's being falsely accused. It's me that feels bad, because my fear is that what they're saying is true. I *am* selfish, willful, demanding, intrusive . . . A BITCH. I thought I'd cleaned this out in therapy years ago, but it's still festering. My task is not to make these people like me, which I've tried fruitlessly. It's about me liking me in the teeth of what they're saying—even if true.

· · ·

Firecrackers start exploding at five in the morning like gunshots. It's Diwali, the Festival of Lights, celebrating the victory of the forces of light over darkness. *Crack crack crack!* Walking to the guesthouse, I cover my ears and fight my way through clouds of smoke and fumes of sulfur. I eat a banana and throw the peel on the road, unthinking. I've joined them, it seems.

At the orphanage Sita tells us we won't be teaching because of the holiday. We sing and play with the kids, dumping a sack of battered toys and incomplete Lego sets on the ground. The kids are ecstatic and play with one toy each, totally absorbed. After lunch, they crowd around a TV set to watch a DVD I've brought from the States, *Beauty and the Beast*. But the DVD player can't read the disc. "Wrong region" flashes on the screen.

I suggest to Mohan and Sita that we drive to a store in Mumbai so I can buy them DVDs that will be compatible. We set out in their Jeep with a decal of Shiva on the windshield. The Raus bring their teenage children: Vikram, fourteen, and Maya, sixteen. The four share one dusty room and bathroom at the home, and every morning I'm struck by how beautiful Sita looks: her bright-colored sari immaculate, her hair shining clean.

The Raus started the orphanage ten years ago when they were working at professional jobs and volunteering in rural villages, helping families in distress. They took three kids into their home, fed them, and sent them to school, which they'd never attended. Word spread that they were taking in children, and before long they had a dozen sleeping on their balcony. Kids were brought by priests, town leaders, or police; each child had an unfortunate story, and the Raus couldn't turn one away. Mohan went online looking for financial support and connected with WSC, which now sends ten teams a year whose donations cover the children's basic costs.

"We have dreams," Sita says. "We want to build separate houses and bathrooms for the boys and girls, expand the school, and offer teacher training." I ask if any kids try to run away. She looks puzzled. "No. If they don't want to stay we send them back to their relatives or the people who brought them here."

Mohan says, "When they visit their relatives, they always come back thinner and sick."

Sita says when a child arrives, the first three months are hardest. "Some are coming from bad places where people would beat them, gamble, and drink. Some children were stealing or begging. We start to teach and direct them spiritually." The children are awakened at five-thirty A.M., and Sita leads chants and prayers three times a day. Mohan says they rarely have to punish a child and don't allow teachers to hit them with sticks as is done in other Indian schools.

"The most important thing," Sita says, "is to give them love and not show partiality. We treat them all the same."

We arrive at the video store and start going through the bins. I find *The Lion King* and hold it up triumphantly, telling them it was my children's favorite movie. Mohan shakes his head. "We don't want cartoons."

I explain, "It's an animated story, with wonderful songs by Elton John."

Mohan says the kids can't identify with animated characters. "They want to see real people, animals, comedies, and scary stories. If it's a cartoon they fall asleep." He holds up a DVD of Charlie Chaplin films. "I think this is good."

"No, no," I say, "it's old, black and white, and there's no sound."

"The children love Charlie Chaplin," Mohan says. "He makes them laugh."

I tell them to pick whatever they want. They choose *Spider-Man, Halloween 2,* documentaries on gorillas and snakes, and Richard Pryor comedies. Back at the guesthouse, Stephen tells me that animated films never go over in India. "*Shrek* was a flop."

. . .

After two weeks at the orphanage, my attitude toward the kids has changed. I've seen children in Mumbai who've been mutilated so they can beg, who may not eat for days and don't go to school because their families can't pay the fees. At Grace and Flower the children get three robust meals a day, attend school and have tutoring, go on field trips, and watch movies. Bob, the pediatrician, conducted physical exams of all the students and found their health "surprisingly good. No serious illness. Nutrition is good. No heart murmurs, enlarged liver, or lymph nodes. A lot of dental problems, but their eyesight is good."

Trudy, who assisted him, says the kids they see in Boston are not healthier. "Many are obese and have early-onset diabetes."

What the children at Grace and Flower are deprived of is what matters most in India—family. There are no grandparents, uncles, and distant relatives to arrange a marriage or show up if there's trouble or to celebrate. "The kids are not in the mainstream," Stephen says. "But the fact that they'll speak English—they're learning it from kindergarten—will give them a boost." He says that every volunteer contributes something "just by showing up and speaking with them."

In the afternoon, the kids gather in the great room for our send-off. Mohan calls each of us to the center of the room and drapes over our heads a gaudy wreath made of gold braid with a big red heart in the center. Mohan describes in Hindi what each of us has done at Grace and Flower. When he speaks about me, I make out the words "Charlie Chaplin."

Row by row the children file past us, shaking our hands and repeating what they've been coached to say:

"Happy journey."

"I will pray for you."

When Wilson comes by he throws his thin arms around my neck. He can write his name now, easily. "Please come back," he says, his eyes fixed on mine.

Saranivas shakes my hand and says, "Cookie jar!" He wants to play one more time before I leave.

It's hard to get into our cars with the kids crowding around us, shouting our names and imploring, "You come back?" At our final meal at the guesthouse, Stephen passes out evaluation forms. I know Pam and I will write about the hostility and lack of team support we encountered, and I can only imagine what the three veterans will write. Bob, the doctor, had said he's not sure he'd come on a trip like this again. "I don't think I'm that skilled at teaching, although I'll miss the kids and never forget their faces." The three veterans plan to return to Grace and Flower next year. Roger says it's been the most rewarding trip he's taken. "My best student hugged me at the end and wouldn't let go. I feel I really made an impact."

I will not be joining the three of them, but I could imagine teaching in different circumstances with a more hospitable group. I also question if it's necessary to live in squalid quarters. Ed Wayne has a cheerful apartment in Belgrade, and Charles and Torkin rent a garden condo in Kampala. Yet the experience of living as people live in third world countries has made an indelible impression.

After gathering my bags I leave the group and take a cab to Le Royal Meridien, where I've booked a room for the final night. I'm feverish and want to recuperate in comfort before traveling on. Saying good-bye to the veterans, I tell them I appreciate their commitment to the children. Kathleen and Roger merely nod but Libby says, with an unctuous smile, "Nice meeting you."

It's been raining all day, and the water has risen so high that the roads are nearly impassable. Le Royal Meridien emerges from the mists like a mirage. There are doormen in white gloves, palm trees, and marble stairs leading into the gilded lobby, where the Bee Gees are singing from a player piano, "Saturday Night Fever." I feel displaced, dizzy, as if I'd been shipwrecked and suddenly dropped at the Plaza Hotel in New York. It's been ten days since I showered in the health club here but it feels as if that occurred in a parallel time stream.

In my room, I slip into a king-size bed with a white duvet and a console beside me that controls the air-conditioning, lights, and TV. There's high-speed Internet at my desk and two phone extensions. I feel pangs that I can move so deftly from the bottom to the top of the economic ladder while the orphans have to stay where they are. In the lobby I'd seen workers crouched on the floor, polishing the marble, and knew I'd spend more rupees on breakfast than they'll earn in a month. I knew also the kind of place they're going home to: sleeping on the floor with the whole family in one room, bathing at a tap with cold water.

As I settle under the duvet, I wonder if my shunning by the volunteers was due to bad luck or social chemistry. We'd come to Mumbai in an effort to redress the caste system but created castes among our group. Leaders at WSC would later insist that my experience was an anomaly and that volunteers are generally "the best people you can meet." What I draw from this is that idealism on paper doesn't always translate to compassion in the trenches; we have to work with our humanness. Those who make commitments to serving people in crisis may not be capable of extending the same warmth to fellow volunteers, just as spiritual teachers aren't always skilled at intimate relations.

I'm still attracted to the wing-it-yourself style of service done by Ed Wayne and Charles and Torkin. They demonstrate that you don't have to wait for an organization, government, or foundation to hire you or fit you into a ready-made program, although many might prefer that. I can foresee doing short-term or part-time projects, but not having that be my primary focus. In our younger years, the movement had two streams: the political activist change-the-world stream and the hippie, spiritual, creative, change-yourself stream. Based on their character, people were drawn to one or the other. A few did both—Abbie Hoffman and Paul Krassner tried to yoke the two in forming the yippies— and some did neither, and my tropism has always been to the creative, inner, spiritual.

Looking back on my time with the orphans at the Grace and Flower Home, I can see those two weeks as a softening-up or breaking-down process for what would come next. Much as I wish it weren't so, I've found that enormous steps are possible when I've been brought to my knees. When I'm down, crying for help and abandoning hope that there's anything I can do about the situation . . . light enters.

I am not thinking of this, however, when I arrive, sick at heart and running a fever, at Le Royal Meridien in Mumbai. Swallowing the antibiotics and immune boosters I've brought along, I press the DO NOT DISTURB button on the console and the room goes dark.

13

My Sweet Lord

Peculiar travel suggestions are dancing lessons from God.

—Kurt Vonnegut, *Cat's Cradle*

The suggestion came, as it often does, from a stranger, Paul Mason, whom I met at an Internet café in Pondicherry called Coffee.com. He was sitting at the computer next to me, and because he looked British, wearing shorts, sandals, and metal-rimmed glasses, I asked in English if he knew the best way to get to Tiruvannamalai.

"I've just been there," he said.

Ten minutes later we were sitting at a table, drinking tea and eating baguettes with butter—the Indian version, which was improbably delicious. Paul was a sculptor from New Zealand, born the same year as I. He was intensely verbal, with a graying beard and small gold hoop in his left ear. He'd been coming to Pondicherry for two-month stretches every few years, creating pieces out of granite quarried nearby, and shipping the work home by boat. Every time he returned to India, he said, he'd go into shock for a week and then remember why he'd come: the exoticism, the visual stimulation, and the spiritual boost. He'd just returned from the holy city of Tiruvannamalai (Tiru), staying at the ashram of Ramana Maharshi, who's believed in India to be one of the country's greatest saints. I'd arranged to spend a week there by e-mailing ashram@ramana-maharshi.org.

Paul pulled from his pocket a small green book, *Thus Spake Ramana,* and smiled. "To the extent that it can be put in words—which it can't—it's in this book," Paul said. He suggested that before leaving for the ashram I visit the foundation of another Indian-born spiritual star, Krishnamurti, in Chennai. "They've got a library of videotapes, and you can hear the speech he gave in 1929 renouncing all religions."

Though Paul was from New Zealand, I felt as if we'd grown up on the same block, read the same books, and had the same tastes, so I was inclined to take his suggestion. I'd heard of Krishnamurti, the spiritual philosopher who died in California in 1986, but I'd never seen him or read his work.

The Krishnamurti Foundation in Chennai was an oasis—a quiet park of enormous banyan trees and an elegant two-story manse—surrounded by streets clogged with traffic, noise, and animals. In the library, there were individual viewing stations with headphones and comfortable chairs. The young Indian man who takes care of the collection suggested I start by watching a documentary of Krishnamurti's life, which I found riveting. In the early 1900s, the mystic Theosophical Society had a hundred thousand members all over the world who were told that there would soon be a new world teacher like the Buddha or Christ, a prophet for the scientific age.

Annie Besant, head of the order, discovered Krishnamurti on the beach near Chennai when he was fourteen, a thin, piercingly beautiful Brahmin boy who had "an emptiness about him." She obtained permission from his father to bring him to London to live with her, study at the finest schools, and be immersed in the teachings of Theosophy. He was presented to and embraced by the society as the long-awaited teacher, but in 1929, speaking at an international conference of Theosophists while thousands listened on the radio, Krishnamurti disbanded the order.

"Truth is a pathless land," he announced, "and you cannot approach it by any path whatsoever, by any religion, any sect." The spoken or written word is not the truth, which cannot be organized, he said. "If an organization be formed for this purpose, it becomes a crutch, a weakness, a bondage . . . and must cripple the individual." For this reason, he was dismantling the order. "You can form other organizations," he said, but that was not his concern. "My only concern is to set men absolutely and unconditionally free."

Krishnamurti told people not to believe what he said but to seek the truth that resides within them. Yet for the rest of his life he traveled to every continent, asserting his ideas. What strikes me as I sit at the viewing station, watching him on film, is that he's not a serene, beaming prophet. He speaks with force and fire, using his whole body for emphasis. His message is revolutionary: All religions are dead—collections of meaningless words, rituals, and superstitions that obfuscate truth. He says a guru should be one who eradicates ignorance, "not someone who imposes his ignorance on others," and warns that "ashrams are like concentration camps." I wonder why Paul wanted me to hear this before going to Ramana's ashram.

In a talk on meditation, Krishnamurti tells people to ask not how to do it, but what it is. "Meditation is when the mind is utterly quiet," he says. "The brain stops thinking, and in the space and silence, something unnamable is experienced." My brain has never ceased thinking except for a millisecond. When I'd told this to Paul, he'd laughed. "At least you have that millisecond." But Krishnamurti's views on organized religion and theology resonate with me.

· · ·

Since my twenties, I've been walking what Joseph Campbell calls "the pathless path," cutting through teachings and traditions, trusting personal experience. There was an upsurge of spiritual seeking in the seventies, when it seemed that everyone I knew in New York was reading *Be Here Now* by Ram Dass, trying vegetarianism, learning to sit on a meditation cushion, running to Chinatown for tai chi and to Central Park for Sufi dancing and to hear a lecture by R. D. Laing. Looking back, some have called it the Fourth Great Awakening in U.S. history, but the previous Great Awakenings in the eighteenth and nineteenth centuries were predominantly Christian revivals, reactions against increasing secularism and social change.

What happened in the seventies and continues to this time is closer in spirit to the New England transcendentalists of the nineteenth century: Ralph Waldo Emerson, Henry David Thoreau, Margaret Fuller, Amos Bronson Alcott, and others who questioned religious dogma and stressed the importance of a direct personal experience of nature and God. Instead of accepting what's been handed down from others, Emerson asked in *Nature:* "Why should not we also enjoy an original relation to the universe?"

Those who took up the quest in the seventies and afterward wanted, like Emerson, an unmediated engagement with the divine. Elizabeth Lesser, who was present at the creation, cofounding the Omega Institute, calls this movement the New American Spirituality, which is eclectic, individualistic, and grassroots rather than top-down. As with designer pizza, people can mix 'n' match, create their own, or stick with straight tomato. Christopher Isherwood described the eclectic seekers of his day as "continually on the lookout for fresh formulations . . . new information which could be fit into their complex individual world pictures."

A wave of teachers and gurus arrived from the East: Swami Satchidananda, who taught that "truth is one, paths are many," Yogi Bhajan, Pir Vilayat Khan, Swami Muktananda, and Chogyam Trungpa Rinpoche, the first of countless Buddhist lamas who were dispersed and blown like seeds from Tibet to root in new soil.

It was young people primarily who went to hear and study with them. Some joined their camps and are now teachers themselves, but the majority stayed for a time and moved on, gleaning what seemed relevant. It was this "gleaning" that made the movement unique. In New York, I attended one group for Hindu chanting, another for Buddhist meditation, learned tai chi, and prayed and sang with the mystic rabbi Shlomo Carlebach.

A significant number eventually returned to the religious traditions in which they'd been raised, looking for the experiential and mystic elements in Christianity and Judaism. A few years ago, I visited the Abbey of Regina Laudis, a Benedictine women's monastery in Bethlehem, Connecticut, and found that a good many nuns are in the boomer demographic. One, Sister Angèle, was raised in a Reform Jewish family in New York, although two of her aunts had converted to Catholicism. Sister Angèle, then known as Joyce, became a manager of opera singers for Columbia Artists Management, traveled to Europe twice a year, and enjoyed a vibrant social life. Wherever she was, she'd sometimes walk into a church to pray or find solace and began to feel a love and connection with Jesus. A friend brought her to visit the abbey, she returned with increasing frequency, converted to Catholicism, and at age fifty became a postulant.

The abbey, established in 1948, is unique because the founder believed that every woman who enters should have a talent or profession and be "equal to or superior to others in her field." The community includes a Shakespeare scholar from Yale, a sculptor who trained in Italy, several lawyers, a Wall Street executive, and a former movie star, Dolores Hart, who starred with Elvis in two movies. They grow their own food and raise cows from whose milk they make an award-winning cheese. The women sing Gregorian chant seven times a day and at two A.M., strive to make every activity a prayer, and the love you feel after a brief stay is palpable.

It was this intense experience of love that drew Sister Angèle to "enter," as they phrase it. A small, gregarious woman with blue eyes and gold-rimmed glasses, Sister Angèle says, "At fifty, you don't feel old, but you know that now is the time to go after what's most real for you." She emphasizes that the nuns she knows don't enter "to escape from the world, but to become more focused on what's essential." The first few years, however, were difficult. She missed seeing friends and family; she'd gone from living by herself, completely independent, to living with forty other women and practicing obedience. Although she was sometimes in tears, she says, "I never thought to leave." She found that obedience "doesn't look like freedom, but it actually gives you freedom and the fearlessness to be who you are." She compares it to ballet, citing Balanchine's theory that the dancer needs a formal structure in order to soar.

After a week at the abbey, I long for such a community: to live in a place of beauty, with love at the core and the society of brilliant women who're also witty and passionate. What stops me is the dogma, which they take literally. Those of us who've gleaned from different traditions are spiritual mongrels, temperamentally incapable of surrendering to outside authority. According to the gospel of Bob Dylan, we "don't follow leaders." The actress Joan Hotchkis states, "I'm allergic to anyone— priest or minister—who tells me how I should worship, where I'll go when I die, or what's the meaning of life." We understand the nature of truth to be relative. Reggie Gray, who teaches Buddhist psychotherapy, says, "No one knows the absolute truth about life, death, and God. I want to find what's true for me, what I can live with. Whether it turns out to be true . . . ?" She smiles and shrugs.

The Graying of Esalen

At retreat centers like Esalen and Hollyhock, the teachers and clients are growing old together. At workshops, it's common to look out on a sea of graying hair and beards. Sharon Salzberg, a founder of Insight Meditation Society in Barre, Massachusetts, says she and her colleagues wonder "if we'll be like the Shakers and die out." Or as Elizabeth Lesser of Omega puts it, "We may go the way of canasta and Frank Sinatra records, and that would be okay. When we started Omega we were hippies, we camped out, and it cost nothing. Now it costs a lot, and maybe twenty-somethings can't afford it. It may not be our job to awaken the next generation. Maybe the workshop is not their model." It's been our model, though, and some of us will keep at it until we're hobbling with our walkers to the hot tub, where they've installed special hold bars.

In the early years, we expected enlightenment to come in a flash— as to Saul on the road to Damascus. Now we say, only partly in jest, "Thirty years of meditating and we're not enlightened? Why keep at it?" Because, I've decided, as with writing, the reward is in the process. Prayer, yoga, and other spiritual practices generate feelings of calmness and joy. And for most humans, enlightenment is not sudden; we'll gain and lose and regain periods of clarity and oneness.

Those who wish to lengthen and deepen these periods are finding that, paradoxically, this requires a change from striving to make things happen to allowing them to unfold. It also requires—and this is a bitch—accepting that pain teaches and tempers us. Ram Dass, who was born before the baby boom and has been the figure holding the lantern, suffered a stroke at sixty-five that left him in a wheelchair with his right side paralyzed and a diminished ability to speak. Ram Dass had been a brilliant and hilarious raconteur who could hold thousands rapt, and after the stroke he spoke haltingly and had trouble accessing words. He lost his faith for a time, then came to see the stroke as "fierce grace," and in his talks now says the work of growing older is to move from "the point of view of ego to that of soul." From the ego view, the stroke was "a horrible thing. People said, 'Poor Ram Dass.' " From the soul view, he says, "the stroke was giving me lessons, advanced lessons. I'd always been the giver, and now I'm learning what it is to need help. That's grace."

Marion Woodman, the Jungian author, believes the soul's voice and urgings become imperative as we get older. "I'm talking about the small voice that says: I want, before I die, to find out who I am in my soul and who that soul is in relation to the divine. I don't have to prove anything." She hits the desk for emphasis. "I don't accept anybody's judgment of me. I am going to find out who I am in my soul, and I'm determined to live it!"

Marion laughs. "This is not easy to do in the world we're in."

Sally Kempton

In 2001, when I was contemplating how to go deeper with spiritual practice, I heard that Sally Kempton, then known as Swami Durgananda, was publishing a book, *The Heart of Meditation*. We'd been journalists together in New York in the sixties, but I'd had no contact with her since 1974, when she became a disciple of Swami Muktananda, took vows of celibacy, and disappeared behind the "guru curtain." I was eager to see her again and sense the effects of a twenty-seven-year commitment to rigorous Hindu practice. I called to suggest an interview about her book, and while she was pleased to hear from me, said, "I don't get to make my own decisions." I was floored that Sally, whom I'd known as an outrageous young woman, a radical feminist who wouldn't take shit from anyone, had surrendered her ability to make decisions. She said she makes personal decisions, but any question involving the Siddha Yoga Foundation, which has two hundred centers worldwide, has to be referred to a committee. Three months later, she called to tell me the decision was affirmative, and we arranged to meet in Los Angeles, where she'd be teaching.

As I wait for her in Pradeep's, an Indian restaurant in Santa Monica, I wonder if we'll recognize each other. I've heard she's gained weight, but the woman who steps inside, clothed in red monks' garb, is thin and has the unmistakable ice blue eyes and high cheekbones I remember from twenty-seven years ago.

We walk toward each other and hug, assuring each other that we appear little changed. "Your hair is still blond," I say.

"The women in my family don't turn gray till they're seventy."

If I was expecting Swami Durgananda to be spacey or robotic, I was immediately disabused. She speaks with the elegant diction and playful irony I recall, but there's a quality that's unfamiliar—a gentleness, an active sympathy. When we'd been friends before, I'd been intimidated and guarded in her presence. I knew she could skewer people with a look or single phrase that would pierce their pose and reduce them to an object of ridicule. In her memoir of feminist outrage, "Cutting Loose," which was published in *Esquire,* she'd confessed to having "a compulsion to seduce men," and a fair number viewed her with lust and terror.

I ask how she moved from radical feminism to following a Hindu male guru. She says that in spite of her literary achievements and cool exterior, she'd felt empty and anxious. "To tell you the truth, I was looking for happiness, but because I was a political-intellectual-left-wing person, I became a feminist first. I couldn't go straight to God. The road was twisty." She says I was the one who connected her with "Baba," as Muktananda was called, but I have no memory of this. When I was living in Venice, California, writing *Loose Change,* I went to a weekend "intensive" with Baba during which he hit me on the head with peacock feathers. I thought some kind of mass hypnosis might be occurring: People were laughing, weeping, and convulsing after being hit with the peacock feathers. Nothing like that happened to me, and I never returned.

When Sally first saw Muktananda, though, wearing an orange robe, a ski cap, and dark glasses, she had what she calls "a classic conversion experience" and was flooded with light.

A waiter brings us plates of curried organic vegetables. Sally says that when she told friends about the state of oneness she'd felt with Baba, they told her it was a high, like a drug high, and she would come down. At the time, she agreed that such a state of unity and joy could not be present all the time.

She takes a bite of curry. "And now it is."

I put down my fork. "Joy is your basic state, every day?"

She nods.

"How long has this been true?"

"About ten years."

I tell her I've had interludes I'd call happy, but there's usually been pain from one sector or another.

"I used to be in pain 98 percent of the time," she says.

I press her to describe this state of joy.

"The closest analogy I have is that heart-melting feeling you have when you're in love, when the world seems fascinating and you take pleasure in simple things." She says there are degrees, and at times she might feel worried or frightened but can bring herself back to that heartfelt joy.

She does seem content, but I can't know how she is when alone or in times of crisis. I'm inclined to believe, though, that years of meditation and cultivating love toward the self and others have brought her this equanimity.

In spiritual life, it's said that one can go deep or one can go wide—deep by staying with one master or tradition and wide by gleaning from many. Durgananda has gone deep and I've gone wide, and as we talk, during our lunch and subsequent visits, it occurs to me that we've each reaped benefits and paid a price. I wouldn't give up what I've had—my children, love with certain men, the exaltation of the creative process—but these haven't brought me the sustained happiness and serenity she claims to own. Durgananda, having chosen to be a monk, feels she has "unfinished business. I still have writing I want to do," she says, and she'd like to experience intimate relations, "the kind of vulnerable intimacy with people that I've been protected from."

Two years after our meeting at Pradeep's, Durgananda, at fifty-nine, renounces her vows, takes off the robe, and goes over the wall—leaving Siddha Yoga to teach and write on her own. It's a stunning move: At a time when many are cutting back on work to take up service or spiritual pursuits, she's becoming Sally Kempton again and creating a start-up. Friends ask, "Are you crazy?" She's moving from a life where every need was taken care of, leaving her free to study and teach, to a life where she's forming her own nonprofit and has to deal with "shopping and doing taxes and getting the car repaired and organizing my time—that's the hardest—after decades of following the ashram schedule." For thirty years she's worn the reddish orange clothes of a monk. The first time she walks into a clothing store, she freezes. What colors to put together? She solves the problem by buying everything black, but after a period of adjustment, she discovers that she can wear jeans and turtlenecks as she did thirty years before.

People are constantly asking why she left the ashram, and she says there are multiple reasons. When she was writing *The Heart of Meditation,* the book had to be approved by committee and published by the ashram, and she longed to be able to write without these constraints. Muktananda had died, replaced by Gurumayi, a woman younger than Durgananda with whom she had a close bond, but Durgananda was moving beyond the ashram tradition. "I'd been nurtured by that tradition, but I'd come to the place where I knew I'd internalized the energy and guidance of the guru. I wanted my freedom back."

She also wanted to "walk among people as one of them," not be on a pedestal. "How could I tell people to integrate their meditation with their daily life when I never had to go to the store?" Most important, she knew she had to leave to grow. Something happens in your fifties or sixties, she says, there's a crisis when you're sighting down the mountain, and "for many, the tendency is to look for security and find a deck chair. What you're meant to do is find a way to challenge yourself, to stay on your edge." She falls silent. "Leaving the ashram put me on my edge. I had to do something hard and new."

It was a risk: She had no pension or savings and little time to prepare for when she might need care. She'd contracted polio at seven, and has to conserve her physical strength. "When I thought about starting a project this big—establishing and supporting myself as a meditation teacher—everything in my system was saying, 'I don't want to!' " Sally laughs. "I like to read and space out in beautiful landscapes, but another part of me is insisting that I do it." She's aware that "I'm doing life backwards. I did the inward part before the career." The advantage of going out on your own at fifty-nine, she says, is that "you tend to get less emotionally involved in day-to-day setbacks. When trouble arises, you know you're gonna get through it." She adds with an antic smile: "I wish I'd known that when I was twenty-five, when I had more physical energy and was cuter."

The Ashram

Sally and I have often taken different trajectories, like planes flying to cities on opposite coasts. Just as she's emerging from the cloister and embarking on a hectic tour of workshops and lectures, I'm in Chennai, India, hiring a car to take me to the ashram of Ramana Maharshi.

We set out at seven A.M. when it's still cool, heading inland past green rice fields where men in *lunghis* are turning the soil with oxen and plows made of branches tied together. It's primitive, pastoral, timeless. Peanuts have been harvested and spread across the road to dry, so that for miles we have to use the shoulder to avoid crushing the peanuts.

There are no road signs so the driver, Raju, stops often to ask directions to Tiruvannamalai. "This is how we are getting places in India," he says. "If people don't know where it is, they will give you some directions anyway, so you have to ask many people." I nod, wondering how many hours this will take.

When I was casting about for an ashram to stay at, Anne Cushman, who co-wrote *From Here to Nirvana,* the best and funniest guide to spiritual India, suggested the ashram of Ramana Maharshi. Several friends of mine concurred. Although Ramana was no longer alive, they said something—his essence, vibration, emanation—was still present and conducive to deep meditation. The other draw was that the ashram sits beneath Mount Arunachala, which according to myth is the god Shiva himself—not his dwelling place, but the god's physical body. In the Hindu trinity, Brahma is the creator, Vishnu the preserver, and Shiva the destroyer who clears the way for regeneration. When Brahma and Vishnu were fighting, Shiva appeared as a pillar of fire with no bottom and no top. Seeing the fire, the other gods ceased their fighting, and Shiva condensed his flaming self into the mountain. For centuries, pilgrims have been coming to walk the ten-mile path around Arunachala. When Ramana Maharshi, a feckless student in a small southern town, had a spontaneous and unexpected awakening, he set out for Mount Arunachala.

I read a biography of Ramana that excited my curiosity. At age sixteen he was struck with a deep-seated fear that he was dying. He stretched out on the ground and began asking: What is death, what will die, what if anything will survive, and who is asking these questions? He felt his personality dissolve, and what replaced it was the awareness of what he called the everlasting Self. He left his home, gave away his money and clothes, did not eat unless he was fed, and for many years did not speak. He was dwelling in what he described as the Self, or pure being, and did not notice when his flesh was being eaten by bugs. Word spread that this young swami had attained realization. Over the years a great number came to see him, and a few, in the presence of his sweetness and simplicity, would experience that same illumination.

Ramana taught a practice called self-inquiry. "Simply ask yourself, Who am I? Use this inquiry to point your mind to the Self. An intuition will rise. Follow that intuition."

I had meditated before with this technique. I would say silently, Who am I? Who is asking the question? Who is hearing the words? I'd been told not to expect an answer but to observe what occurred. I identified with the observer, however, who seemed to have my personality, attitudes, and judgments, even humor. I tried asking, Who is the observer? and, Who is observing the observer? And that's where I was stuck. No intuition came; something subtle perhaps, but what was it?

●   ●   ●

By afternoon, Raju manages to find the way to the ashram, a compound of white stone buildings with peacocks on the roofs, monkeys climbing tree trunks, and barefoot people from all parts of the world streaming through the gates. At the office, a man in a long white dhoti hands me the ashram schedule and a key to my room. It's two blocks away, and when I reach the door I open it warily. To my relief, the room is clean and simple, with its own bathroom and a Western toilet. There's even hot water from a faucet down the hall. After the volunteers' flat in Mumbai, carrying a bucket of hot water to my room is a thrill.

As I walk back to the ashram tucked at the base of Arunachala, the mountain looks aflame, glowing red in the setting sun. A billboard from a bank reads, "Welcome devotees of the Great Sri Ramana Maharshi!" He's called "Bhagavan" here, which means "Lord," and at six P.M. there's a *puja,* or devotional ceremony, at his tomb in the back of the cavernous meditation hall.

About two hundred people are sitting cross-legged on the marble floor, half Indians and half foreigners. In front of the tomb or *samadhi* shrine, five priests are chanting Hindu scriptures. The priests wear nothing but a loincloth and a red cord across their chest. They're all fat, with potbellies, stripes of gray ash on their foreheads, and hair pulled back in a stubby ponytail. As they chant, devotees fall to the floor and prostrate themselves before the tomb. Dozens of others walk around and around it. Some look lost or in a trance, others are moving fast, pumping their arms as if they're racewalking. Round and round they go like the tigers that circle the tree in *Little Black Sambo.* I join them for a few laps and have the odd sense of watching myself from a distance. *What on earth is she doing?*

The priests finish chanting and prepare for the *puja.* One brings a bucket of water and slops it on the floor of the shrine. Then he ties silk scarves around statues of Shiva and Ganesh, who has an elephant's head and a man's body. Other priests drape garlands of flowers over the statues and put *bindis,* or colored dots, between their eyes.

They draw a yellow curtain closed. People in the hall strain forward and stand on their toes to catch a glimpse of—what? A priest rings a loud bell and yanks the curtain open. The crowd surges forward with excitement as if a performance is beginning, but all that happens is: A priest carries a fire offering—a round tray with a small fire burning on it—to the statues, then takes the tray out to the hall. He places it on a table and everyone crowds around it, making scooping gestures with their hands as if to take the flames inside.

With Krishnamurti's words ringing in my ear—that "truth is a pathless land" and religious rituals "obfuscate the truth"—the *puja* looks like so much claptrap. I sit down at the side of the hall and try to tune in at a deeper level, below the adorning of statues and chanting of words I can't understand. Sally Kempton had told me that when she walked into the hall, she sat and cried for three hours. Another friend, the architect Evans Woollen, said, "You will not be prepared for the power of the energy in that room." But I'm not feeling any power or energy. Have I been inoculated by Krishnamurti?

At seven-thirty I join the group waiting by the dining hall for dinner. We sit on the floor in rows with a banana leaf in front of us. Men come around with buckets and ladle out rice, dahl, and four kinds of colored liquids that spill over the banana leaf onto the floor. They bring us cups of water, and when the cup is empty, they fill it with soup, then yogurt. But I don't want to drink the water, which means no soup or yogurt. All I have is rice, which I scoop off the wet banana leaf with my fingers. I feel dizzy. Later we will wash our banana leaves in a communal sink of gray water. I can't believe I thought I could do this for six months. So much for the ashram fantasy. This trip to India, I see, is a total bust. What does that mean, what does it tell me about my focus in the years ahead, if I'm crossing off organized volunteer projects and study in an ashram? I think of calling Raju on his cell phone—he won't have reached Chennai yet—and telling him to turn around, please, come back and get me.

⋅ ⋅ ⋅

The next morning, I decide to skip the milk offering to Bhagavan at six forty-five and walk next door to a café called the German Bakery. It's run not by Germans, but by an Indian family who live in a thatched hut and serve food on tables in their garden. A woman in a sari, Kantha, brings me a menu that is supposedly in English. "I can make anything you like," she says. I ask for hard-boiled eggs with cooked spinach, the Indian bread called naan, and tea with lemon. While she cooks, I sit back under the palm trees and read the menu. There are six kinds of "Spa Katy" listed. What could that be? Spa Katy? Spa cuisine conceived by someone named Katy? *Right.* I repeat the words aloud until I get it: spaghetti. There's also pizza, stir-fried vegetables with tofu, and "Snakes." Snake meat? Python? It turns out to be snacks.

With the first bite of perfectly cooked eggs and spinach and warm bread, I begin to relax. Everything is shifting. I don't have to eat the liquids poured on banana leaves on the floor with my fingers. I can take my meals here. I walk to the ashram, meditate in the hall, then step out front to help with "Poor Feeding." Sadhus—men who've renounced the world, money, and all material possessions to seek God—form a line, all of them dressed in orange cloth and holding little tin pails with tops and handles. I join the serving line; as the sadhus file past, someone scoops rice into their pails and I pour lemon-pickle sauce over the rice. After the sadhus are finished, the poor men from the village come down the line, then the women, some of whom don't have pails but hold out plastic bags or leaves.

When everyone has been served, the young Indian man next to me, Santhosh, asks if I want to see the caves where Ramana Maharshi lived. We follow a stone path up the mountain, which is surprisingly green and lush, with tamarind trees and sweeping views of the great Shiva temple in Tiru with its enormous white pyramid roofs, covered with intricate carvings from the ninth century. I learn Santhosh is a research scientist. At twenty-seven, not yet married, he lives with his parents and comes to the ashram every few months "to feed the soul." He asks if I've been married. "Twice," I say.

"Have you been in love with both your husbands?"

"Yes. And you, Santhosh, have you been in love?"

"Not yet, madam, because if I have been in love, my mother will beat me." His parents are looking for a bride, advertising with services and spreading the word through relatives. "It might take a year," he says, to find a woman from the right caste, the right family, who's educated and pious. Meanwhile, his mother doesn't want him coming to the ashram because she's afraid he'll become a sadhu before she can get him married.

We laugh about this as we approach the cave where Ramana lived for seventeen years. I have to crouch to reach the inner chamber, which has pictures of Bhagavan lit by candles. Sitting on the floor in the darkness, I can hear the chaotic honking of traffic in the city below, drums, bells, peacocks screeching, and men chanting. But I fall in and out of a sleep-like state. I can sense my body letting down, becoming receptive. I feel as if I'm being cradled by soft arms—could this be the energy my friends spoke about, or is it the effect of being in a cave? I don't really care. I tell Santhosh I find the cave more intimate and charged than the meditation hall with the priests chanting and conducting fire ceremonies. He says this is where people sat with Bhagavan in silence. "There was no daily regimen of offerings and prayers. No marble hall, either. All that came after he was gone."

* * *

The next morning I get up at six to do the ten-mile walk around Arunachala. The road is cool and shady with overhanging trees, and every ten feet there's a shrine, statue, temple, or trident—one of Shiva's symbols—stuck in the ground with a lime impaled on the middle prong. Shiva is the god of change, and the symbols associated with him are sexual: the snake, the trident, and the lingam—a phallic column pointing straight up. There are at least seven lingams on this road, and at the first, a pillar of black granite, a group of men are chanting in an adjacent hut.

Two devotees emerge from the hut, wash their feet carefully at a spigot, and place a banana leaf heaped with food at the base of the lingam. To them it's not a stone phallus but the living presence of God, and today I don't see their behavior as nonsensical in the way I saw the potbellied priest sloshing water around the tomb of Ramana. Bliss is rolling in. I feel sparkly and giddy, as if champagne bubbles are coursing through my veins. I hear the words "Lighten up," and start to laugh. I want to play with the children nearby and roll on the ground with the monkeys who have tiny pink bodies and wrinkled little faces like old men.

I make my way along the road, stopping at every shrine to breathe in whatever may be present. There are statues of almost every deity in the

Hindu pantheon: the blue god Krishna, the monkey god Hanuman, and Shiva's son Kartikai, riding on a peacock. This is Shiva's country, Shiva is the mountain and the mountain is always on the right, sometimes shrouded in clouds and then reemerging. I'm very happy. I've caught the rhythm of this place now and don't believe the time I've allotted to stay here will be enough.

*   *   *

At the Manna Café where foreigners hang out, I'm eating organic lentil soup and crusty bread. The foreigners seem to fall into two age groups—under thirty and over fifty—on either side of the child-raising years. They come from countries all over Asia, Europe, and the Americas, and there's a large contingent of Israelis. Many come every year for "the season," November to March, when it's not oppressively hot. The women wear punjabi—long tunics over slacks—and the men wear dhotis—like wraparound skirts—and silk V-neck shirts. An exotic-looking Italian man with green eyes and dark hair goes barefoot but carries blue plastic sandals in his knapsack in case the road becomes too rocky or hot. Most of them go native—renting flats with no hot water and an Indian-style toilet outside. They can live on $100 a month and when the money runs out go back to their native countries and earn enough to come back.

When I ask what they do here for five months, they look at me as if I'm benighted. They say they meditate, work on creative projects, study, or just sit with the many saints and teachers who pass through or have ashrams in Tiru. They get together to make music and chant on Sundays and dance on Friday nights. They invite me to a dance on a terrace by the ashram, and I'm surprised by the number of unattached men. This may be the only place I've visited where women don't complain, "There are no men." Some came to India in the seventies as hippies and stayed. They may not be terrific at making money or sticking with you for the long run, but the boys can dance. They leap and whirl, improvise and switch partners, and everyone of every age and gender dances with everyone else. "There's so much going on here, you have to pace yourself," the Italian says.

I see what he means from the posters on the walls of the Manna Café announcing classes, workshops, concerts, poetry readings, volunteer projects, and massage. One draws my attention: a photo of a man with a white beard and glasses who's called Arunachala Ramana. The poster says he's "an American disciple of Bhagavan—back in India for a limited time." A. Ramana, as he's also called, says he teaches the self-inquiry meditation of Ramana Maharshi. This interests me because no one at the ashram teaches it, and this may be an opportunity to move beyond the place where I've been stuck. To attend one of his *satsangas,* or teaching sessions, though, you must first have an interview conducted on Thursdays upstairs at the Manna Café.

It happens to be Thursday, so I climb the stairs and find a woman with a boyish haircut, Jan Sundell, interviewing three newcomers: a twenty-year-old Israeli boy who's come to India "to experience the grace of the guru," an American nurse in her fifties from Santa Cruz, California, and an Indian shopkeeper from Pondicherry.

Jan goes over the rules for the *satsanga* to be held tomorrow from nine to eleven A.M. You must make a reservation. You must attend an orientation session at eight-thirty. You must be on time or you won't be admitted, and you must stay for the entire session. "Ramana does not like it when people get up and leave, even to go to the toilet, because it's disruptive to the flow and disturbs everyone." She warns that he's controversial, a Texan who wears shorts and T-shirts and uses "adult language."

I don't care if he says "fuck," but I've never been to a *satsanga* where you had to be interviewed first and make a reservation. This man is a control freak; it doesn't smell right.

Jan is asking questions from a printed form and says she'll convey the answers to A. Ramana.

"What is most important in your spiritual quest?

"Do you know what it is to be with a living guru?

"Do you have a question for Ramana?"

When she comes to me, I say I know nothing about him or his organization, and I'm not sure it's for me. She says he was born Dee Wayne
Ray in El Paso in 1929, sought the truth from a young age, and became
enlightened in a bookstore in Houston in the 1970s when he "acciden-
tally" came upon a picture of Ramana Maharshi.

Jan is staring at me and asks if we've met before.

"I don't think so."

She asks what I do, where I went to school—no overlap there—but
we both grew up in Los Angeles. "Were you in Girl Scouts?" she asks.

I startle. "Briefly."

Jan was a big-time Girl Scout. "My mother was a professional—in
the Scout organization."

"Did you go to Camp Ocito?" I ask, dredging up the name of the
Girl Scout camp I attended miserably for three summers. *Ocito* was the
Native American word for a bear that once roamed the mountains
where we slept on cots in tents.

Jan rises from her chair. "Of course I did!"

"I still remember the songs," I say.

"You remember 'The Little Ocito'?"

We begin to sing together: "The little Ocito comes at night to you,
and you . . ." all the way through verses and choruses with hand gestures
and sound effects. How strange is that? Singing Girl Scout camp songs
from Big Bear, California, in the holy city of Tiruvannamalai?

This is an omen.

· · ·

"Should I go?" I ask two Australian women, Susan and Lily, whom I
have dinner with that night. They're not keen on A. Ramana when they
hear the name of his organization—AHAM, the Association of Happiness for All Mankind—and glance at a book he wrote, *Living Free.* Both

women are former teachers in their fifties who remind me of English ladies in an E. M. Forster novel. When they buy stamps at the post office, I ask why they don't use e-mail. Susan turns and brings her face close to mine. "There's nothing like a letter!" Lily says she writes and receives at least one personal note a day.

Susan has come to Tiru because she's always wanted to write and never had the courage. Last year she decided, "I'm going to chuck my job, take the money I've saved, and have a go at the writing. If I leave it for longer, it will be too late." She left her husband behind in Melbourne and rented a flat in Tiru. The marriage of thirty-three years, she explains, "had gotten frozen. I'm hoping that when I return things will shift a bit."

I ask why she had to travel to India to write instead of shutting herself off somewhere in the Outback. Susan says she wants to explore the human need for sacredness. "In India, it's everywhere. But have we lost the sacred in the West?" She lights a cigarette. "In Melbourne we make football sacred—not your version but a combination of Gaelic and aboriginal football."

Lily, who's wearing a lavender punjabi and a big powder blue sunhat, came to Tiru to visit Susan at a time when her own career as a teacher seemed to be ending. She doesn't know what she'll do next. "I don't mind uncertainty," she says. "The question is, where do I put my energies, my commitment? It's not about filling time—I could do that easily. It's about vocation."

I ask if they want to come to the *satsanga* with me tomorrow, but Susan is appalled that you have to pass an interview first.

I nod. "I don't think I'll go."

.   .   .

I wake up knowing I should go. I've learned you can never tell where the next message will come from, and in any case, this is research.

Unlike Bhagavan's ashram, which is open to all, the AHAM ashram has high gates and a guard who checks for your name on a list. This is ashram luxe: a spectacular piece of land on the road that circles Arunachala so the red-coned mountain looms over the property. All the buildings are new, elegant, spotless. Birds call from the trees, and butterflies flit about the gardens of tropical flowers that are meticulously tended by the Indian staff.

We leave our shoes at the gate and walk down a red dirt path to the terrace where Elizabeth MacDonald, AHAM's senior trainer, gives the orientation. "He's already tuned in to your presence," she tells the four of us who are new. "His grace is consuming you now even if you're not aware of it." I ask how this ashram and the one Ramana has in North Carolina are supported. She looks uncomfortable. "The AHAM trust owns the land, and it's supported by . . . donations, tithing . . ." Her voice trails off. She tells us there'll be an hour of meditation, then Ramana will answer questions. "He likes a good argument, so don't be shy."

Before entering the meditation hall, we're asked to step into a marble footbath and dry our feet on a mat. In the hall are wicker basket chairs with plush green cushions—a sharp contrast to the cave in which Bhagavan sat on the dirt floor with devotees. I sit in the first row facing two altars—one to Jesus and one to Bhagavan. By nine A.M., when the front gates are locked, sixteen people are sitting in the basket chairs, three of them Indian and about two-thirds women. A side door opens and Ramana walks in. He's towering, overweight, with a tattoo of the state of Texas on his left arm. He lights incense and sits down between the altars, laces his fingers together, and closes his eyes.

I struggle with the self-inquiry meditation. The "Little Ocito" song —that damned tune from Girl Scout camp—keeps running through my head. I can't make it stop, so I give it my attention, and it plays on and on. Who is singing it? Who is hearing it? Who wants it to stop? Who is asking these questions, and who is observing the one who asks? I become fidgety and bored and am relieved when Ramana rings a bell at the end of the hour.

"Welcome to AHAM," he says with a melodious southern drawl. For twenty-six years, he says, he's been introducing people to "the simple yet pure teaching of Bhagavan Ramana Maharshi." He begins by telling us, "You already *are* the Self." He says we don't have to look, seek, struggle, go anyplace. "Just let go of the wrong ideas about who you are and you'll be free and happy. Now."

Right.

He reads the question submitted by Prem, the Indian man from Pondicherry. "There is something separate from the body/mind. How do I find it?" Ramana stares at Prem, who sits ramrod straight and cross-legged in his basket chair. "Stop imagining that you are *not* the Self. How many selves are you?"

Prem looks blank.

"How many? Come on."

"Only one."

"And you can't find it?" Ramana laughs, a Santa Claus–like chuckle that makes his belly shake. "Stop believing you are your body, your mind. You are the awareness that *sees* your body and your mind, but you can't see *you.*"

He looks about the room. "Are you with me?" A few say yes. I shake my head no.

Ramana tells Prem, "When you let go of everything that you're not, what's left?"

Prem doesn't respond.

"Thoughtless awareness," Ramana says.

Well, yes. I've heard teachers and monks speak about awareness—the force or consciousness that animates and connects all living things. I've even had moments—milliseconds—of experiencing that consciousness but it ain't happening now.

"These are just words," Ramana says. "Words are not it. *You* are it."

Prem breaks into a smile—something has pierced him.

Ramana speaks to the group. "This is not just for Prem. You don't have to search anymore for your Self, unless you're addicted to the search." He mimics one of the foreigners in Tiru. "I just *love* to come to India every year to continue my search." People laugh. "Are you ready to find?" he asks in a booming voice. "Are you ready to get it?"

Ramana calls my name and reads the question I submitted at the interview: "How do I get beyond identification with the observer?" He looks at me. "Has your question been answered?"

"No," I say. "Is the observer the same as the awareness you speak of?"

"Yes," he says immediately.

"But the observer seems to have a personality, an identity, to think about what it observes."

He gives me one of his long stares. "Your problem is, you think you are your body. You think you are your mind."

"I have moments of knowing I'm not my body," I say.

He drops his head and looks at me over his glasses. "With all due respect, you're still identified with it. You can say the words, but you still believe you're that body in that chair."

"I go back and forth."

"Quit going back and forth," he bellows. "Do it now. Let go."

I lean forward and say in a clear, strong voice, "If we're not the body and not the mind, why don't we know that? Why are we hardwired to believe we are this body, because all of us do?"

"That's your mind." He chuckles. "You're addicted to thinking. Nothing wrong with that. Just tell the truth—you're addicted."

I shrug. "I'm always doing it."

"Remember what the Bard said? 'There is nothing either good or bad but . . .' " He pauses, and we all finish the line from *Hamlet:* " 'Thinking [Ramana draws out the word *think . . . ing*] makes it so.' "

I have more questions—as each is answered, more arise like bubbles in a carbonated drink, but I tamp down the lid. I want to feel what it is to have no thoughts—if such a thing is possible.

"Stop identifying with your thoughts," Ramana says. "Just watch them. You don't have to identify with them. You're the awareness that is watching your thoughts. Are you ready and willing to do that?"

"Yes," I say.

I don't hear what he says next. Tears are rolling down my face, and relief washes over me. Relief . . . as if I'm home. Love swells and expands "like gold to airy thinness beat." No thoughts. . . . I observe there are no thoughts, and the spell shatters like glass, but I can drop back again to stillness, just breathing.

It's hard to write about these states because when I look for words, the state transmutes to something else. As I write this, I am not in that awareness. But when I meditate and sometimes when I'm going about my day—washing dishes, talking on the phone—I can open a wedge between me and what I'm thinking, watching the thoughts rather than being absorbed and agitated by them. When strong emotions—anger, sadness—take over the body and brain like a dybbuk, I find that if I step into awareness for a moment and watch the rage or tears, the grip loosens. I see that my thoughts and feelings are like smoke, gathering and dispersing, real but with no solidity, and this is freeing.

I'm grateful to A. Ramana, though I feel no compulsion to join his community. I'd been meditating, asking, reflecting, and had worked my way out to the edge of the plank, where I was poised on my toes. He gave me the push that sent me, like Dumbo with the feather, into the air.

· · ·

I came back from India by stages, like a deep-sea diver who stops at different levels to decompress. From Tiru I took a car to Pondicherry, where I met up with Paul Mason, the sculptor who was about to fly back to New Zealand. From Pondicherry I drove to Chennai, then took a plane to Mumbai and a final night at Le Royal Meridien. I remembered that when I'd first arrived in India, the buffet breakfast at the Meridien for 300 rupees—$6—seemed reasonable. Now it seemed outrageous. I'd eaten in Tiru for less than 100 rupees a day. From Mumbai I flew to Frankfurt, caught another plane to Chicago, then Denver, and forty-five minutes later I turned the key in the front door of my home in Boulder. But it took much longer for me to fully arrive.

At the stop in Pondicherry, Paul and I find rooms in a bed-and-breakfast, the Residence Shalimar, run by a Kashmiri man and his French wife, who's an extraordinary cook.

"How are you feeling?" I ask when I see Paul.

"Old."

He's just taken the train to Madurai to see the Meenakshi Temple and developed a 104-degree fever in the middle of the night. He lay shivering under the blanket, imagining being taken to an Indian hospital and seeing the headline in the New Zealand paper: MASON DIES IN INDIA.

"That's dramatic," I say.

"I go in for that," he says. "It's hard being here when you're not twenty-five." He has a feeling he may not come back to India again.

I've been feeling that also, I say. "Is that why you sent me to hear Krishnamurti?"

He laughs. "I don't know why I told you to go there."

I say Krishnamurti pointed me in the direction I'd been groping toward on my own, but he put up lights I couldn't miss. "It's a pathless land. I don't need to go anywhere, look for a teacher or guru, or seek out experiences the way I've done for years."

I tell him what happened at A. Ramana's ashram and how it's affected my meditation.

"Are you hooked on self-inquiry?" he asks.

"That was Bhagavan's method, and as Krishnamurti said, anyone who tells you how to do it is not setting you free."

Paul laughs and makes a gesture that says, Touché. He looks at A. Ramana's picture on the cover of *Living Free* and says, "That's a nice story."

"What do you mean? It's the past, it's become a story that I'm telling, and whatever state or understanding I've reached will change?"

He shakes his head. "I mean the message you need to hear can come from the most obscure place."

"That's why I went."

Eliana, the French innkeeper, calls out that lunch is ready, and we walk barefoot to the dining room.

"You do look well," Paul says. "You haven't stopped smiling."

14

When We're Sixty-four

How can one accept living, with time bearing down on us so unbearably, like the load on an ass? . . . One ought to rebel.

—Eugène Ionesco, *Mémoires en Miettes*

It seemed by chance that I came to read Carolyn Heilbrun's book. At a time during my fifties when I was struggling with insomnia, I went looking for a book in the Health and Sexuality section of the bookstore. As I scanned the shelves, a title caught my eye: *The Last Gift of Time: Life Beyond Sixty.* I pulled out the slim paperback and sat down on a bench. It was written by Heilbrun, whom I'd heard of but hadn't read—the feminist scholar who also wrote, under the name Amanda

Cross, a popular mystery series featuring a female English professor. The first page I flipped to had a quote from Cicero:

> Since (nature) has fitly planned the other acts of life's drama, it is not likely that she has neglected the final act as if she were a careless playwright.

The book was only tangentially about health or sexuality, so how it came to be placed here was mysterious. I began reading it and forgot about the book I'd been searching for. I bought *The Last Gift of Time*, kept it by my bedside for years, and gave it to many as a present: a smart, biting, and witty memoir on the unexpected pleasures of aging.

In the preface, Carolyn writes that she decided at a younger age that she would commit suicide at seventy. She anticipated that her sixties would be "downhill all the way" and believed it was better to "leave the party while it's still fun," before she was too sick or weak to pull it off.

Carolyn was a literary lioness, a female professor in the vaunted English Department at Columbia when it was an all-boys school and "men were the only models we had." Wearing glasses and her brown hair in tight natural curls, she created and fought for the legitimacy of feminist literary studies. "She *was* the field," one of her students says. She brought new feminist interpretations to Virginia Woolf and the Bloomsbury group and wrote books like *Writing a Woman's Life* that inspired a mass audience. She raised three children and had a circle of friends and students—now professors—who saw her as "muse, nurturer, and mother of us all."

When she turned seventy, Carolyn looked back on her sixties with surprise: It had been her "happiest decade." After a lifetime of solitude, she'd made brilliant women friends with whom she had standing weekly dates to walk and talk or eat a take-out dinner. At sixty-eight, although she had two homes—an apartment in Manhattan and a farmhouse in the Berkshires where she'd spent summers with her family—Carolyn bought a home of her own in upstate New York, a retreat where she could sit by the fire and think. She stopped wearing dresses, pantyhose, and heels and wore only slacks, stopped giving parties, and saw friends only one-on-one. She was exhilarated by the conversations she could have with her adult children and made peace with her husband of more than four decades. "Many husbands, many men, are boring, certainly more boring than women," she wrote, but "now that I have got used to my husband . . . now that I know he will never become a poet of love or be likely to remember what I said yesterday . . . I have found life good, and I do not accept the possibility of his desertion." She realized that she had fixed seventy as her exit year when it was far away and, having attained it, decided to keep living. She found it "powerfully reassuring" to know that each day she could ask, "Do I choose death or life? I daily choose life," she wrote, "the more earnestly because it is a choice."

I made the same agreement with myself on days when I felt so despondent I couldn't leave the house. I only have to endure this until I'm seventy, I thought. Whatever pain I'm in, it will be over at seventy, and knowing this—knowing there was an end point—made it possible to roust myself and go on. Timothy Quill, MD, a professor of medicine at the University of Rochester, helps people who have terminal diseases die at the time they choose. At a conference on "The Art of Dying," Quill said that people with a fatal illness manage to stay alive longer if they know they have the ability to leave. "It's like being shut up in a small room," he said. "You can tolerate it longer if you have the key to get out." I expected, of course, that at seventy I would modify my agreement as Carolyn had, and I took hope knowing she was still out there, feisty and affirming life.

In the fall of 2003, when I began research for *Leap!,* I told my agent, Joy Harris, that I planned to interview Carolyn Heilbrun.

Joy was silent a moment. "She died."

"What?"

"She killed herself two weeks ago."

It was a blow to the stomach; I'd lost someone I'd never met but who couldn't be replaced. Others, I learned, who hadn't known her but read her work felt the same. Carolyn was a model of a woman leading a life of the mind—independent, productive, and exuberant—into her seventies, and this is where the road led?

I regretted that I hadn't arranged to interview her sooner and became compelled to look into her death. I learned that people over sixty-five, along with those between fifteen and twenty-four, are the two groups at greatest risk for suicide in this country. Carolyn's suicide at seventy-seven raises questions that people close to her are "thinking hard about." Did she kill herself in despair, or was it an act of principle? Is there such a thing as "rational suicide"? Carolyn believed there was. She didn't share her thoughts with friends or family before she took her life. Was she pulling away, preparing to die, or did she just not give a damn? If one's work is, as she wrote that hers was, "the essence of life," does life become worthless when work wanes?

· · ·

Carolyn gave no sign to anyone that she was ready to die. She was healthy and active, her memory was sharp, and she'd just written an essay for a scholarly journal. Her children, husband, and the close friends she had standing dates with every week were shocked. Her daughter, Margaret, who was then forty-six and had a nine-year-old daughter, said she knew her mother's ideas about suicide, knew "there might be some time in the future that Mommy's going to do this, but not now." Margaret adds, "I can't say I was nervous when she approached seventy. She had a busy, interesting life, she had more friends than she'd ever had, and I actually thought, Okay, so much for that notion. She sees it was an idiotic idea."

Susan Heath, a British woman who had been Carolyn's student, friend, and later her editor, says, "I knew she wanted to be the author of her ending, but I'd been lulled into thinking we'd have more years. We'd keep having dinner every Thursday night at her kitchen table. Suicide had gone off the radar screen."

The week before she died, Carolyn went to a book party for her son, Robert, an attorney who was having his first novel published. He'd named his hero after Carolyn's father, Arch Gold. Carolyn left the party without saying good-bye to her children, which they say was typical. That weekend her husband, a retired professor of economics, drove to the country for several days, taking their dog. On Tuesday, Carolyn met Mary Ann Caws at their appointed time to walk in Central Park—a ritual they'd been doing for twenty-six years. Mary Ann, an English professor who also studied the Bloomsbury women, says Carolyn didn't seem low or distracted. They stopped to pet dogs, even the scraggly mutts, to whom Carolyn insisted on giving as much attention as the pedigreed beauties. When they parted, Carolyn would always ask, "Will you be here next Tuesday?" Mary Ann says, "I can't remember for sure, but the last time, I don't think she did ask." Two days later, Susan Heath took the subway to Carolyn's apartment on Central Park West for their Thursday dinner. The doorman said he thought Mrs. Heilbrun was out of town because she hadn't picked up her mail. Susan went cold. Carolyn had never missed a dinner without calling. "We've got to get the superintendent and go in," she said. She walked into the kitchen: nothing. She opened the door to the bedroom. Caroline was on her bed with a plastic bag over her head. A note on the bureau said, "The journey was over. Love to all."

Carolyn had taken pills, tied the bag over her head, and gone to sleep. Mary Ann Caws recalled that Carolyn had told her that if she killed herself, she didn't want to botch the job as had Virginia Woolf and Dora Carrington, two of the Bloomsbury women, requiring them to do it a second time. "She explained that when the mind wants to finish, the body fights back. That's why you need the plastic bag."

Susan Heath says Carolyn was not in mental anguish like Virginia

Woolf. "She was not Sylvia Plath. And she did not want to be rescued. She knew how and when to do it and arranged it so I would find her, I hope because she trusted I could handle it."

Why, then, on a crisp October day in her favorite season—fall—with her e-mail box full of loving messages from people she liked to see, did she plan her death so carefully and successfully? Victoria Rosner, a former student of Carolyn's who teaches at Texas A&M, says one explanation is that it was the "fulfillment of a promise she'd made with herself—an act of principle." Carolyn had strong convictions, and one was that people have a moral right to choose when they die. "I think it was a mistake," Victoria says, "because I want her here."

Others are poring over Carolyn's writings to determine why and when she decided to die. The clearest statement is in the last piece she wrote, submitted the week before she died to the *PMLA*, the journal of the Modern Language Association. The subject is *The Ambassadors* by Henry James and what it reflects on the predicament of "those of us coping with retirement and old age." Carolyn had retired from Columbia in 1992 in protest against what she viewed as persistent and pernicious sexism in the English Department. After leaving, she found that rereading books was dreary because her thoughts could no longer "be put to practical use, either in teaching or publishing."

Making a radical turn, she began studying science. She liked to quote T. H. White that the only cure for sadness is "to learn something." Carolyn read about Galileo, Newton, Einstein, and Darwin, who was her favorite and about whom she hoped to write. But after several years of reading, she felt no work was crystallizing. She came to believe her writing was finished, and so, therefore, was she. At the end of the *PMLA* essay, she describes proposing to a male colleague that they edit a book of "stringently honest essays—about how retired academics are coping with our unfamiliar state," but he declined. She states that the present essay is what she would have contributed "to the volume that will never be."

Reading this bleak essay underscored for me that the essential re-
quirement—the urgent task—of the years ahead is to ensure there are
sources of meaning and fulfillment other than work. Carolyn wrote that
if Strether in *The Ambassadors,* after being forced to retire, continues to
write, "he will write . . . not for recognition . . . but to render his obser-
vations and the skill for observing he has now acquired, into new words
in a new pattern." She herself, apparently, could find no satisfaction in
this.

Were there no other pleasures strong enough to tether her—the delight that others take in their children and grandchildren, friends, nature, music, or spiritual inquiry? It seems not. Carolyn did not relish
spending time with her grandchildren because they were too young for
serious conversation. She would not tolerate her husband deserting her,
but she deserted him without a word. She showed up for her son's first
book party but then rained, big-time, on that parade. Her daughter,
Margaret, hoping her mother had written her a final letter, watched for
days and none arrived. "To my grave I will feel guilty," Margaret says.
Although she frequently met her mother for drinks at a neighborhood
bar and usually brought a present—sharp ginger cookies or the score to
a piano quintet—Margaret thinks, "I should have seen her more often."

Nancy K. Miller, one of Carolyn's closest friends, edited a series of
books with her on gender and culture for Columbia University Press.
When I spoke with her two months after Carolyn's death, Nancy, who's
Distinguished Professor of English and Comparative Literature at the
City University of New York, said, "I'm in a phase where I'm angry at
her. I feel her decision was erroneous—not good judgment." Nancy had
heard Carolyn argue many times that you have to kill yourself "when
you feel good and still can." But Nancy believes that "what she left out
of the equation is: You're not only by yourself." Nancy says feminist
scholars have come to understand that "the female self tends to exist in
relation to others." She asks why Carolyn didn't have those relational
bonds. "What had happened to Carolyn that she couldn't feel she

needed other people and other people needed her and that was valuable?" Nancy adds, "When you look out the window, it's a beautiful day, you're in good health, and lots of friends want to see you, do you say, 'No, I'm killing myself because I don't want to arrive at a place in the future where I can't'?" Nancy shakes her head. "That's where the 'rational' drops out."

Betty Friedan puts the question in *The Fountain of Age:* "Should the choice of when to die be a basic human right?" Friedan says she believes, as Carolyn did, that "the 'right to die' may be as essential to the personhood of age as the 'right to choose' . . . is essential to the personhood of women." But I find the analogy specious. We can choose when to have children, but once they're born, we don't decide when they'll die. And we don't choose when we're born (although some Eastern religions hold that we do), so what gives us either a divine or basic human right to choose the moment we die? How would one determine when the time is right and the reason sufficient? If it's permissible for people to check out when they wish—to spite someone or after receiving a poor grade on a test—would that not tend to undermine the worth and honor of being alive?

When I met with Susan Heath, who'd found Carolyn dead in her apartment, she said, "I don't understand this concept of rational suicide. What are the terms we would see as rational?"

"If you're a Buddhist monk and set fire to yourself as a political protest?"

Susan considers this.

"Or terminal illness," I add, "when you're in excruciating pain and there's no cure?"

"That's essentially it," Susan says. "If you're mentally disturbed and kill yourself, we say you're crazy and it's not rational. Then we get into a circular argument: If you commit suicide, you must be crazy."

Susan questions why Carolyn, who loved writing and thinking, "didn't leave a written record of her thought process at the end." Nancy

Miller finds it sad that Carolyn, who'd spent her life "being an example, wasn't interested or willing to be an example for the last part of the journey."

Willing or not, however, no one can be an exact model or example. Carolyn was eccentric and unique, and as Susan noted, "She thought differently from everyone else about almost everything." An author's life is rarely as inspiring as his or her words. Suicide is a blow that inflicts lasting wounds on the living, and yet I'm reluctant to judge the action anyone else feels pressed to take. As a neighbor of Carolyn's, Steve Isenberg, pointed out, "Who knows what kind of tunnel Carolyn was down at the end and what if anything could have had meaning?"

For myself, I know that at my lowest point, when I played and replayed in my mind driving my car off a steep road because I'm a notoriously bad driver and there would be room for doubt as to whether it was an accident, I knew I could not press down on the gas. I could not leave a mess—and the message that they were not enough—for my children. I would prefer to endure the darkness, read *The Last Gift of Time,* and let the words lift me, rather than take and carry out Carolyn's agreement literally.

. . .

Facing and preparing for death comes with the territory ahead. Patricia Johnson, MD, who runs a clinic in North Carolina, says the people she sees approaching the end in nursing homes "weren't prepared. Our generation likes to prepare." Indeed. Jim Hart, the poet who's married to Carly Simon, follows the Franciscan tradition and contemplates death for half an hour every morning. Tibetan Buddhists practice dying daily—moving through the *bardos,* or states they believe will follow the death of the body—so that when it comes, the experience will be familiar. But this assumes that what they're practicing is in fact what will occur. Ram Dass, when he suffered a stroke at sixty-five, had spent years working with dying people, sitting at their beds to help them meet death without fear. "I'd always projected deep thoughts and profound experiences onto these people," Ram Dass said. But when his legs gave out and he collapsed on the floor, "they said I was dying, and I didn't have any profound thoughts. I was looking at the pipes on the ceiling. And I'm Mr. Spiritual!" He laughed. "That showed me: I still have work to do." He said that if you see death as "the moment when you engage the deepest mystery of the universe, then you prepare for that moment, so that you'll be open, curious, equanimous."

On the other hand, Sherwin Nuland, MD, suggests in *How We Die* that the brain cannot conceive of its own demise. "None of us seems psychologically able to cope with the thought of our own state of death," he writes. The sculptor Damien Hirst titled one of his pieces *The Physical Impossibility of Death in the Mind of Someone Living.* Joan Didion, whose husband of forty years, John Gregory Dunne, died at the dinner table of a heart attack, wrote about her shock and grief in *The Year of Magical Thinking.* When I interviewed her before the book was published, I asked how writing it had affected her sense of mortality. Joan paused and made a circling motion with two fingers, round and round. It's a moment when John might have answered the question for her. "I know I'm going to die," she said, "but not really. John's death made me look at it for John, but not for myself. There's almost nothing that can make me accept the fact that death will occur to me."

I've practiced Tibetan meditation, visualized myself dispersing into light, and tried to remind myself, as Carlos Castaneda wrote in his books, that death is always on our left, an arm's length away, but that knowledge doesn't enter the bloodstream, the cells. I was startled in 2004, reading an article about how Hispanics and Asians are gaining in population and whites are becoming the minority in the United States, when I came to the words, "As the baby boomer generation begins to die . . ." That was a jolt: This *whole generation* is going to die. This self-reflective group will all be gone, wiped out, cease to exist. I'd considered my own death, but not that my entire cohort would vanish like the flap-

pers, the Victorians, the Athenians of classical Greece. Young entrepreneurs are already vying for our corpses, creating green, PC funeral parks
where "the 4.1 million baby boomers . . . expected to die by 2040" can
be buried in a natural landscape with no chemicals or cement.

At the same time that we can't fathom this, I'm betting that it won't
hurt to prepare. What would that entail? The first step, according to
Reb Zalman, is to do a "life review," which he says is like "looking down
from a hot-air balloon at the panorama of your life" to see the overall design and how what we view as mistakes helped move us toward the
point we were meant to reach.

I meet with Reb Zalman in his office—strewn with computers,
cords, voice recorders, and electronic gear—at Naropa University, where
he's Professor Emeritus of Religion. Wearing a tan knit yarmulke, tan
slacks, and matching suspenders, he tells me the Spiritual Eldering Institute, which he founded, runs workshops for conducting a life review.

"Just thinking about that makes me anxious," I say. I don't want to
relive all the times I made a hash of things, fucked up, yelled at my children, argued over nothing, married a man for the wrong reasons, and
turned down a job that would have led to wealth and opportunities. Oy!

Reb Zalman laughs and says it's best to do this not alone but with a
friend who unquestionably loves you and can help you acknowledge
what you've learned and forgive yourself. When he revisits his first marriage, when he was a young Hasid in Brooklyn and the union was
arranged by a marriage broker, he says, "I want to kick that young Zalman in the ass! I wasn't marrying because of what I wanted and needed,
but to gain the approval of my peers." He and his first wife proved not
to be compatible, "but we really tried to love each other, for close to
twenty years. And when I look at the children I had with her . . ." He
smiles. Seen from the long view, he says, the marriage helped propel him
from the nest—the insular Hasidic world. Had he not divorced his wife
and left the community, he would not have traveled widely, met leaders
from other traditions, and launched the Jewish Renewal movement.

If conducting a life review seems overwhelming, he tells me, start by doing what he learned at yeshiva—a weekly moral review. On Friday before Shabbat, he says, he looks back at the week and examines his conscience. "If you don't review the week, it melts into gray soup. Then you have to dig much harder later to remember what happened." If you develop the habit of weekly review, he says, "it's easier to remember something you've already remembered." This makes sense, but I haven't managed to do it yet.

Life review, as I see it, is one technique for coming to terms with what you've done and haven't done. The voice that taunts me when I'm low says I haven't used my talents well, and why did I waste twenty years writing TV shows that were never produced? I know others who're acquainted with this demon. Steve Isenberg, who was an intellectual star as a student at Berkeley, became New York mayor John Lindsay's chief of staff in the sixties, then went into newspaper publishing with no experience and became an executive at the *L.A. Times* and *Newsday.* Now teaching literature at the University of Texas, Steve says, "There are certainly times when I feel I didn't drive on every piston, didn't take the best route, didn't have the wingspan I wanted. I'd like to have run one of the largest U.S. newspapers, but that won't happen because I'm too old and my family, regrettably, doesn't own the paper. On the other hand, how many people ever walk through the door I did and get the ride I got? Does life have only one winner's circle?" Steve, who's tall with receding hair that once was jet black, says that in his high school yearbook, the words by his picture were "Berkeley, politics, law." "I became an English major and thought seriously about becoming an English professor. So here I am coming around on the road not taken."

Even the most talented and accomplished seem to wrestle with acceptance. Tom Hayden has learned to "swat" any voice that says "you should have" or "you could have." Ray Manzarek of the Doors faces down his critics—inner and outer—who say, "You don't have the chops anymore," by responding: "Fuck you. Did you ever do *one thing*?"

When I repeat this to my sister, Terry, who lives in Hawaii, where she teaches tai chi and volunteers at Kaiser Foundation Hospital, she calls back and says, "I got really depressed after thinking about that. I mean, what great thing have I done?" Her voice quavers. "I haven't done one great thing."

I tell her Ray didn't say "great," he said "one—"

"But then," Terry continues, "I remembered what Mother Teresa said: 'We cannot do great things, only little things with great love.' "

I take in a breath. Terry and her husband, Gary, have been married thirty-one years and have a gift I've long admired for finding laughter every day, bringing people together, and turning a small moment into a celebration. "Your great thing," I say, "is love."

· · ·

And the end of all our exploring . . . life reviewing and forgiving . . . will be to arrive at the state Erik Erikson describes as "ego integrity":

> It is the acceptance of one's one and only life cycle as
> something that had to be and that, by necessity, permitted
> of no substitutions.

Acceptance is the key, after which come lightness and detachment. Helen Luke, in *Old Age: Journey into Simplicity,* describes this process as "a gradual letting go, through which alone the emptiness comes, into which the glory may enter." I have not quite arrived at this state of acceptance and emptiness, but I can pick up the scent of it, catch its sight behind the curtain that flutters in the wind.

Time accelerates: The week begins and it's over. The new year comes, I learn to write the date, and just as I'm getting used to the number we're making plans for the next numbered year. Already? You turn fifty and celebrate—throw a party or go off on an adventure. A woman I know in Atlanta took six friends to look for grizzlies at night in Yellowstone. You feel great, look great, little seems to be changing. Then sixty arrives with a thud. William Styron calls it the "hulking milestone of mortality." You notice that people in the news, the doctors you see, the stockbrokers you consult, the others sitting near you in restaurants—are all younger. You've scaled the peak, you're sliding down the other side of the mountain, and the changes in your body are more significant than at any period since adolescence.

People mark the hulking milestone in different ways. Joan Borysenko told me, "We need to do a ritual—help push you into a new energy." Jon Carroll, the columnist for the *San Francisco Chronicle,* said the month before turning sixty he realized, "You have two choices. You can pretend you're not freaking out. I tried that. Or attempt some kind of ceremony." He and his wife, Tracy Johnston, flew to Pátzcuaro, Mexico, where people were celebrating the Night of the Dead. Jon and Tracy stayed up all night with generations of Mexican families, sitting in the graveyard among skulls made of sugar with names written on them, flickering candles, and baskets of food and wine. Jon wrote his mother's name on a skull, and Tracy wrote her father's. A Mexican grandfather was showing his granddaughter how to place flowers on a grave, understanding that she would one day do this for him. Everyone talked, drank, and sang, but by four in the morning all was silent. When the first streaks of pink appeared in the sky, they began speaking again in a noisy burst, passed around their bread and fruit, and Jon and Tracy walked back on the dirt road to town. "There was this enormous lifting of spirits," Jon recalls, "a real moment of release. For me, it was the beginning of a more healthy approach to getting old. It's all . . . acceptance."

A different ceremony—a celebration of giving—is being improvised by Laura Baudo, head of the Tomorrow Foundation in New York. Laura plans to gather her friends and ask them to "do research and identify an individual who would benefit from a grant, free and clear." It could be a teacher, she says, an artist, or a mother who can't afford child care but has a visionary idea and needs funds to make it happen. Laura says, "I want to give my friends the joy of giving, and it'll be so much fun to see who they come up with."

Others may choose to ignore turning sixty. Jude Blitz, a psychotherapist who's been wild of heart since high school, tried to blow off her birthday because "I hate getting fucking old." But her son said he was flying in, and she thought, This must be important. Her husband, Tom Daly, rented a hall in a church for a party, and they danced to songs Jude loved: "Celebrate," "Jump!" "I Heard It Through the Grapevine," and "Joy to the World." Jude asked her friends over sixty to go up onstage, and about fifteen out of eighty people did.

"Then I walked up the steps," she recalls, "and my codger friends were there to welcome me. They took me in their arms, and I felt I was leaving on a ship, going out to sea. I could hear the band playing. I waved good-bye to everyone below. They were all younger, and I could see they were happy being younger, and they should be. I was in my place. Part of me was sad, because I don't look or feel so old, but the truth is, I'm moving into another country."

. . .

It's the spring of 2006, and as I sit at my desk, looking out at the lilacs coming into bloom, I feel both hopeful and nervous. When I began working on *Leap!*, I was in free fall, not knowing what I'd do with my time or where and with whom I'd live. I thought I needed to search for a new vocation—teaching? health care? But I've found that what suits me, what I need at the center of my days, is to study and create, regardless of how the work is received. But will I be able to write for the sheer pleasure of putting "new words in a new pattern"? This book has been so engrossing that it's given shape and propulsion to my days. I tell Sally Kempton, "I'm afraid it's a temporary fix. When the research and writing are over, I'll be back where I was before."

Sally says with a playful laugh, "It's all a temporary fix."

The truth, I must acknowledge, is that I'm not in the same place I was when I began; the incidents and accidents of the past three years have made me half in love with uncertainty. Once again, I have no idea what work I'll do next or what companions will be with me, but I'm not fighting and raging against it. Expectancy is in the air.

Certain points have clarified, the first being that we're more individuated than when younger, and what becomes clear for me may be utterly different than for you. I'd like to stay as healthy and attractive as I'm able, to do simultaneously what Thomas Moore suggests: accept age and cultivate the Venusian. I'd like to mentor a young person and work for progressive change. I intend to live with people of shared affinity in some form of community, let down barriers to love, and find sensuality in unexpected places. I want to treasure wildness and spontaneity and take surrender as a daily practice. I've found there's strength in yielding; in fact, strength and yielding wrap about each other like the black and white symbols of yin and yang. It's the strong who are able to yield gracefully, and those who yield gain strength.

The country ahead, from the extensive scouting I've done, is not arid but rich and unpredictable. It's Reb Zalman learning to hang glide and speak Arabic at eighty. It's Marcia Seligson founding a musical theater company at fifty-seven; Tom Hayden rallying us to give the system hell; Joan Borysenko and Gordon Dveirin choosing to marry a fourth time and walk the rest of the way together; Beverly Kitson building the first library in a Costa Rican town; Jane and Bob Fyrberg, at sixty, adopting a baby.

It's also contracting illness, losing loved ones, and finding the courage to keep on keeping on. When we were young, "The time to hesitate is through" meant: Let's fuck now. Today, it means, not just in regard to sex: How many chances do we have left? And this adds a fierce and exquisite flavor to every endeavor.

It's possible to attain both serenity and intensity. Many speak of "a creeping happiness" that's not tied to external circumstances, and a diminution of fear. Mark Twain wrote, "Twenty years from now you will be more disappointed by the things that you didn't do than by the ones you did do. So throw off the bowlines. Sail away from the safe harbor." In short: It's never too late, and don't wait. We'll sleep when we're dead.

· · ·

On a Sunday, when the Flatiron Mountains jut out against a cloudless sky, I take Andy Weil to the Boulder teahouse for lunch. Avatar of health that he is, Andy orders tofu and Vietnamese rice noodles, while I eat lavender duck. When we walk outside afterward, we see people of different ages clustered around a man in a wheelchair who wears a yellow golf sweater. The skin sags on his face like Yeats's tattered coat upon a stick, and wisps of white hair blow across his scalp. Yet I see a soul who was a child, played ball, fell and stood up, made his way to this Rocky Mountain town, and raised children through blizzards and drought and perfect days like this when the magpies sing and he sits in the sunlight with the family he's created. I try to picture Andy, me, and some of our friends in wheelchairs, living in a place where our kids and grandkids visit, although I know there will be moments—I've had them already—when I can't remember my children's birthdays. I picture a place where there are animals and a garden and we can still do many of the things we love: sing, make each other laugh, meditate, enjoy good food, books, and films we've seen before but are watching as if for the first time.

I nod toward the man wearing the yellow golf sweater. "That could be us one day, wheeling along."

Andy looks at the man, looks back at me, then raises an eyebrow. "I'll race you."

ACKNOWLEDGMENTS

Almost all my friends are in this book, and I wish to thank them for accepting that our friendship often leads to being written about. As the screenwriter Ron Koslow once joked, "Sit on the couch in Sara's house and you're fair game." I thank each one of you for your good humor and love.

I'm also grateful to my support team during publishing: my agent, Joy Harris; my editor, Nancy Miller; my *consigliere,* Woody Wickham; my editor at *O: The Oprah Magazine,* Liz Brody; my bestower of flowers, Jeff Grossberg; and the divine Annie Gottlieb, who read several drafts with attention and insight.

INTERVIEWS

From 2003 to 2006, I interviewed more than 150 people for this book and related articles. I took detailed notes during interviews and, in almost every case, recorded them as well. Most people agreed to have their real names used, but a few requested anonymity and appear under invented names, with potentially identifying details changed. The cast list below excludes those whose names have been changed.

By the time I completed the book, however, the people I'd interviewed at the beginning were three years older, and many had altered their status or opinions. Some had married, some split up, some quit or were fired from jobs they'd sworn to keep doing, and some who'd retired changed their minds and went back to work. I considered updating everyone's story before turning in the book, but I knew that by the time it was published, the sands might have shifted again. I've chosen to keep the interviews intact (and cite the ages people were then) because they reveal where each person was standing at that moment.

Cast

Sr. Angèle Arbib, OSB, nun, Abbey of Regina Laudis

Antell, Darrick, MD, plastic surgeon

Atchley, Robert, PhD, head of gerontology at Naropa University

Baudo, Laura, philanthropist, writer

Baxt, Bob, DDS, dentist

Baxt, Cindy, bookkeeper

Blitz, Jude, therapist, aikido teacher

Borysenko, Joan, author, medical scientist, psychologist

Campbell, Bebe Moore, novelist, commentator on NPR (died in 2006)

Carroll, Jon, columnist, *San Francisco Chronicle*

Caws, Mary Ann, PhD, Distinguished Professor of Comparative Literature, City University of New York

Drake, Annie, cofounder, South Pacific Real Estate Services, Costa Rica

Durrett, Charles, architect, founder of the cohousing movement in the United States

Dveirin, Gordon, PhD, organizational psychologist

Engle, Adam, director, Mind Life Institute

Evans, Jodie, cofounder, CODEPINK

Firestone, Tirzah, rabbi

Fonda, Jane, actress

Fyrberg, Jane, MD, retired emergency room physician

Gass, Judith Ansara, MSW, teacher, therapist, artist

Gass, Robert, ED, leadership coach, consultant, musician

Glick, Daniel, journalist

Goldberg, Danny, ACLU officer, former CEO of Air America, record company executive

Goodman, Kathy, art dealer

Goodwin, Cathy, career coach

Gray, Reggie, psychotherapist

Hart, Jim, poet

Hayden, Tom, political activist, served eighteen years in the California legislature

Heath, Susan, editor

Heilbrun, Margaret, library director, archivist

Hibbard, Chris, psychologist, professor

Holzman, Jac, founder of Elektra Records, entrepreneur

Hotchkis, Joan, actress, performance artist

Howard, Christopher, relocation tour guide and author, Costa Rica

Iman, model, head of IMAN Cosmetics

Isenberg, Steve, former publisher, professor of humanities at University of Texas

Jennings, Terry, Ro-Hun therapist, tai chi instructor

Johnson, Patricia, MD, founder and director, Tallulah Health Center, Robbinsville, North Carolina

Johnston, Tracy, writer

Joseph, John, MD, plastic surgeon

Kamer, Frank, MD, plastic surgeon

Kempton, Sally, meditation teacher, formerly Swami Durgananda

Kennedy, Jayne, actress, first black woman to be a network sportscaster

Kidder, Tracy, Pulitzer Prize–winning journalist

Kitaen-Morse, Beverly, PhD, psychologist

Kitson, Beverly, former Peace Corps teacher, founder of the David Kitson Library, Costa Rica

Krassner, Paul, humorist, satirist

Leach, Jim, president, Wonderland Hill Development Co.

Lesser, Elizabeth, cofounder, Omega Institute, writer

Lewis, Barry Meyers, English teacher

Lietaer, Bernard, financial systems engineer

Liu, Aimee, novelist

Manzarek, Ray, pianist, the Doors

Mason, Paul, sculptor

Materson, Dick, MD, retired doctor of physical medicine and rehabilitation

Materson, Rosa, physical therapist

Meade, Michael, poet, drummer, mythologist

Miller, Nancy K., PhD, Distinguished Professor of English and Comparative Literature, Graduate Center, City University of New York

Molloy, Jim, electronics consultant, silver jeweler

Moore, Thomas, author, former monk

Muir, Caroline, tantra and Divine Feminine teacher

Muske-Dukes, Carol, poet, novelist, professor

Newman, Tracy, singer-songwriter, TV writer-producer

Paterno, Vicky, MD, pediatrician

Philbrook, Bud, founder and head of Global Volunteers

Quinn, Janet, professor of nursing, University of Colorado

Ram Dass, spiritual leader

Rechtschaffen, Stephan, MD, CEO, Omega Institute

Rosenberg, Jack, PhD, psychologist

Rosner, Victoria, PhD, assistant professor of English, Texas A&M University

Russell, Annie, community builder, Wonderland Hill Development Co.

Salzberg, Sharon, meditation teacher, writer

Schachter-Shalomi, Rabbi Zalman, rabbi, teacher, author

Schiff, Robin, screenwriter, director

Seligson, Marcia, founder and artistic director, Reprise! musical theater company, Los Angeles

Simon, Carly, singer-songwriter

Simon, Peter, photographer

Steinberg, Charles, MD, AIDS doctor, Uganda

Steinem, Gloria, feminist leader

Stermitz, Tom, tango teacher

Tiegs, Cheryl, model

Tucker, Michael, actor

Wakefield, Dan, novelist, essayist

Wakefield, Torkin, cofounder, BeadforLife, Uganda

Wayne, Ed, humanitarian, Serbia

Weil, Andrew, MD, author, director of the Integrative Medicine program at the University of Arizona

Welch, Raquel, actress

Whitt, Jan, associate professor of journalism and literature, University of Colorado

Wickham, Woodward, consultant to nonprofit foundations, former vice president of the John D. and Catherine T. MacArthur Foundation

Woodman, Marion, Jungian analyst, scholar, writer

Woollen, Evans, architect

Zerner, Donna, book editor, writer

Zimbelman, Nina, metaphysical teacher

Zuckerman, Mort, publisher, New York *Daily News* and *U.S. News & World Report*

Additional Interviews

The following people gave their time and thoughts in generous conversations and interviews. Although they're not quoted in the book, their ideas contributed to the overall picture. I thank:

Regina Barrett, Deborah Barry, Judy Blatt, Jacob Brackman, Deborah Brackman-Tomasini, the Rev. Rosalyn L. Bruyere, Kyle Callahan, Betsy Carter, Phil Catalfo, David Chernikov, Ellen Chesler, Rick Cotton, Tom Daly, John Davis, Barb deGroot, Paul DiMarchi, Dery Dyer, Tracy Ehlers, Alyne Ellis, Janine Fafard, Farrah Fawcett, Tom Fineman, Mark Gerzon, Charles Gohmann, Trudy Goodman, Meg Grant, Randy Gritz, Amy Gross, Jeff Grossberg, Christina Hager, Sam Hamra, MD, Tom Hast, Barry Horowitz, MD, Eve Ilsen, Gary Jennings, Craig Karpel, John Kaye, Rachael Kessler, Ron Koslow, Mother Lucia Kuppens, OSB,

Christine Lavin, Mel Levine, Suzanne Braun Levine, Terrence McNally, Gerry Marzorati, John Metzger, Rose Moberly, Marc Nordstrom, Jim Palmer, Jan Peterson, Mike Pettiford, Agnes and Jo Pinheiro, Tom Pollock, Carol Poston, Murray Richtel, Richard Sann, Bob Shayne, Steven Smith, Carlos Torres, Nancy Warner, Margaret Whitt, Dale Willman, Patty Yanitz, and Jacob Young.

NOTES

1. The Long and Winding Road

4 **Image of the three suggests the picture of Dorian Gray:** Oscar Wilde, *The Picture of Dorian Gray*, first published London, 1891.

8 **Turning fifty at the rate of one every seven seconds:** AARP. The figure is based on AARP analysis of Census 2004 Interim projections for boomer data by single year of age.

8 **52 percent voted red in the last presidential election, and 47 percent voted blue:** Greenberg Quinlan Rosner Research, results of three thousand respondents who indicated they voted in the 2004 presidential election in surveys conducted November 2–3, 2004.

2. The Narrows

13 **The most instructive words I found were in a tape:** Marion Woodman, *The Crown of Age: The Rewards of Conscious Aging*. Louisville, Colo.: Sounds True, 2004.

16 **What the Buddhists call the second arrow:** Numerous essays and books explain the Buddhist concept of the second arrow in emotional suffering. A succinct description may be found at www.insightmeditationcenter.org/book/14.html.

26 **Major law firms have a mandatory retirement age:** Surveys by consulting firms such as Edge International and Hildebrandt show that 40–70 percent of law firms have mandatory retirement ages. See www.thirdagecenter.com/Lobster%20Pot13.htm.

27 **Destitution, writes Anne Lamott:** Anne Lamott, *Plan B.* New York: Riverhead Books, 2005.

3. Sweet Surrender?

32 **Life was not yielding to "intelligence and effort":** Fitzgerald wrote that in his youth, "life was something you dominated if you were any good. Life yielded easily to intelligence and effort . . . —And then, ten years this side of forty-nine, I suddenly realized that I had prematurely cracked." F. Scott Fitzgerald, *The Crack-Up.* New York: New Directions, 1993.

41 **The bronze statue by Cyrus E. Dallin, *Appeal to the Great Spirit:*** May be viewed at www.dallin.org/pages/spirit.html.

4. The Body Electric

43 **Whoopi Goldberg says she was shocked:** Interview in the documentary *Searching for Debra Winger,* directed by Rosanna Arquette.

54 **"If you look at national morbidity and mortality rates, comparing MD anesthesiologists with nurse anesthetists":** Michael Pine, MD, MBA, Kathleen D. Holt, PhD, You-Bei Lou, PhD, "Surgical Mortality and Type of Anesthesia Provider," *AANA Journal* 71, no. 2 (April 2003): 109.

A list of published studies comparing anesthesia outcome by provider can be found by clicking on www.aana.com and, in the search box on the right, typing "morbidity."

56 **For decades, plastic surgeons have been arguing:** Denise Mann, "Face Off," WebMD Medical News, May 15, 2001. See www.my.webmd.com/content/article/32/1728_79750.

57 **Dr. Antell did his own study on twins:** Darrick Antell, MD, "The Largest Series in the World of Facelifts on Identical Twins with a Comparison of

SMAS Techniques," *Plastic and Reconstructive Surgery,* September 1, 2005, p. 28.

63 **I'm seventy-eight . . . and I had sex last night":** Helen Gurley Brown, "Don't Give Up on Sex After 60," *Newsweek,* May 29, 2000, p. 55.

5. Change Is Gonna Come

67 **Reb Zalman had plunged into a depression:** Zalman Schachter-Shalomi and Ronald S. Miller, *From Age-ing to Sage-ing: A Profound New Vision of Growing Older.* New York: Warner Books, 1995, p. 1.

79 **Robbinsville is a conservative, red-voting community:** Robbinsville, N.C., community profile, www.epodunk.com.

82 **I think of the Dalí painting:** Image may be viewed at www.latifm.com/salvador_dali/salvador_dali_exhibition11.htm.

6. Sea of Love

85 **Edith Wharton called "the flower of life":** Edith Wharton, *The Age of Innocence,* originally published 1920.

101 **Gloria said she herself was finished with sex:** Claudia Dreifus, "Ms. Behavin' Again," *Modern Maturity,* May/June 1999.

105 **Was this an eerie and ghoulish coincidence:** Carol Muske-Dukes, "In a Heartbeat," *O: The Oprah Magazine,* November 2001, p. 198.

7. The Second Sexual Revolution

112 **The consensus among the literary lionesses:** Francine du Plessix Gray, "The Third Age," *The New Yorker,* February 26 and March 4, 1996, p. 188.

113 **Frightened when I read an interview with Hanif Kureishi:** Lynn Hirschberg, "Questions for Hanif Kureishi," *New York Times Magazine,* May 23, 2004.

113 **AARP survey reveals the shifting landscape:** Susan Jacoby, "Sex in Amer-
    ica," *AARP* magazine, July and August 2005, p. 63.

125 **Lydon stated that the clitoris was the center of all orgasms:** Susan Lydon,
    "The Politics of Orgasm," in *Sisterhood Is Powerful,* Robin Morgan, ed. New
    York: Vintage Books, 1970.

8. Get a Job

136 **Seven out of ten in the forty-six to sixty-four age range say they expect
    never to stop working:** RoperASW for AARP, *Boomers Envision Retirement
    II,* research report, May 2004. States that "79% of boomers plan to work in
    some capacity during their retirement years." See www.aarp.org/research/
    work/retirement/aresearch-import-865.html.

148 **People fifty-five and older . . . account for 30 percent of self-employed
    consultants and entrepreneurs:** Study by Challenger, Gray & Christmas,
    Inc., reported in *Forbes.*

154 **Nina Wise . . . asserts that humans are the only animals who create art:**
    Nina Wise, *A Big New Free Happy Unusual Life.* New York: Broadway Books,
    2002.

9. School's Out

161 **More than 75 percent of boomers plan to work beyond age sixty-five:** *The
    New Retirement Survey,* conducted for Merrill Lynch by Harris Interactive in
    collaboration with Age Wave, February 2005. See www.ml.com/index.asp
    ?id=7695_7696_8149_46028_46503_46635.

10. Our House

181 **About a third of people over sixty-five are expected to do the endgame in
    nursing homes:** Betty Friedan, *The Fountain of Age.* New York: Touchstone,
    1993, p. 510.

184 **I'm reminded of young people who started rural communes in the 1960s
    and declared them "open land":** Sara Davidson, "Open Land: Getting

Back to the Communal Garden," *Harper's* magazine, June 1970. See www
.saradavidson.com under "Articles."

185 **cohousing being constructed for people over fifty:** Charles Durrett, *Senior Cohousing: A Community Approach to Independent Living.* Berkeley, Calif.: Ten Speed Press, 2005.

199 **Beacon Hill Village in Boston:** AARP bulletin, December 17, 2005; and Jane Gross, "Aging at Home: For a Lucky Few, a Wish Come True," *New York Times,* February 9, 2006.

11. Revolution No. 9

200 **"The energy of a whole generation comes to a head":** Hunter S. Thompson, *Fear and Loathing in Las Vegas.* New York: Random House, 1971, pp. 67–68.

206 **took on Democrats and the entire American Left:** Danny Goldberg, *How the Left Lost Teen Spirit.* New York: RDV Books, 2005.

213 **he was on what Joseph Campbell called "the pollen path":** Bill Moyers and Joseph Campbell, *Joseph Campbell and the Power of Myth.* Burlington, Vt.: Mystic Fire Video, DVD, 2001.

Joseph Campbell, *The Inner Reaches of Outer Space: Metaphor as Myth and as Religion.* New York: New World Library, 2002.

13. My Sweet Lord

244 **Annie Besant . . . discovered Krishnamurti:** Mary Lutyens, *Krishnamurti: The Years of Awakening.* New York: Avon Books, 1975.

245 **Emerson asked in *Nature*:** Ralph Waldo Emerson, *Nature,* in *The Collected Works of Ralph Waldo Emerson,* vol. I. Cambridge, Mass.: Harvard University Press, 1971.

245 **Elizabeth Lesser, who was present at the creation:** Elizabeth Lesser, *The Seeker's Guide: Making Your Life a Spiritual Adventure* (formerly titled *The New American Spirituality*). New York: Random House, 1999.

245 **Christopher Isherwood described the eclectic seekers:** Christopher Isherwood, *My Guru and His Disciple.* New York: Farrar, Strauss & Giroux, 1980.

254 **I read a biography of Ramana that excited my curiosity:** Arthur Osborne, *Ramana Maharshi and the Path of Self-Knowledge.* New York: Weiser Books, 1995.

267 **Love . . . expands "like gold to airy thinness beat":** John Donne, "A Valediction: Forbidding Mourning," in *The Complete Poetry and Selected Prose of John Donne.* New York: Modern Library, 2001.

14. When We're Sixty-four

270 **"How can one accept living":** Eugene Ionesco, quoted in Simone de Beauvoir, *The Coming of Age.* New York: W. W. Norton, 1996, p. 463.

271 **"Since (nature) has fitly planned the other acts of life's drama":** Marcus Tullius Cicero, *De Senectute (On Old Age),* quoted in Carolyn Heilbrun, *The Last Gift of Time: Life Beyond Sixty.* New York: Ballantine Books, 1997, p. 1.

273 **The two groups at greatest risk for suicide:** Abigail Trafford, *My Time.* New York: Basic Books, 2004, p. 244.

275 **She liked to quote T. H. White that the only cure for sadness:** T. H. White, *Sword in the Stone,* quoted in Carolyn Heilbrun, *The Last Gift of Time: Life Beyond Sixty,* p. 53.

277 **Betty Friedan puts the question:** Betty Friedan, *The Fountain of Age.* New York: Simon & Schuster, 1993, p. 538.

278 **Ram Dass, when he suffered a stroke:** From the documentary *Ram Dass, Fierce Grace,* directed and produced by Mickey Lemle, 2001, available on DVD.

279 **Young entrepreneurs are already vying for our corpses:** Patricia Leigh Brown, "Eco-Friendly Burial Sites Give a Chance to Be Green Forever," *New York Times,* August 13, 2005.

282 **The state Erik Erikson describes as "ego integrity":** Erik Erikson, *Childhood and Society.* New York: W. W. Norton, 1950.

282 **"a gradual letting go, through which alone the emptiness comes":** Barbara
A. Mowat, Folger Shakespeare Library, quoted in Helen M. Luke, *Old Age:
Journey into Simplicity.* New York: Parabola Books, 1987, p. x.

282 **"The hulking milestone of mortality":** William Styron, *Darkness Visible.*
New York: Vintage Books, 1990.

RESOURCES

Giving Back

Civic Ventures (www.civicventures.org): a national nonprofit that "seeks to tap the talents and skills of older Americans."

Corporation for National and Community Service (www.nationalservice.org)

Cross-Cultural Solutions (www.crossculturalsolutions.org): volunteer programs abroad lasting from one to twelve weeks

Foster Grandparent Program, through Corporation for National and Community Service's Senior Corps (www.seniorcorp.org)

Global Crossroad (www.globalcrossroad.com): volunteer and internship programs in twenty countries

Global Volunteers (www.globalvolunteers.org): two- and three-week service trips in United States and abroad

Habitat for Humanity (www.habitat.org)

Mentor (www.mentoring.org): promotes mentoring young people at risk

Peace Corps (www.peacecorps.gov)

Volunteer Abroad (www.volunteerabroad.com): international volunteer organization that will match you with the country and type of work you wish to do

Planning for the Next Stage of Life

2young2retire (www.2young2retire.com): resources for planning for an
   interesting, fulfilling retirement
Atlas: The Unretirement Revolution
   (www.orangerec.com/atlas/home.html)
Second Journey (www.secondjourney.org): a nonprofit dedicated to creating a new vision of aging

Housing/Communities

Aging at home: Beacon Hill Village offers a model (www.beaconhillvillage.
   org)
Cohousing Association of the U.S. (www.cohousing.org)
*Creating a Life Together: Practical Tools to Grow Ecovillages and Intentional
   Communities,* by Diana Leafe Christian, forword by Patch Adams.
   Gabriola Island, B.C.: New Society Publishers, 2003
   (www.newsociety.com)
ElderSpirit (www.elderspirit.net): the first senior cohousing in the United
   States; works with groups who want to set up similar communities
More Than Shelter for Seniors (www.mtsfs.org): apartment communities
   that focus on creative arts
Wonderland Hill Development Co. (www.whdc.com): the largest devel-
   oper of cohousing for both multigenerations and seniors

Spiritual Practice

The Abbey of Regina Laudis, Bethlehem, Connecticut
   (www.abbeyofreginalaudis.com)
Contemplative Outreach, Inc. (www.contemplativeoutreach.org): Christ-
   ian Centering Prayer
Insight L.A. (www.insightla.org; www.mindfulnessandpsychotherapy.org):
   Trudy Goodman, Buddhist meditation and psychology teacher
Insight Meditation Society (www.dharma.org): Buddhist retreats
Jewish Renewal (http://www.aleph.org/renewal.html)

Nina Zimbelman, spiritual teacher, Gleanings Foundation
(www.gleaningsfoundation.org)
Omega Institute (www.eomega.org): workshop and retreat center
Sally Kempton, Awakened Heart Meditation teacher
(www.sallykempton.com)
Spiritual Eldering (www.sage-ingguild.org)

Expatriate Living

Boomers Abroad (www.boomersabroad.com)
EscapeArtist (www.escapeartist.com)
Christopher Howard, *The New Golden Door to Living and Retirement in Costa Rica.* San Jose: Costa Rica Books, 2005 (www.liveincostarica.com)
International Living (www.internationalliving.com)

Fitness and Sports

Masters ski racing (www.ussa.org/PublishingFolder/3029_3033.htm)
Masters sports (www.readysetgofitness.com/links/masters_sports.shtml)
Senior baseball (www.baseballnews.com/senior/index.htm)

Sex and Sensuality

Divine Feminine workshops for women and men (www.divine-feminine.com)
Source School of Tantra (www.sourcetantra.com)
Taoist sensual practice for men and women, Saida Desilets
(www.jadegoddess.com)

INDEX

LEAP!

Sara Davidson

A Reader's Guide

Reading Group Questions and Topics for Discussion

1. Have you been through what's described in *Leap!* as "the Narrows"? What was it like? Why does Davidson call it "the Narrows"? What different strategies do people in the book use to find their way out?

2. Why was "surrender" painful for the author? Did her understanding of surrender change?

3. Have you considered having plastic surgery or decided against it? Did reading the author's report on a face lift affect your thinking?

4. After resisting the changes that befall her, Davidson visits a friend in North Carolina who's clearing trees to build a community. What happens on that visit that prompts Davidson to yield to change? How do you respond to change?

5. The author explores whether we're "hard-wired" to seek a romantic partner. What would you conclude, based on the material presented? What is your own experience?

6. Davidson discovers a great range of sexual behavior after fifty, from those who give it up to the actress who refuses "to go unfucked to my grave." What intrigued or disturbed you about her reporting on sexuality?

7. The author says we're a society of workaholics, but the imperative now is not merely to work but to align yourself with your purpose, your truth. How would you go about doing that?

8. When her TV career collapses, Davidson searches for a new vocation and becomes frustrated. The turning point comes when a high school teacher asks her: If you *knew* the world was going to end in two days, what would you do? Ask the question of yourself, and see what arises. Whatever that is, are you doing it now? How can you restructure your life to include more of it?

9. Why does the author take a tour of Costa Rica and visit a cohousing community?

10. What examples of "giving back" inspired you?

11. Why do you think the volunteers in India turned against Davidson? What impact did that have on her?

12. The author travels to an ashram to pursue her spiritual quest. What does she learn?

13. Why does Davidson include, in the final chapter, a description of Carolyn Heilbrun's suicide? Is there such a thing as "rational suicide"?

14. What's the purpose of a "life review"? What are the rewards?

NOTE: If you purchase *Leap!* you may download the free *Leap!* workbook, which has exercises to help you define what's right for you in the years ahead. Go to *www.saradavidson.com* and click on "Free Workbook."

Sara Davidson wrote the definitive book about the boomer generation coming of age—*Loose Change*—an international bestseller. As a journalist, novelist, screenwriter, and radio host, she's earned a reputation for writing cutting-edge pieces about the way we live. Davidson is the author of six books, including *Cowboy* and *Real Property;* a contributing editor of *O: The Oprah Magazine;* and has written for *The New York Times Magazine, Esquire, Harper's, The Atlantic, Reader's Digest,* and *Rolling Stone*. She has created dramas for television and was co–executive producer of *Dr. Quinn, Medicine Woman*. Currently living in Boulder, Colorado, she can be contacted at www.saradavidson.com.